The Elements of
C Programming
Style

Other McGraw-Hill Books of Interest

The Elements of C Programming Style

Jay Ranade

Alan Nash

McGraw-Hill, Inc.

New York St. Louis San Francisco Auckland Bogotá
Caracas Lisbon. London Madrid Mexico Milan
Montreal New Delhi Paris San Juan São Paulo
Singapore Sydney Tokyo Toronto

Library of Congress Cataloging-in-Publication Data

Ranade, Jay.
    The elements of C programming style / Jay Ranade, Alan Nash.
        p.   cm.
    Includes index.
    ISBN 0-07-051278-7
    1. C (Computer program language)   I. Nash, Alan, date.
    II. Title.
    QA76.73.C15R36   1992
    005.13'3—dc20   92-28692
                                                               CIP

1 2 3 4 5 6 7 8 9 0   DOH/DOH   9 8 7 6 5 4 3 2

ISBN   0-07-051278-7

*The sponsoring editor for this book was Jerry Papke, the editing
supervisor was David E. Fogarty, and the production supervisor was
Donald Schmidt.*

Printed and bound by R. R. Donnelley & Sons Company.

To my daughter
Sheena S. Ranade
J.R.

To Rosemary
A.N.

Contents at a Glance

Contents

Preface

What is this book about?

Once you learn the C language, how do you get to the point where you can produce good C programs? Knowing the language syntax is necessary, but not enough. You need to know how to combine the separate components into a meaningful whole. Learning the basics of the C language is easy. It can be done in a few days. The next step, learning how to produce good C code, is difficult. It can take many years.

This book provides a shortcut. It provides clear, concise, and specific advice that will help you create good programs. Much of the advice provided in this book may be obvious to expert C programmers. Most C experts have learned and unconsciously apply many of the rules presented here. However, it probably took them many years to learn these rules. The purpose of this book is to explicitly state the rules that most C experts apply (or should apply) to create good programs.

This book has been strongly influenced by three excellent classics: *The Elements of Style* by William Strunk and E. B. White, *The Elements of Programming Style* by Brian Kernighan and P. J. Plauger, and *The C Programming Language* by Brian Kernighan and Dennis Ritchie. It strives to emulate the spirit of the first two to become a deserving sequel to the last one.

Who is this book for?

This book is for anybody working with the C language. It is for students and beginners learning the C language, intermediate C programmers, expert C programmers, and managers of C programmers.

For the student or beginner, this book provides strong and specific guidance. It helps to put diverse C tools and techniques together to create programs. Instead of providing many different, conflicting, and vague suggestions, it provides clear-cut rules.

For intermediate C programmers, this book provides the opportunity to consolidate some of the rules learned with time, to revise some erroneous notions and practices, and to learn new and useful rules that would otherwise require further years of practice. It also provides a challenge and an opportunity to stop and think. Even if there is some disagreement with the rules presented here, intermediate C programmers might gain further insight into why and how they do things.

For expert C programmers, this book provides entertainment, food for thought, and formalization of some of their acquired knowledge. Experts, by definition, do not need much advice. Nor do they often run into suggestions that they have not already applied or discarded. While most of the rules in this book will, at best, elicit an "aha" or "of course," a few will (we hope) provide new and useful advice. Some rules will generate strong disagreement, probably with good reason. Experts are usually strongly opinionated people. While some disagreement is inevitable with a book of this sort, we hope the expert will not condemn this book if only a few rules conflict with his or her opinions. This book can help train less experienced co-workers.

For the manager of C programmers, this book provides a strong starting point for a style manual. The book can serve as a standards manual on its own or with additional notes. In the additional notes, modifications to the rules can be suggested to conform to personal taste or company standards. The book can then be given to the programmers with the notes. The book can also be used to generate discussions on the subject.

What do you need to know?

This book assumes that you have a decent understanding of the basics of the C language. We assume that you have read *The C Programming Language* by Brian Kernighan and Dennis Ritchie or some other introductory text about the C language. We also assume that you have worked with C and that you have some programming experience. Strong C knowledge is required for a full understanding of Chapters 16 and 17.

We do not dwell upon things that should be obvious to you. We intentionally do not over-explain the examples. Working through them might be a useful exercise.

Many bullet points and examples have been written anticipating that you would recognize them from previous experience. If that is not the case, read the discussion.

Why a book on style?

While many books have been written on C syntax, C techniques, the C library, and C algorithms, few books have been written on C style. Even though the interested programmer can get a lot of advice on individual language components, library components, or techniques, he or she still has to go through years of painful work to discover practical rules to create good code.

Large quantities of ugly C code have been produced, mostly by intermediate-level programmers. Straightforward application of a few rules would have turned most of that code into at least decent code. Over and over we have had to provide the same basic advice to less experienced programmers. Next time, we will just hand out this book.

Why rules?

We have chosen to adopt a paternalistic attitude, and provide rules phrased as strong imperatives, following the approach of *The Elements of Style*. Vague statements and generalities are difficult to apply and easy to forget. Discussion of all possible options and conflicting points of view stimulates further thought but seldom provides much guidance. Specific rules are easier to apply and remember, and some can even be applied to improve a program without knowing much about it.

What if you disagree?

If you find some rules too simple or trivial, please put up with us. Many programmers either do not know them or need to be reminded. Since one of our goals is to formalize existing expertise, we have included obvious, but useful, rules for the sake of completeness. Do not resent a rule just because it seems too obvious.

If you disagree with a rule, read the discussion. If you still disagree with the rule, do not use it. Every programmer has personal preferences.

If you do not disagree with a rule, but use a different approach, think about whether the approach suggested in the rule is at least as good. Remember: we do not want to confuse other readers by discussing too many alternatives. If one of our rules will help to produce good code, it is good enough.

How is this book organized?

The book has been divided into five sections.

In Part I we cover the project cycle. We provide rules on design, testing, debugging, and optimizing. Most of the advice in this part can be applied to other languages.

In Part II we provide general programming advice. Most of it can also be applied to other languages. We cover visual organization, comments, data objects, numbers, and input and output.

In Part III we provide rules on C usage. We cover expressions, statements, functions, parameters, arrays, pointers, and the preprocessor.

In Part IV we review two key aspects of the language: operators and the Standard C Library. In this part, instead of providing specific rules, we examine each operator and each header in the Standard C Library. We do not fully describe each of them. Instead, we bring to your attention the key points, the unusual features, and the potential dangers. These two chapters, especially the chapter on the Standard Library, are the most difficult chapters in this book. A higher level of C expertise (compared to the rest of the book) is necessary to understand them.

In Part V we include two special chapters. In one of them we present an alternative style to be used when coding for non-C programmers (that is, programmers who understand the basics of C, but are not fluent in it). In the other, we present several idioms and techniques to demonstrate elegant C code.

Finally there are several appendices. There are answers to the exercises provided at the end of most chapters, and appendices covering operator precedence and C keywords.

Each chapter has an introduction, a series of rules (except for the chapter on idioms and techniques), and usually a set of exercises. The exercises are designed to test the knowledge acquired in the chapter. They usually require straightforward application of the rules presented in the chapter. When working on them, concentrate mostly on what has been taught in the chapter. In keeping with the assumption that you have at least moderate C knowledge and that application of the rules should be straightforward, the code in the exercises is presented without much explanation of what it does. Often, it is not necessary to understand exactly what the code does in order to improve it.

Each rule is presented with a title, a few bullet points to highlight the key concepts associated with it, one or more examples (in most cases), and a discussion.

Where do I go from here?

The process of learning how to produce better code never ends. There is always more to be learned. To further improve your programming skills, read good code, have other people review and comment on your code, discuss rules and techniques with co-workers, and read good books and journals.

As a starting point, here is a list of a few books that could help you improve your programming style:

American National Standards Institute. 1990. *American National Standard for Information Systems — Programming Language — C.* New York: American National Standards Institute.

Dijkstra, E. W. 1976. *A Discipline of Programming.* Englewood Cliffs, N.J.: Prentice-Hall.

Kernighan, B. W., and Plauger, P. J. 1976. *Software Tools.* Reading, Mass.: Addison-Wesley.

Kernighan, B. W., and Plauger, P. J. 1978. *The Elements of Programming Style.* 2d ed. New York: McGraw-Hill.

Kernighan, B. W., and Ritchie, D. M. 1988. *The C Programming Language.* 2d ed. Murray Hili, N.J.: Prentice-Hall.

Knuth, D. E. 1968–81. *The Art of Computer Programming.* 3 vols. Reading, Mass.: Addison-Wesley.

Plauger, P. J. 1992. *The Standard C Library.* Englewood Cliffs, N.J.: Prentice Hall.

Wirth, N. 1986. *Algorithms and Data Structures.* 2d ed. Englewood Cliffs, N.J.: Prentice-Hall.

Acknowledgments

A book on style is the result of a long learning process. Several people indirectly influenced the contents of this book through their excellent published works. It is impossible to remember all of them. The ones who come to mind are: Edsger Dijkstra, Brian Kernighan, Donald Knuth, P. J. Plauger, Dennis Ritchie, William Strunk, E. B. White, and Niklaus Wirth.

We are grateful to those who read the manuscript at different stages of completion and provided valuable suggestions: Lance Greenberg, Leonard Kasendorf, Bruce Ladendorf, Christopher Martin, Theodore Nadeau, Rosemary Rooks, and Saba Zamir. Their friendly and meticulous criticism helped to shape this book.

We are particularly indebted to Richard Schmeidler, who spent many hours reading the drafts and providing invaluable advice. His remarkable thoroughness and precision have greatly improved the text.

We are grateful to all our other friends and colleagues who provided support and advice.

Jay Ranade
Alan Nash

We would like to receive your feedback. You can write to us at the following address:

Jay Ranade Series
P. O. Box 338
Grand Central Station
New York, NY 10163-0338

If you write, please be as specific as possible. Tell us which rules you like the most, which rules do you agree with, and which rules you disagree with and why. Feel free to suggest additional rules.

1.1   Good style vs. bad style

This book provides many rules to write programs in "good style," that is, to avoid "bad style." The concept of style is a somewhat vague one. Good, experienced programmers tend to produce good programs. If asked why they use a particular style, they will often not know the answer. For the experts, good style comes naturally. If pressed, however, they might provide valid reasons to justify their style. When confronted with a bad program, they might feel that something is wrong, even before they can think of the reasons.

Style is usually developed with experience. Many different bits of information acquired during a long career crystalize into a specific style. It is the purpose of this book to present some of the rules that many experts apply unconsciously, and to provide some of the reasoning behind them.

1.2   Your audience

When you write code, just as when you write English, you have to keep your audience in mind. The writing should be tailored for the audience. If your audience is highly experienced in C, it would be a waste of your and your readers' time to avoid using sophisticated techniques and to explain every little boring detail. On the other hand, if your audience is inexperienced in C, it would be prudent to comment about anything unusual and to avoid some of the most complicated features of the language.

This situation is similar to what occurs when you write English. If you are writing an article for a technical journal in a specialized field, you should avoid explaining basic concepts (which your audience knows) and you should use the available technical terms for precision and conciseness. If, however, you are writing for a magazine targeted at the general public, you should explain clearly all key concepts and underlying assumptions, and avoid technical terms.

Some of the potential readers of your programs are you, your managers, people reporting to you, other C programmers, and non-C programmers. Keep in mind that often the most important reader is: you. You are the one who will be looking at that function over and over until you get it to work. You are the one who will have to understand what this or that line of code does, a year after writing the program, when the system suddenly starts misbehaving.

In most cases, it is impossible to determine *a priori* who your audience will be. You should, nevertheless, make some assumptions. Assume certain (reasonable) levels of knowledge for your audience in several areas, then proceed to code accordingly. These assumptions might even be included in the comments or in a separate document. Once these assumptions are made, be consistent. Do not "shift levels." The experienced C programmer does not need to be reminded that within `if(p=malloc(size))` there is an assignment to `p`, not a comparison. Nor does the beginner deserve to be exposed to statements such as `*p++ = (*pfun)(a,b) <= TMAX;` unless he or she is intentionally reading code for experts.

When making decisions about your audience, do not assume too low a level of C proficiency unless there is a specific reason. When writing English, it is a good idea to avoid fancy words that can be easily replaced, but it is not a good idea to avoid words that most adults know. You can't provide for every case. There might be readers beginning to learn English, people with limited vocabulary, etc. Trying to write for the widest possible audience results in loss of richness of expression. The majority of your audience, who can understand many words, should not be addressed in a fifth grade vocabulary. If the reader does not know C, in most cases it should be his or her responsibility to acquire the required proficiency. The readers of C programs should, and usually will, be C programmers. Do not penalize them by trying to accommodate beginners, programmers from other languages, or managers.

It is a key concept of this book that, in most cases, at least moderate C proficiency should be expected of your audience. Accordingly, we assume that you have at least moderate C proficiency.

1.3   Notations

Languages such as English are very useful to deal with most everyday situations. Ordinary languages, however, provide very limited capabilities for some specialized situations. Mathematics is a prime example. A system of symbols has evolved over the centuries to express mathematical concepts. By using these symbols, sophisticated mathematical statements can be expressed clearly, precisely, and concisely. To express some of those statements in ordinary language, hundreds of sentences would be required. Not only would conciseness be lost, but also clarity and precision would be diminished.

A system of symbols that allows you to express concepts in a specialized field is a *notation*. Notations are more effective than ordinary language in many situations. Programming languages are notations. While there are some advantages in making a programming language somewhat English-like, this should not be pushed too far. After all, programming languages are designed to express operations that are mostly outside the field of everyday experience. English is a general-purpose language; it is inadequate to express the complex operations required when programming.

The C language, like many other notations (mathematical, musical, etc.), is difficult for a beginner or outsider to understand. Once mastered, however, it is easier to read than equivalent text. Readability should therefore be measured not by how similar the program is to text, but rather by how effectively the notation is used to express operations clearly.

It is a key concept of this book that this notation (the C language) should be mastered and exploited.

1.4   Two bad extremes

Two extremes should be avoided. Do not write code that uses only the most basic features of the language when more sophisticated features would be useful. This is equivalent to writing about a technical subject and avoiding the use of sophisticated technical terms. Your audience, which knows those terms, is left wondering why so many words have to be used to explain concepts for which more adequate terms exist. This practice of "coding for everybody" is justified only when the audience is *known* to lack the necessary C proficiency.

On the other hand, do not try to pack into every statement as many C tricks as you know. C offers sophisticated features to be used when necessary, not to be abused. Use advanced features to solve complicated problems. Often, simpler techniques will be adequate. Do not repeat the mistake of those who try to demonstrate their intelligence by using every complicated word they know as often as possible. Clear and concise expression can be often achieved without sacrificing simplicity.

1.5   A pragmatic approach

The rules presented in this book should allow you to produce good code. That is the ultimate objective of most programming methods. Of course, the methods differ in exactly what they consider good code. But, independent of the particular approach, most experts agree on what constitutes good and what bad code in most situations. (There might, however, be vehement disagreement in some situations.)

If a particular rule (from this book or from anywhere else) would result in bad code, it should not be applied. Rules should be applied consistently but not slavishly. A good example is the structured programming approach. Strict structured programming requires each unit (function, loop, condition, etc.) to have only one entry point and one exit point. It also prohibits the use of goto. Strict adherence to structured programming results, in general, in good code. In some cases, however, very ugly code can be generated by blind adherence to some of its rules. (For example, not allowing more than one exit point per function can create complicated situations.)

Consistency is very important. Blind obedience is not.

1.6   Applying the rules

The advice given in this book should be easy to apply. In many cases, you should be able to look at a code fragment, realize that a specific rule has been broken, and modify the code to conform to that rule without understanding what the code fragment is supposed to do. In other cases, a more complete understanding of the system might be needed.

The rules are intended to be simple, direct, and unambiguous. Exceptions are usually noted explicitly, although most rules should be understood to carry an implied "whenever possible" or "whenever reasonable." The rules should be applied unless either one of the noted exceptions occurs or a very good reason, not contemplated in the noted exceptions, exists. In case of doubt, apply the rule.

Within some rules, suggestions are given. Suggestions, always explicitly identified as such, are not equivalent to rules. They are provided to further clarify the rule and to give you a starting point. Feel free to disregard them.

1.7   About the C language

C is an excellent general-purpose language. It does not have the elegance
of LISP, the cleverness of Forth, or the clarity of Pascal. It is, however, one
of the most widely used and best supported computer languages. C maps well
into most machine languages, allowing compilers to produce efficient code. C
is a small and simple language; it offers a minimal framework without
complicated built-in features. Additional features are provided as separate
functions.

C is a real-life language. It was not designed for teaching (as Pascal and
BASIC were) or for a specialized use. It was designed by a programmer
(Dennis Ritchie), for programmers. It has bad spots, as most languages do,
but they are few. And while at first it seems ugly (too many strange
operators), it eventually reveals a subtle elegance. It is a language that works.

1.8   The ANSI standard

The C language was first introduced to the general public with the
publication of *The C Programming Language* in 1978. Since then, it has been
slowly polished, and currently it is a mature language. In 1983, the American
National Standards Institute (ANSI) established a committee to produce a
standard for the language. In December 1989, the standard was approved.
Long before that, the ANSI Standard C draft was already a de facto standard.

The ANSI committee introduced a few important modifications or
extensions to the language. It also introduced several small changes while
pursuing its goal of unifying existing practice. The ANSI committee produced
a standard not only for the language, but also for some of the core functions
provided in most environments (the Standard Library).

Standard C is a complete and useful language. In contrast with other
language standards, it does not cover just a limited core of the functionality
provided by most implementations. Most modern implementations fully
support the Standard. Furthermore, they seldom provide much additional
functionality except by the use of additional functions or libraries. Therefore,
very portable programs can be written in C.

All the rules in this book refer and conform to the current ANSI C
Standard. New revisions of the Standard will probably be published, most
likely as extensions that minimally affect programs conforming to the current
Standard. A few possible rules have been left out of this book because they
do not conform to the Standard. For example, a feature not in the Standard
that we particularly like is the ability to create a comment at the end of a line
by using a double slash (//). We hope that this feature will make it into the
next revision of the Standard.

1.9   Portability

Since Standard C is a very portable language, portability should be considered when writing a program. In many cases a program will be naturally portable, as a consequence of being written in Standard C. On other occasions, however, implementation-dependent features might be used intentionally or inadvertently, limiting portability. Sometimes decisions have to be made as to whether to sacrifice portability for the sake of efficiency.

In general, do not sacrifice portability for small gains in efficiency or ease of coding. However, do not make big sacrifices for portability when portability is not required. Portability is not treated separately in this book. Rather, it should be a natural result of using Standard C and of avoiding implementation-dependent features. Implementation dependencies and unusual features that might have a significant impact on portability are explicitly noted.

1.10   Conclusion

Many rules are presented in this book. Many of them deal with variations on the following key concept: elegant programs are achieved through consistency and simplicity.

PART I: **The Project Cycle**

CHAPTER 2: **Program Design**

Good program design is not easy to learn or to teach. This is very unfortunate, since a good design is the key ingredient of a good program. If your design is poor, having elegant code will not help much. Good design takes time, experience, and ability, among other things. This chapter suggests just a few basic rules as a starting point.

In this chapter we use two key words: "clients" and "users." We consider the person or persons who requested the system (and who will usually be directly or indirectly paying for it) to be the client or clients. The person or persons who will be using the system we consider the user or users. We will often use plurals in both cases for simplicity, even though there actually might be only one client or user.

The users might or might not be your clients. Your clients might have requested you to write a system that they will provide to the users.

Sometimes, you will be either the client, the user, or both.

2.1   Make sure you understand the functional requirements

- Whenever possible, get functional requirements in writing.

- Functional requirements are seldom accurate, clear, or complete.

- Emulate the program verbally; whenever possible, prototype.

- If in doubt, ask; clients do not always express clearly what it is they want.

- Avoid intermediaries; try to deal directly with the clients.

- If possible and appropriate, try to interact with the users.

- Participate in the functional design; it is likely to save you work in the long run.

- If possible, write the requirements yourself and have them approved.

To do a good design, you need to understand the requirements. This is a key step, overlooked by many programmers. It is not enough to have a good idea of what the system is supposed to do. You need to know what the system has to do *exactly*.

Of course, this is not always easy to do. Sometimes, the system is simple, and just a few verbal indications are enough. More often, the system is complex, and several discussions are necessary to establish what it is supposed to do. If you are lucky (or unlucky, depending on the quality of the document) you might receive a written functional specification. Often, the clients do not express clearly what they want, and it takes several iterations to outline the functionality.

Gathering requirements is a tedious process. We all want to start with the "actual work" (analysis and coding) as soon as possible. Defining functional specs is often not your job, and you do not want to do it. However, unclear or incomplete specifications will haunt you later. If you do not understand exactly what it is that you are supposed to create, your analysis will be incomplete, your delivery dates will be inaccurate, and, eventually, you will have to do the work that you did not do in the beginning.

Go to any lengths to make sure that you understand the requirements. It will save you work in the long run. Insist on having them in writing; maybe you will get them. If possible, participate in the drafting of the functional specifications document or write the specifications up yourself and ask the responsible party to review and approve them. This way, you enhance your chances of understanding the document. Try to deal with whoever will eventually be using your system. If that is impossible, deal with a responsible party. Ask as many questions as necessary. Emulate your program verbally: ask the clients to give you sample input and, based on your understanding of the functionality, tell them exactly what output your system will provide. Be as precise as possible. Get to the point where *you* could be the system. Clear up any misinterpretations and repeat this process until you can consistently provide the clients with the desired output. Create prototypes or use preliminary versions of your program to demonstrate the functionality and to confirm that your program does what your clients want.

2.2   Try to negotiate difficult requirements away; present alternatives

- Question any requirement that seems too difficult to implement.

- The clients might be unaware of the difficulties presented by certain requirements and might be willing to accept alternatives.

Often, the functional design is made by people who do not know the technical implications of their decisions. They might choose option A because is just slightly "nicer" than option B, without realizing that option A might be tremendously more difficult to implement.

If you run into a requirement that is difficult to satisfy or that will take a significant percentage of the total work, present an alternative to the clients. You might save yourself some work and give the clients a more cost-effective solution.

Both you and the client can benefit from your participation in the functional design. You can provide the necessary technical background while making sure that no "impossible" requirements will be dumped on you. You can help the client to see the technical difficulties and the possible shortcuts.

2.3   Do not impose unreasonable limits; limit only what you need to limit

- Do not impose unnecessary limits.

- Pass on the environmental limitations as transparently as possible.

- When imposing a limit that is not dictated directly by a physical constraint, try to make the limit much higher than what is expected in normal use.

When coding a program, you might have to impose some limits. Try to impose only limits that are strictly necessary or limits that are far above what the users can reach. Always look for implementations that do not set a limit. For example, some languages implement strings as a one-byte or two-byte length followed by the text itself. This limits the length of the string to 255 or 65,535 characters. C, instead, uses null-terminated strings. While null-terminated strings suffer from the disadvantage that their length cannot be immediately determined, they have the big advantage of not imposing any limit on the string length. This latter type of implementation is to be preferred.

When you do have to impose limits, try to make them as reasonable as possible. For example, do not limit the number of lines in a text file to 100 because you have 3K available and the average line length is 30 (or worse, because the maximum length is 30). Instead, limit the size of the file to 3K. In other words, try to pass on the limitations as transparently as possible. If you have to limit something that will be placed on the heap, do not limit it in advance to 40K. Instead, accept as much data as possible and reject data when no more space is available on the heap. If you want to make sure that 50K will be left available on the heap, determine the amount of free memory first, then accept data.

It is extremely annoying to run into a limit that does not have a good reason to exist. An arbitrary limit is a nuisance to the users and often makes more work for the programmer who must enforce it.

2.4   Keep your code simple

- Do not write convoluted code.

- Do not try to demonstrate how smart you are.

- If you do something in a complicated way, make sure there is a good reason.

Writing good and clear code is a difficult art. It is usually mastered with experience, although some programmers never master it. Pay attention to your code. Do not be satisfied with code that just works. Make sure it is not unnecessarily complex. Learn as many tricks and techniques as you can, but use them only when they are called for. Do not try to pack as many tricks as possible into one statement.

Writing good and clear code can be compared to writing clear and precise prose. It is useful to have a large vocabulary and to use it effectively. But using every sophisticated word you know as often as possible to impress your audience is very bad practice.

Reread your own code often and rewrite it when necessary. Try to identify unclear or inelegant areas and improve them. Share code with other programmers. They might give you useful suggestions.

2.5   Outline your code in C

- Use top-down techniques, bottom-up techniques, or a mixture of both.

- Outline; leave details to be filled in later.

- Attack key functions early on.

- Create function prototypes but leave functions empty.

Try to get a clear picture of how the whole program will flow as soon as possible. (This is known as top-down design.) Attack the key functions, those that might have repercussions throughout the whole program, early. (This is known as bottom-up design.) Both approaches are useful and can be used together. Leave details for later.

Outline your code in C; a more generic pseudo-code is not necessary. Use function names or comments for functionality not yet delineated. Create prototypes for complicated or low-level functions and "use" them in the code without worrying yet about their implementation. While "using" them you might discover that you need to alter their functionality.

2.6   Let each function do one job well; do not force two unrelated jobs into one function

- Do not create "Swiss army knife" functions. Have several specific functions rather than one fat, multipurpose function.

- Break a complicated function into several simpler ones.

- Make sure you can explain what a function does in a few sentences; if you can't, consider restructuring your code.

- Compress two or more tasks into one function only when that substantially increases efficiency or when the tasks are very often used together.

Do not pack too much functionality into one function. Make sure that each function does one simple task and can be described in a few sentences. If you need a long explanation of what the function does (including ifs, excepts, or in this or that case), consider breaking your function into smaller and simpler functions. Simple functions are usually more efficient and easier to use. Complicated functions are great when they do exactly what you need, but they seldom do. Often, you will end up using a small part of the function's functionality and pay the price in efficiency, code size, and complexity of use.

In a few cases, packing two or more somewhat unrelated tasks into one function can be appropriate. Pack more than one task into a function when doing so greatly increases efficiency, or when those tasks are very often used together.

The Standard Library functions are excellent examples of how functionality should be packaged. Note that most of them perform a single simple task and can be fully described in a few sentences.

2.7   Hide unnecessary details from higher-level functions

- Hiding details allows underlying functions to change without affecting the rest of the program.

- Hiding details diminishes complexity at higher levels. Higher-level functions deal with a more abstracted view of the underlying reality.

Functions are the building blocks of programs. Each function should hide some details of its functioning and provide its callers a higher level of functionality. Constantly dealing with all the underlying detail makes analysis extremely difficult.

2.8   Do not hide too much from higher-level functions

- Hiding too much diminishes efficiency.

- Hiding too much limits functionality accessible at the higher level.

- Hide only when necessary and useful.

Do not always hide all the underlying detail from the users of a function. Sometimes, users of a function may need to know some of the underlying details. Hiding too much results in limited functionality.

For example, a function that reads the keyboard and returns an ASCII value corresponding to the key pressed will satisfy many requirements. However, sometimes it will be necessary to know the exact key that has been pressed (scan code on the PC) to differentiate between keys returning the same ASCII value, or it might be necessary to know whether a key has just been pressed or released. A keyboard handling module that completely hides this information from the caller is taking away functionality that should be accessible.

2.9   Do not make your code too specific; generalize

- When possible, create general rather than specific functions.

- When appropriate, depend on parameters rather than global variables.

- Consider other situations where you might need similar functionality.

- Make your functions independent of the specific application.

- Whenever reasonable, do not embed key parameters into your code; instead, put them into configuration files.

Always strive for generic rather than specific solutions. Whenever it is possible to generalize without increasing the length or complexity of the code, do so. Often, making a function more generic does not require any additional effort. Sometimes it requires less.

Consider using parameters instead of global variables if that will increase the flexibility of the function. Think about how else a function could be used. Try to avoid special cases. Handle special cases outside of functions that will be used in other contexts.

Put key system parameters in configuration files instead of hard-coding them into your code. Allow the possibility of changing the behavior of the system without recompiling.

2.10   Keep functional requirements in mind

- Make sure you provide all that was requested.

- Do not provide functionality that was not requested before discussing it with the clients.

- Do not provide any extra functionality before studying its possible consequences.

It is easy to break this obvious rule. You might get so absorbed in coding for the most difficult requirements that you might forget a few trivial ones. You might spend a lot of time working on a program to provide more general functionality or some extra feature. Or you might work hard to support a requirement just to have the client tell you that it is not what was required. Avoid all these pitfalls. Provide *all of* and (in general) *only* what was required. If you have good ideas for additional functionality, talk to the clients and make sure they want the additional functionality. If you are planning to provide functionality beyond the original requirements, make sure that you are aware of the implications. Often, additional functionality requires extra work now and in the future (extra features might require extra maintenance work).

Exercise

1. Write a short functional specification of the Standard C Library function
    strchr(). Be clear and concise, and try to cover all possible alternatives.
    Do not refer to any documentation. This function takes two parameters, a
    pointer to char (s) and a char (c). It returns a pointer to the character c
    within s, or NULL if c is not found.

Testing is part of creating a working system. However, most developers neglect this important area. Testing is often done superficially, almost as an afterthought. Developers usually want to demonstrate that their system works, not find bugs. The bugs in the system will not cease to exist because they have not been found during testing. Sooner or later they will affect the user.

Testing is a difficult art. It requires a different set of skills and a different mental attitude than analysis or programming. Not all good programmers are good testers.

Do not underestimate the importance of good testing. Incorporate testing in your project plans and dedicate attention to it.

3.1   Unit test

- Test independently those functions that can be tested by supplying test arguments.

- Test functions in small groups when individual testing is not possible. Make every possible attempt to check the functions that depend heavily on other functions by causing them to call as few other functions as possible.

- By testing each unit independently you can detect errors that would not be detected in a system-wide test. A system-wide test can check only a limited subset of all the possible combinations.

Units should be tested independently whenever possible. A complete system test exercises only a small part of all the possible conditions. Even if the system seems to work, errors in infrequently used paths might remain. These errors might then appear under unusual circumstances, and might be very difficult to detect. Unit testing makes your code more robust.

To exercise all paths of a complete system, you need to perform at least as many tests as the product of the number of paths for each unit. This is almost always impossible. To test each unit separately, you need only a number of tests equal to the sum of the number of paths for each unit. For example, in a system with ten units, each with four possible behaviors, 40 unit tests are required vs. 1,048,576 (4^{10}) system-wide tests.

To unit-test functions, create short test programs that provide the appropriate arguments and check the return value. If the function uses global variables and has significant side effects, try to approximate the correct environment. If that is not feasible, test several functions together as a small unit.

3.2   Use test scripts

- Create and maintain a list of *what* to test and *how* to test it.

- In addition to test results, provide information on *what* was tested and *how*.

- In every script, specify what input should be provided, what constitutes right behavior, and what constitutes wrong behavior.

- Test scripts allow you to be consistent in your testing.

When you test, it is very important to know *what* to test and *how* to test. When testing several releases of the same software (a very common occurrence), it is important to be consistent. The same tests (and possibly some additional ones) have to be performed over and over.

Test scripts allow you to accomplish these objectives. A test script is, in its most basic form, a list of things to test, clear instructions on how to perform every test, and specifications of what is success and what is failure.

Test scripts help you ensure that the same things will be tested in the same way. Test scripts allow you to be concrete in your test report. You can state that tests 3, 15, and 17 have been completed successfully, instead of "the release looks pretty good." Test scripts also make transfer of information easier. Developers can learn exactly what was tested, and how. New employees can learn the testing procedures and do the tests themselves, instead of relying on the local "testing guru."

A hazard of standardized testing is code that is only thought through for the standard cases. The presence of a test script should not preclude some impromptu testing for each release.

3.3   Automate testing

- Automated testing is fast and consistent.

- If you are testing functions, use a test program.

- In test programs, use `assert()` to catch errors and print a message on successful completion.

- Use a batch file (UNIX script).

- Modify the functions that obtain keyboard input to read data from a file. In that file, provide keystrokes as if a user has typed them.

- Use a keyboard emulator (software or hardware).

- Use a screen capture program.

Example:
```
int main()
{   static char s[] = "abcdefabc";
    assert(!strchr(s,'k'));
    assert(strchr(s,'a')==s);
    assert(strchr(s,'b')+1==strchr(s,'c'));
    assert(strchr(s,'f')==s+5);
    assert(strchr(s,'\0')==s+strlen(s));
    printf("\nstrchr() tested OK.");
}
```

Notes: This sample fragment tests the function `strchr()` for correctness. The first `assert()` tests a case where `strchr()` should return NULL. The next three statements test cases where the character should be found. The last `assert()` verifies that `strchr()` returns a pointer to the end of the search string when a null character is supplied.

Since you are working with a computer, use it. Let it do some of the testing for you. By automating part of the testing, you can save time and achieve higher consistency.

When testing a function, create a program to call the function with several different sets of parameters and verify the result. After you make several modifications to a library of functions, run the tests for the entire library to make sure that everything is working correctly.

To test full programs that are not too screen-oriented, use batch files (UNIX scripts). They can run your programs with the right input and then run a program to verify your output.

For screen-oriented, highly interactive programs, use a keyboard emulator program and a screen capture program. A keyboard emulator generates keystrokes that appear to the program as if they had been typed by a user. There are software and hardware keyboard emulators. Software emulators simulate the keystrokes by intercepting system software. Hardware emulators replace the keyboard and, to the program, are undistinguishable from a real user. Screen capture programs allow you to save screens or portions of screens. Some of them provide a rudimentary language to interpret the data on the screen and make decisions accordingly.

3.4   Test for special cases and extreme values

- Programs and functions fail much more frequently on extreme values and on special cases than on normal values.

- In general, at each range or domain boundary, try a value within the range or domain and a value outside the range or domain.

- Provide values to test all, or the most important, special cases.

- For real numbers, try at least a big negative value, a small negative value, minus one, zero, one, a small positive value, and a big positive value (e.g., -1.0e30, -1.0e-30, -1.0, 0.0, 1.0, 1.0e-30, 1.0e30).

- For integer values, try at least *XXX*_MIN, minus one, zero, one, and *XXX*_MAX (e.g., INT_MIN, -1, 0, 1, INT_MAX).

- For strings, try a null string (i.e., "") and a very long string.

Example:

```
/* testsqrt.c  This program tests sqrt() for
               special cases and extreme values. */

#include <assert.h>
#include <math.h>
#include <stdio.h>

int main()
{   double x;

    errno=0;
    sqrt(-1.0e30);
    assert(errno==EDOM);

    errno=0;
    sqrt(-1.0e-30);
    assert(errno==EDOM);

    errno=0;
    assert(sqrt(0.0)==0.0);
    assert(!errno);
```

```
x = sqrt(1.0e-30);
assert(0.999e-15<x);
assert(x<1.001e-15);
assert(!errno);

x = sqrt(1.0e30);
assert(0.999e15<x);
assert(x<1.001e15);
assert(!errno);

printf("\nsqrt() tested OK.");

}
```

Most programs and functions produce valid results for input that conforms to certain constraints. Input violating some of these constraints will generate invalid results. If the transformation that the program or function is modeling is not defined for a given input, a *domain* error occurs. On the other hand, if the transformation is defined, but the result cannot be represented by the program or function, a *range* error occurs. For example, when -1 is supplied to a square root function, a *domain* error occurs. When 1.0e10 is supplied to an exponential function (e^x), a *range* error occurs.

If a program or function works correctly for a few random values well within its domain, it will probably work correctly for most others too. Once the basic algorithm is correct, most of the problems are found at the boundaries and at special values. To test boundaries, provide pairs of values, one right inside the range and domain, the other outside the range or domain. Also test some special values. At the very least, try a big and a small negative number, a big and a small positive number, zero, and one.

Do not test for values for which there is no defined behavior. Test only for values for which the behavior is at least partially defined. If the behavior is totally undefined for a certain value, it is impossible to determine whether the observed behavior is correct. However, even though if a program or function cannot return a valid result for a given value, its behavior might still be defined (e.g., it might return an error code). For example, the function sqrt() should set errno to EDOM for negative arguments.

3.5   Have somebody else test your program

- The developer is usually not predisposed towards discovering bugs in his or her program.

- The developer tends to test the cases that he or she provided for, missing potential errors or nonconformance to functional specs.

- A person not involved in the creation of the program is easier to motivate towards finding bugs.

- A person not involved in the creation of the program can naively (but profitably) test areas that the developer would not have thought of.

Few people are inclined to break what they create. Finding bugs in one's system is often perceived as breaking or diminishing one's creation. Most developers do not enjoy finding bugs. When developers test their systems, they usually test with the hope of not finding any bugs.

This is not a good attitude for a tester. A person testing a system should want to find bugs. In any complex system, bugs should be assumed to exist. The tester's mission is to find bugs; anything that could uncover a bug should be recklessly pursued. Not to find bugs is failure. To be effective in this role, the tester should not be involved in the creation of the tested component. Very few developers, if any, can achieve the necessary detachment.

When choosing a person to test for you, make sure that he or she is motivated to find bugs. If possible, provide some incentive based on the number and severity of the bugs found.

Independent testing has another big advantage. A person who did not participate in the creation of the system will not be prejudiced towards testing only the areas that are considered important by the developer or the areas that are known to be implemented. Instead, he or she might discover missing features that the developer did not consider important enough or forgot about, and might test implemented functionality in a different way, discovering additional bugs.

3.6   Test for off-by-one errors

- Off-by-one bugs are very common.

- Off-by-one bugs might go unnoticed for long periods of time.

- Scrutinize conditions; make sure that a < is not used instead of a <= and vice versa.

- Scrutinize use of the ++ and -- operators; make sure that ++a is not used instead of a++, or --a instead of a--.

Wrong code:
```
char *memcpy(void *dest, const void src, int n)
{   char *d,*s;
    *d = dest;
    *s = src;
    while(0<=n--) *d++ = *s++;
}
```

Notes: This function copies one byte more than it should. --n should be used instead of n--, or < should be used instead of <=. This bug might go undetected until n is set to the size of the destination object and an important data object is allocated immediately after the destination object. This version of memcpy() will then destroy the contents of the first byte of that adjacent data object.

Off-by-one bugs occur frequently. Sometimes programmers implement the main idea of an algorithm correctly, but fail in small details. Common errors are using <= where < should be used or vice versa, placing the decrement or increment operator incorrectly (e.g., ++a instead of a++), and testing against 0 instead of 1 and vice versa.

Off-by-one bugs can go unnoticed for a long time. The effects might affect the execution of the program only when a very special case occurs.

When testing for off-by-one bugs, try extreme and special values. Verify that the program or function is doing exactly what was intended. That is, if n bytes have to be copied, verify that n bytes are indeed copied (instead of n-1 or n+1).

3.7   Make sure that your code "does nothing" successfully

■ Many programs or functions have to "do nothing" in some cases. Make sure there are no unexpected side effects.

Wrong code:
```
            char *memcpy(void *dest,
                         const void src,
                         unsigned int n)
        {  char *d,*s;
           *d = dest;
           *s = src;
           do
           {  *d++ = *s++;
           } while(--n)
        }
```

Notes: This function does not behave correctly when the number of bytes to be copied (n) is zero. In a two's complement architecture, it copies 2*INT_MAX+2 bytes.

For certain input, some code sections have to do nothing. The net result should be similar to not having executed the code at all; no errors should be reported since no error occurs. Since in most cases code is expected to do something, the special case of doing nothing is often overlooked.

Test your programs for these cases. Make sure that when nothing should be done, nothing is indeed done.

Exercises

Write short test programs to test the following functions of the Standard C
Library:

1.   `strstr()`

2.   `memmove()`

3.   `ceil()`

CHAPTER 4: **Debugging**

Debugging is a difficult art. It requires the ability to create theories that agree with the observed facts, and act upon them. Most programmers do not like debugging. They assume that their programs should work correctly the first time. They do not like to hear about bugs.

Do not try to dismiss bug reports because the effects are difficult to reproduce or because you think that the reported behavior is impossible. Keep an open mind. Remember that some bugs cause very subtle and erratic effects. The more pertinent and detailed information you gather, the easier it will be to find the bug. Use effective tools for debugging.

There are many causes of bugs. Some of the most common are: dynamic memory allocation problems, array overruns, off-by-one errors, assignment to pointers that point to the wrong address, signed/unsigned confusions, type conversion problems, and incorrect function parameters.

4.1   Think

- Try to find a possible explanation for the observed facts.

- Rule out explanations that obviously conflict with some observations.

- Do not ignore some observed bugs (especially those difficult to reproduce) hoping that they will go away with the next version.

- Do not consider bugs that "went away" to be fixed. Make sure there is a good explanation for every bug and its fix.

- Do not blame the hardware or the system software without good reason.

Tools can make debugging easier and more effective, but usually will not pinpoint the bug. Deductive reasoning is still the key component of effective debugging. Use tools and techniques to gather data. Sometimes, the data will clearly show where the bug is.

To find difficult bugs, an approach similar to that of science is required. You must first create an explanation that fits all the observed facts. Then you might need to perform additional experiments or look at more data and see if they fit your explanation. Usually once a complete explanation that fits the observed facts is found (when there is sufficient information), the bug will be easily fixed.

Discipline is also required. Do not ignore or distort some facts because they do not fit with your theory. If some facts do not agree with your explanation, find a better one. Do not choose unlikely explanations; specifically, avoid an all too common tendency to blame the hardware or the system software.

4.2   Use a good source-level software debugger

- A good source-level debugger should, at least, allow you to single step through your source code, see the contents of any data object, and set breakpoints.

- Seeing exactly what your code is doing can save you time.

- Software debuggers do not work well under some circumstances.

Many programming environments now include a source-level debugger. A good source-level debugger should allow you to see what is happening throughout the execution of your program. It should allow you to single step through your source code, examine data objects, and set breakpoints.

Some source-level debuggers might allow you to see and single-step through the generated machine-language code, see the contents of the function call stack, change the values of data objects, single-step over or into a function, etc.

A good source-level debugger can make debugging much simpler. Seeing what is happening makes it easier to find difficult bugs. It saves you from having to either guess at what your program is doing or insert many printing statements to follow the program's execution.

Software debuggers, however, have some limitations. They slow down the execution of your program, making it difficult or impossible to solve timing-related problems. Software debuggers also alter the memory map. Bugs that overwrite memory might disappear or cause different symptoms. Also, software debuggers might not fit in memory with your program or might conflict with other software in the working environment.

4.3   If necessary, use a good hardware debugger

- A hardware debugger can analyze your code without affecting it. Everything stays in the same location.

- A hardware debugger can detect exactly when a particular memory location is accessed.

- A hardware debugger usually does not slow down your code much.

- A hardware debugger allows you to do a post-mortem, that is, to analyze the system after a fatal error.

Hardware debuggers, also called In-Circuit Emulators (ICEs), usually work by replacing the CPU in the target machine by a complex system that emulates the CPU. This system is usually connected to a second computer, the host machine, which controls the emulator. Because the debugger replaces the CPU, it can control and respond to many low-level events. The environment of the target machine is virtually unaltered, a great advantage over software debuggers. ICEs usually allow real-time execution of software in the target machine, another critical advantage. Errors that disappear or change behavior with a software debugger because of memory allocation or timing dependencies can normally be reproduced while using an ICE.

ICEs also allow you to detect events such as read from, write to, or execution of a certain memory location. An ICE is particularly good for finding out what code is transferring control to a particular code segment or what code is overwriting a particular memory area. Many ICEs provide source-level capabilities, although usually more limited than those of software debuggers. Since the host machine runs independently of the target machine, ICEs allow you to examine a target machine after a fatal error.

The main drawbacks of ICEs are their cost (much higher than the cost of software debuggers) and the need for two machines.

4.4   Print debugging output to a file

- On many occasions it is not desirable to disrupt the normal screen presentation.

- By saving the debugging output, you can compare different runs.

- A user can be instructed to turn debugging on, run the program, and then give you the debugging file.

- If the system might crash, open and close the debugging file periodically to ensure that the data are written to disk. Closing the file is usually more secure than using `fflush()`.

Writing debugging information to a file is a common technique. It has several advantages over other methods of providing debugging information. First, it does not disrupt the screen. Second, it can be used in many environments where a hardware and software debugger cannot be used. Third, the debugging information can be compared to previous runs. Fourth, the debugging information can be generated at a remote location by an end user, who can then deliver the information to you. And fifth, there is no delay introduced by human screen reading.

You might need to open and close the debugging file periodically to ensure that the data are actually written to disk. Otherwise, if the system crashes, a buffer might be left unwritten to disk, or the file might be left unreadable. This is because some operating systems (e.g., MS-DOS) might write the data to disk without updating the file length until the file is closed. Keep in mind that in many systems `fflush()` does not ensure that the data will be written to disk. The Standard only guarantees that (for a given stream) "the `fflush` function causes any unwritten data for that stream to be delivered to the host environment to be written to the file." The Standard uses an almost identical sentence in the description of `fclose()`. In practice, however, `fclose()` is usually at least as likely (and probably more likely) to write the data to disk.

4.5   Use macros and functions for debugging

- Buy or create a package of debugging macros and functions.

- Use macros and functions to print the value of expressions, to print the current location, to verify that certain conditions hold, etc.

- Macros and functions make it easier to control debugging output. Debugging can be easily turned on or off (if necessary, with no recompilation) or eliminated from the code.

Instead of:
```
y *= z+bn(n,i);
fprintf(fdbg,"The value of y *= z+bn(n,i)"
            " is %lf",y);
```

Use:
```
#ifdef NDEBUG
    #define EXPR(t,q) (q)
#else
    #define EXPR(t,q)                              \
        (fprintf(fdbg,"\n%20s(%4i) %s --> " t,     \
                    __FILE__,__LINE__,#q,q))
#endif
...
EXPR("%lf",y *= z+bn(n,i));
```

Notes: The macro EXPR() in the second form can be used around almost any expression statement. (It cannot be used around expressions using the comma operator unless this operator occurs within parentheses.) When enabled, it prints the source filename, the current line number, the expression text, and the result of the expression. It is easier to use EXPR() than to add a call to fprintf() into the code as in the first form.   EXPR() is also more secure than an additional fprintf() since the expression has to be typed only once. With EXPR() there can be no doubt that the printed result corresponds to the printed expression. With the first form there is always a chance that the text in the fprintf() will be slightly different from the evaluated expression. EXPR() also ensures a consistent message and can be easily enabled, disabled, or modified.

Parentheses are not used around parameters in the macro (as Rule 15.1 suggests) because they are not necessary for any legal use of the macro.

Note that t must be a string constant; it cannot be any other expression. Because of this, the macro is not similar to a function and its name is in uppercase, following the convention suggested in Rule 15.4.

Do not add debugging statements such as `fprintf()` directly into your code. Instead, create or buy a package of debugging macros and functions and use the macros in your code. This has several advantages. First, your debugging output will be consistent. That will allow programmers from other teams to understand it and will make it easier to read. It will also make your debugging output easier to enable, disable, or modify to suit particular requirements. Second, the debugging output will be more reliable. Debugging macros can eliminate the need to repeat text, minimizing the possibility of a mistake. Third, it is easier to insert some debugging macros into your code than to insert several debugging statements to accomplish roughly the same purpose. And fourth, because of the ease of use, debugging macros and functions can provide many sophisticated capabilities. They can, for example, print the source filename, line number, and exact time for each line of output. (This allows unequivocal identification of where and when a given statement or expression was executed.)

Among other things, debugging macros and functions can print the values of expressions, function entry and exit messages, values of supplied arguments, and return values.

4.6   Intercept the dynamic memory allocation functions

■ Dynamic memory allocation bugs are among the most difficult to fix.

■ Use sentinel values on each side of the allocated block to detect overruns.

■ Keep statistics on allocated dynamic memory.

■ Make sure that free() and realloc() have a valid pointer.

■ Find total memory allocated by following an allocation chain.

Example:
```
#define NPVOID      (sizeof(void *))
#define malloc(s)  dbg_malloc(__FILE__,__LINE__,s)

#define M_VAL1 0xde
#define M_VAL2 0xad

static char *dbg_mstart=NULL;
static char *dbg_mend=(char *)&dbg_mstart;

void *dbg_malloc(char *file, int line, size_t size)
{  char *p;
   size += NPVOID+14+4;
   p = malloc(size);
   *(char **)dbg_mend = p;
   (char *)dbg_mend  = p;
   *(char **)*p =      NULL;
   sprintf(p+NPVOID,"%9s %4i",line,file);
   p[NPVOID+15] = p[size-2] = M_VAL1;
   p[NPVOID+16] = p[size-1] = M_VAL2;
   return (void *)(p+NPVOID+14+2);
}

#define malloc(size) \
        dbg_malloc(__FILE__, __LINE__, size)
```

Notes: dbg_malloc() allocates a bigger block than requested. It uses the first few bytes to store a pointer to the next allocated block. To maintain the allocation chain, it updates the two global variables: dbg_mstart and dbg_mend. (dbg_mstart points to the first allocated block, and dbg_mend points to the last allocated block.) Next, it writes the line number and filename from which the malloc() was called to the next 15 bytes. It then writes recognizable sentinel values at the beginning and end of the allocated block. Finally, it returns a pointer to the location immediately after the pointer and the initial sentinel values.

The sentinel values delimiting the memory block may allow the detection of buffer overruns. (The sentinel values at the beginning of the block serve to detect overruns of previously allocated buffers into this one.) The allocation chain can later be traversed to detect buffer overruns or to provide information on memory allocation. Inability to traverse the allocation chain to the end is also an indication of possible buffer overruns. The filename and line number relate each memory block to the source code responsible for the allocation.

Bugs related to dynamic memory allocation can be very difficult to find. A library of functions replacing `calloc()`, `malloc()`, `free()`, and `realloc()` can help. The replacement functions can perform several housekeeping and verification tasks to make the debugging process easier. They can detect overrun of an allocated buffer by surrounding the allocated block with sentinel values. They can detect pointers that do not correspond to an allocated block, or pointers whose block has been overrun. (This can be achieved by checking the sentinel values associated with the pointers passed to `free()` or `realloc()`.) They can also provide detailed information on dynamically allocated memory (total allocated memory, total allocated blocks, biggest/smallest allocated block, etc.) by tracing the allocation chain.

You can either buy such a library or create one. Several companies offer such debugging libraries. It is not, however, too difficult to create one. By using just a few simple techniques, you can provide a significant level of protection and information reporting. When allocating memory, allocate a memory block bigger than requested. Use the extra memory to write information to maintain a chain of allocated memory blocks, to identify the allocated block, and to detect overruns. When freeing or reallocating memory, check this information for correctness. Also, provide functions to traverse the memory allocation chain to provide information on dynamic memory allocation and to verify correctness. These functions can even be called on every `malloc()` or `calloc()` to verify the integrity of allocated memory.

4.7   Intercept `string.h` functions

■ The functions in `string.h` (especially the ones starting with `mem`) are frequently involved in buffer overrun bugs.

■ By intercepting them, you can compare the number of bytes to manipulate with `sizeof(destination)`, store usage statistics for later evaluation, flag unusually long buffer copies, etc.

Example:

```
#define memcpy(d,s,n)                          \
        (assert(sizeof(d)==sizeof(void *) ||   \
                (n)<=sizeof(d)),               \
        assert(sizeof(s)==sizeof(void *) ||    \
                (n)<=sizeof(s)),               \
        memcpy(d,s,n))
```

Notes: This macro verifies that `memcpy()` is not used to copy from or to a data object smaller than the number of bytes copied, unless that data object has the size of a pointer. In that case, copying is permitted, since the data object is most likely a pointer.

If a parameter of `memcpy()` is a pointer and not an array, copying should be allowed since `sizeof` provides the size of the pointer, not of the area pointed to. Otherwise, in the following example only the first of the two correct copy operations would be allowed:

```
char a[100],b[100],*p;
...
p = a;
memcpy(a,b,100);
memcpy(p,b,100);
```

Buffer overrun bugs occur frequently. A buffer overrun occurs when data are copied beyond the boundaries of a data object (for example, when 55 bytes are copied to an array of 50 characters). In most environments, this is not detected immediately. Instead, data are copied to the memory adjacent to the data object whose boundaries are overrun. If a data object is allocated in that memory, its contents will be altered. This condition will not be detected until that data object is used, and even then it might not be noticed.

Memory overrun bugs are difficult to resolve. Corruption of some data objects might cause subtle and variable effects. Changes in the program affecting memory allocation, or the use of software debuggers, might change the symptoms or make the bug disappear. Even when corruption of a particular data object has been established, finding the bug might be difficult. This is because there is no easy way of finding the line of code causing the problem. (Some of the techniques presented in this chapter, especially using a hardware debugger, might help.)

Since the functions in `string.h` are frequently used for copying and manipulating blocks of memory, they are often involved in memory overruns. By intercepting these functions to check their parameters, many potential problems can be detected early.

4.8   Print entry/exit, arguments, and return value for key and suspect functions

- Verify that correct arguments are supplied.

- Find whether a function is called unexpectedly or not called at all.

- Check return values.

- Indent function entry/exit messages to show call hierarchy.

- If possible, print the location of the function call.

Example:

```
#ifndef DEBUG_H
#define DEBUG_H

#define dbg_tvar(t)      t  dbg_ ## t

dbg_tvar(char);
dbg_tvar(int);
int dbg_level;

#define dbg_printf (printf)

#define DBG_CALL_VOID(func,param)                     \
    (  dbg_printf("\n%20s(%4i)%*s >" #func             \
                "()",__FILE__,__LINE__,                \
                dbg_level*2,""),                       \
        dbg_level++,                                   \
        (func) ## param,                               \
        dbg_level--,                                   \
        dbg_printf("\n%20s(%4i)%*s <" #func            \
                "()",__FILE__,__LINE__,                \
                dbg_level*2,""),                       \
        (void) 0                                       \
    )
```

```
#define DBG_CALL(fmt,ret,func,param)              \
    ( dbg_printf("\n%20s(%4i)%*s >" #func         \
                 "()",__FILE__,__LINE__,          \
                 dbg_level*2,""),                 \
      dbg_level++,                                 \
      dbg_ ## ret = (func) ## param,              \
      dbg_level--,                                 \
      dbg_printf("\n%20s(%4i)%*s <" #func          \
                 "() --> " fmt,__FILE__,          \
                 __LINE__,dbg_level*2,"",          \
                 dbg_ ## ret),                      \
      dbg_ ## ret                                  \
    )

#endif
```

Notes: This example shows complete code for a header that allows
            you to print a message on entry and a message on exit for any
            selected function. If the function returns a value, the exit
            message will print it.

            To use this header, follow these steps:

            1. #include the header in your code.

            2. To trace a function, add a #define.
               For example, for a function add accepting two ints
               and returning int, use:
```
#define add(a,b) \
        DBG_CALL("%i",int,add,(a,b))
```

            3. Make sure that the name of the function in its
               definition or in any declarations is surrounded by
               parentheses. For example: int (add)(a,b);

            If you want to deactivate tracing of a given function, simply
            remove or comment out the #define created in step 2. If the
            function does not return any value, use DBG_CALL_VOID
            instead of DBG_CALL and omit the first two parameters used
            in DBG_CALL.

            When tracing is activated, the macro will generate messages
            (on entry an exit) such as

```
    test( 114) >add()
    test( 114) <add() --> 23
```

Due to lack of space, we cannot describe how this code works in full detail. Instead, we will highlight the major points.

The macro `DBG_CALL()` takes four parameters: `printf()` format, return type, function name, and parameter list. It expands into a complicated expression that prints an entry message, calls the specified function, and then prints an exit message. The expression evaluates to the return value of the function. To accomplish this and to print the return value, a temporary variable is used. All your function calls will be replaced by this big expression. To avoid replacement of the function name in the function definition, you should enclose the function name in parentheses.

`dbg_printf` is `#defined` to `printf` in this example for the sake of simplicity. Replace it with a function to print debugging to any destination and in any format you like. The `#defines` for each intercepted function can be expanded to print function parameters.

It is often very useful to intercept some or all functions and print a message whenever any of them is entered or exited. It is also useful to print the values of some or all arguments supplied to certain functions and to print their return values.

This can be accomplished in two basic ways. You can replace the function call with an expression that prints an entry message, an exit message, and the return value. Or, you can print these messages from within the called function without altering the function call. The first of these methods is shown in the example. It has the advantage that the location of the function call can be identified, but the disadvantage that it might introduce substantial overhead. The second method is simpler, but it requires a modification of every function to be traced.

By intercepting key functions, you can trace the flow of your program. This allows you to find many difficult bugs. You can even add additional checking into your macros (e.g., you can examine a memory area that is being overwritten). One small change in the header and a recompilation will scatter the desired check throughout your program.

4.9   Use a lint program

- A lint program can detect many potential errors that most compilers won't.

- Lint programs detect errors before run time, making the debugging cycle faster.

- Lint programs are easy to use and require little time.

Lint programs thoroughly examine your source code and provide warnings of possible errors. A lint program can warn you of declared but unused variables, unreachable code, useless constructs such as if(...);, mismatched argument lists, dangerous type conversions, etc. Several companies provide lints of varying levels of functionality. (The functionality of a lint is not clearly specified, as opposed to the functionality of, for example, a compiler.) Some modern compilers incorporate part of the functionality normally found in lint programs.

Since a lint is used as a compiler would be, it does not require the longer debugging cycle (edit, compile, link, test) required for other debugging techniques. A lint program is easy to use and can detect difficult bugs before their effect is observed.

4.10   Use a C beautifier program

■ A C beautifier can help you catch structural problems (mismatched braces, `if ... else`, etc.) before run time.

■ A C beautifier can make it easier to read the code of somebody following different or inconsistent indentation practices.

This incorrect code:

```
for(i=0; i<n; i++);
    if(i<a[i]) return BAD_ELEM;
```

would be rearranged as

```
for(i=0; i<n; i++);
if(i<a[i]) return BAD_ELEM;
```

or

```
for(i=0; i<n; i++);
if(i<a[i])
    return BAD_ELEM;
```

Notes: The rearranged code clearly shows that the `if` is not within the `for` loop as intended. This immediately draws your attention to the semicolon after the `for`.

A C beautifier is a program that accepts source code and reformats it to conform to one of a set of standard indentation styles. It can be very useful in identifying control-flow problems masked by indentation that does not conform to the code logic. (Notice that we are not suggesting the use of a C beautifier as a tool to format your source code permanently. After running the beautifier to identify problems such as the one in the example, the rearranged source code can be discarded.)

4.11   Use a cross-reference utility

■ A cross-reference utility can help you find unexpected references to data objects or functions.

A cross-reference utility provides you with a sorted list of identifiers. It usually gives you, for each identifier, a number indicating how many times the identifier appears and the line number of every place where the identifier appears. Some implementations provide the function name of every function where a given identifier appears. Some can also differentiate locations where data objects are modified from locations where data objects are just referenced.

A cross-reference listing shows you a totally different view of your program, allowing you to detect errors that might otherwise pass unnoticed. For example, it allows you to see clearly where a global variable is accessed or modified.

4.12   Print stack contents when necessary

■ Printing the stack on function entry allows you to see the function's parameters without the need to print each of them explicitly. This is particularly useful for functions with a variable number of arguments.

■ Printing the stack helps you detect trashing and overrun of local variables.

■ Call history can be reconstructed from stack contents.

■ Stack printing can be useful to debug raise()/signal() and longjmp()/setjmp() use.

Example:
```
/***** Implementation dependent *****/
#define    STACK_OFFSET  2
#define    STACK_GROWTH  1

void  print_stack(char *stk, int n)
{  int *p;
   sprintf(stk,"Stack: ");
   for(p=(int *)&stk + STACK_OFFSET;
       n;
       p += STACK_GROWTH,n--)
     sprintf(stk+strlen(stk)," %04x",*p);
}
```

Notes: This function prints the top n int-sized elements on the stack to the character array pointed to by stk. This is a highly implementation-dependent function. It works under MS-DOS when compiled with Microsoft C 6.0, for the large model. For some other implementations, this function can be made to work by adjusting STACK_OFFSET and STACK_GROWTH. STACK_OFFSET should contain the offset between the parameter stk and the beginning of the stack *before* the call to the function (in int-sized elements). STACK_GROWTH should be 1 or -1 depending on the direction of stack growth.

This function works by obtaining the address of the parameter stk, then printing the contents of memory STACK_OFFSET ints after that location to the character array pointed to by stk. n ints are printed to stk starting at this location and proceeding in the direction indicated by STACK_GROWTH. The contents of stk can then be printed to the screen or to a file.

Most implementations of C pass parameters through the stack and store the return address in the stack. Accessing the contents of the stack is easy in most implementations, but it requires the use of highly implementation-dependent techniques. To print the stack, you need to determine whether the stack grows towards high or low memory. Then, you need to find the address of the current top of the stack. The address of the top of the stack can be obtained by creating a function that declares at least one automatic variable (automatic variables are usually stored in the stack), and taking its address. By adding or subtracting a fixed, implementation-defined quantity (to skip the information pushed on the stack to call the function), you can obtain the address of the top of the stack *before* the call to the function. You can then print the stack by traversing it as if it were a char or int array. The example illustrates how to do all this for Microsoft C 6.0 under MS-DOS. Please note that all these techniques are highly implementation-dependent and therefore non-portable.

By printing the stack on carefully chosen occasions within your program, you can determine argument values, automatic variable values, call history, etc. Deciphering these requires a little extra effort, since the stack contents will usually be printed in some unformatted manner. Integer argument values and automatic variables can usually be easily read. Other types might be difficult to read.

A sophisticated facility can be coded to print a call history with function names. This can be achieved by generating a table of function names and addresses. This table can then be used to find the names corresponding to the return addresses on the stack.

Stack printing can also be used to investigate bugs that cause a function to return to the wrong address. This can happen, for example, when an automatic array is overrun, causing a return address on the stack to be trashed.

Despite the fact that the stack contents can be difficult to interpret, printing the stack can be very useful. It is easy to do, and it can be activated or deactivated as needed. Only some of the information on the stack has to be decoded. Sometimes, even that information needs to be only partially decoded. A wrong pattern can often be easily detected.

4.13   Use `assert()`

- `assert()` can help you discover "impossible" conditions.

- `assert()` makes your code more secure.

- `assert()` makes it easier to find bugs by limiting the possible causes to search for.

- `assert()` can be easily disabled.

- Write your own `assert()` equivalent to handle special requirements.

- Since asserts can be disabled, do not put expressions that need to be evaluated because of side effects within asserts.

Example: `assert(!*p && p-s==strlen(s));`

Notes: This statement verifies that p is pointing to the end of the string s. If it isn't, the program will abort with an error message.

This rule is included here, even though it is partially treated in Rule 17.1, for the sake of completeness. For a functional description of `assert()`, see Rule 17.1.

Frequent assertions in your code make your code more robust. Debugging also becomes easier, since you can rule out many hypotheses knowing that certain conditions held when the error occurred.

CHAPTER 5: **Optimizing**

You can optimize several areas of a program or of a programming project. You can optimize speed, memory utilization, readability, and other factors. Many of these factors conflict with each other to some extent.

The first important decision is *what* to optimize. Once this decision has been made, decide *how* to optimize. To help you in making these decisions, try to estimate how large the possible gains are.

Optimize intelligently. Use tools to assist you in the process.

5.1   Make it work first, optimize later

- Do not worry too much about efficiency details in the first pass; just make the program work. Keep a loose eye on performance.

- Do try to use a reasonable algorithm from the start.

- Do analyze high-level performance issues when designing the program.

- It is usually easier to optimize when working code exists. Working code gives you a starting point and a clear definition of the problem.

- Optimizing every detail from the start makes coding more difficult. It distracts you from the real objective: working code.

The first and key objective when writing a program is to make it work. Good performance is important, but, in most cases, it comes a distant second. An inefficient program that works correctly is almost always better than an efficient program that does not work correctly. (Sometimes, however, performance is so important that an inefficient program is just unusable.)

When writing a program for the first time, do consider efficiency, but only at a high level. Look for an algorithm that will provide reasonable performance. Once you have a working system, optimize. If you worry too much about efficiency from the beginning, you might take too long to have a working system. Having a working system soon is very important. It allows you to make sure that you understand the required functionality correctly. Also, many dimensions of the programming problem are not obvious until you make a first coding pass. When you have a working system, it becomes clearer what and how to optimize.

5.2   Optimize for speed only the code that takes a significant percentage of total execution time

- Usually, most of the execution time is spent in a few small portions of the code.

- Blind optimization of all the code is not very effective and requires great effort.

- Before optimizing, estimate what the improvement in speed will be. Optimize only if it is worthwhile.

Optimize the way you optimize. Trying to improve performance for every statement in a program is foolish. The execution of most of those statements probably takes a negligible portion of total execution time. Instead, concentrate your efforts on a few key portions of your code. Usually, a small percentage of the total number of lines of code is responsible for most of the execution time. (In Rule 5.8 we recommend using a profiler.)

Before optimizing, make sure it will be worth it. Make rough estimates of the improvement in efficiency.

5.3   Optimize for memory only the data objects that take a significant percentage of total memory

- Usually, most of the memory required for data is taken by a few large arrays.

- Blind optimization of all data objects for memory is not very effective and requires great effort.

- Before optimizing, estimate what the expected improvement in size will be. Optimize only if it is worthwhile.

This rule is the data object counterpart of Rule 5.2. Trying to improve memory use for every data object in a program is foolish. Most of those data objects probably take a negligible portion of total memory. Instead, concentrate your efforts on the few big data objects. Usually, they take most of the total memory.

Before optimizing, make sure it will be worth it. Make rough estimates of the expected memory savings.

5.4   Do not repair bad code, rewrite it

- Code that caused problems in the past is likely to cause more problems in the future.

- Bad code that almost works might need endless repairs. Rewriting it will usually save you time in the long run.

Sometimes you will run into bad code that almost works. It might be somebody else's code, or it might be your own code. It might be bad because of poor analysis, shifting requirements, poor understanding of the requirements, slow evolution by fix upon fix, bad implementation, lack of time, tiredness, or any other reason. Your goal is to turn this "almost works" into plain "works."

There are at least two possible approaches. You can introduce yet another fix and hope that the ugly monster will behave. Or, you can rewrite the code.

Rewrite the code.

Fixing bad code that already has fixes upon fixes is dangerous business. At first sight it seems to be the most efficient solution because it apparently requires very little effort. Usually, however, once that first fix is made, other problems appear. New fixes are then made. Still more problems appear. After a few cycles, so much time and energy have already been spent that it becomes even more difficult to abandon the code that still does not quite work. Working code always seems to be just a little fix away.

Make a clean start. It will usually save you a lot of time and effort.

5.5   Periodically step back, look at your code, and rewrite it

- When possible, rewrite your code at least once. The first pass acquaints you with the subtleties of the problem. The second pass allows you to write good code for a problem that you now understand well.

- As a system evolves, modifications upon modifications clutter the original code. Code and data objects that once made sense become unnecessary or inefficient. A rewrite allows you to clean up the mess.

Consider the first coding pass a means for understanding the requirements and the subtleties of the problem at hand. Consider your first version of the working system as a prototype. Once you understand what to do and once you have a decent idea of how to do it, do it well.

Write your programs at least twice. Remember, coding takes a small portion of total project time. System integration, testing, and maintenance usually take much longer. A program that starts with a good design and a clean implementation often evolves (due to additional or shifting requirements) into an over-patched system. If you take the time to stop and reread your code, you will often be surprised ("Did I write that?"). While there might be excellent historical reasons to justify existing convoluted code, you should use your current knowledge to write better code. It will usually more than pay for itself by reducing maintenance time.

5.6   Do not sacrifice clarity for insignificant gains in efficiency

■ Clarity is very important. Sacrifice it only when the gains are big.

Do not get carried away when optimizing. Do not resort to programming tricks that obscure your code unless they result in a substantial gain in performance. Often, the loss of clarity is not worth the small gain in efficiency. If performance is really an issue, look for ways of improving speed or memory utilization that do not impair clarity.

5.7   Optimize by finding a better algorithm

- "Tweaking" of code without changing the underlying algorithm seldom improves performance by more than one order of magnitude.

- A better algorithm can improve performance by several orders of magnitude.

- Look for a better algorithm; often there is one.

You can improve performance in several ways. You can change the hardware on which the system runs. You can make small adjustments here and there. Or you can change the algorithm.

All of these approaches should be used when necessary. However, note that, in most cases, the improvements brought about by changing hardware or by "tweaking" code are relatively small. To improve performance 100 times would require incredible changes in hardware or amazingly lucky tuning of your code. On the other hand, improvements of 100 times or more are not uncommon when changing to a better algorithm.

When optimizing, always look for better algorithms. If performance is paramount, make sure you are using the best possible algorithm. Consult some of the many books that have been written on the particular subject, and spend some time analyzing the problem carefully (you might discover a better way of doing it).

5.8   Use an execution profiler

- A profiler can tell you exactly what portions of your code take most of the
  execution time.

An execution profiler is a tool that analyzes a program as it runs. It then provides information on where in your code the execution time is spent. An execution profiler is very useful when optimizing for speed. With it you can easily identify the key areas of your program to work on.

Execution profilers were once relatively rare. Today, they are widely available and are even included in some commercial software development packages.

PART II: **General Programming Advice**

CHAPTER 6: **Visual Organization**

Like many other modern languages, C is extremely flexible about the format of source code. A C program is a sequence of tokens, some of them separated by white space. Any combination of white space characters (space, tab, newline, comments) can be used in most cases where white space is required. There are two notable exceptions. New lines have special meaning within macro definitions and are not allowed in string literals.

You could write your program in a few very long lines, using just one space to separate tokens. This is not recommended. Instead, you should use the flexibility provided by the language to make your code clear, elegant, and pleasant to look at.

6.1   Use a consistent indentation scheme

■ Always indent the same number of characters per level.

■ Locate braces consistently.

■ Indent statements after if, else, while, for, do ... while, and switch consistently.

Instead of:
```
for(p=pstart; p<pend-1; p++)
   if(*p=='\t')
        do
        {   *q++ = ' ';
        } while(++pos%TAB);
    else {
        pos++;
        *q++ = *p;
    }
*q = 0;
```

Use:
```
for(p=pstart; p<pend-1; p++)
   if(*p=='\t')
        do
        {   *q++ = ' ';
        } while(++pos%TAB);
    else
    {   pos++;
        *q++ = *p;
    }
*q = 0;
```

Notes: In the first form, two different conventions are used in positioning braces, and the number of characters per indentation level is not constant.

There are several styles of indentation. You can place the opening brace on the same line as the statement that it belongs to, or in the following line. You can make the opening brace stand on a line by itself, or combine it with the first statement of the block. You can align the braces with the statements inside the block delimited by them, or with the statements outside the block. You can indent one, two, three, four, eight, or any number of spaces.

Most indentation styles are variations on the following three ways of positioning braces:

```
if(n<0)                 if(n<0)                 if(n<0) {
{                       {                           error(BAD_NUM);
    error(BAD_NUM);         error(BAD_NUM);         return;
    return;                 return;             }
}                       }
```

Each of these styles has its ardent supporters. We do not recommend any particular indentation style. What we do recommend is consistency. Choose one style and adhere to it strictly. Make sure you handle each case (including switch, if, else if, while, for, and do ... while) in a consistent manner. For example, in this book we:

- Indent 3 spaces.
- Indent statements inside braces; align braces with outer statements.
- Put the first statement of the block on the same line as the opening brace.
- Put a single statement following if, else, while, or for (but not do) on the same line, if possible.
- Put break on the same line as case when the case contains only one statement.
- Keep a chain of if ... else if ... on the same indentation level.

6.2   Use blank lines consistently

■ Separate each type of logical unit with a consistent number of blank lines.

■ Do not arbitrarily insert blank lines into your code.

■ Make your blank lines meaningful; do not overuse.

Instead of:
```
if(!newfield) return;

if(save_select(current))

{  if(modified(current, nfld))
   {  insert(current, newfield, nfld);
      tfields++;
   }
}

else

...
```

Use:
```
if(!newfield) return;
if(save_select(current))
{  if(modified(current, nfld))
   {  insert(current, newfield, nfld);
      tfields++;
   }
}
else
...
```

When you read a book, you expect a consistent use of blank lines. For example, paragraphs may follow each other with no separating blank line, sections may be separated by two lines, chapters may start on a new page, and titles may be separated from text by one line. When writing code, give your reader the benefit of consistent line spacing.

6.3   Do not use too much white space

- Large amounts of white space will not make your code more readable.

- White space dilutes your code. Too much white space forces the reader to look at several pages to understand a simple task.

- Some well-placed white space can be very effective; too much of it loses effect.

Instead of:
```
switch(disp-BASE_DISP)
{
    case 1:

        disp = env->width;          break;

    case 2:

        disp = -env->width+1;       break;

    case 3:

        cursor = next_field();     break;
}
```

Use:
```
switch(disp-BASE_DISP)
{   case 1:  disp = env->width;        break;
    case 2:  disp = -env->width+1;     break;
    case 3:  cursor = next_field();    break;
}
```

If you use large amounts of white space, your code might *look* more readable. This is because each page will hold less code, and therefore there will be less complexity *per page*. The total complexity of the program, however, will not be decreased. The reader will have go through more pages to understand any given part.

A similar thing applies to books. Books with much white space seem to be more readable, and, *per page*, they are. However, more effort from the reader is required to go through a certain amount of information if that information is spread out over several pages than if it is confined to a few. Most books do not have too much white space. White space is used sparingly to separate groups of related items. If you use too much white space in your programs, its effect on the reader will be greatly diminished.

6.4   Use a consistent naming convention

- Create some minimal conventions.

- Do not choose your names independently of each other; make them work together.

- Use a consistent abbreviation scheme.

- Use classical short names.

- Assign a standard meaning to some words.

Instead of:
```
char   buffer[500], mssge[80];
void   read_instance(void), SaveCurrent(void);
void   get_line(void), write_line(void);
int    index1, index2;
int    dirctry, vsble;
```

Use:
```
char   buffer[500], message[80];
void   read_instance(void), save_current(void);
void   read_line(void), write_line(void);
int    i, j;
int    drctry,vsbl;
```

Notes: Each pair of names in the first form does not follow a good convention. Pair 1: the second name is abbreviated and the first one is not, even though the difference in length is only two characters. Pair 2: an underscore is used in the first name but not in the second, and capitals are used inconsistently. Pair 3: get is used as the opposite of write. Pair 4: the names used are too long; i and j are better generic names for indexes (assuming they are temporary variables). Pair 5: the names are abbreviated inconsistently.

When creating names, some decisions have to be made repeatedly. Should you separate words with an underscore? Should you abbreviate this way or that way? What word should you use for output: "write," "print," "put," "display," or "show"? How should you identify pointers, parameters, global variables, typedefs, local variables, etc., that refer to the same object?

Create conventions to simplify this decision making and to guarantee consistency. You can use an existing convention, such as "Hungarian notation," or create your own. (Hungarian notation is a system that uses the first few characters of a name to provide some information about the named object, such as its type and scope. It is called Hungarian notation because at first sight the names seem "foreign" and because its creator, Charles Simonyi, is Hungarian.) If you create your own convention, make sure to address all of the issues mentioned above and others that appear in everyday programming. Once your notation is defined, stick to it.

Being consistent saves you time and effort. It saves you from wondering whether a name had an underscore between words or not, and how the name was abbreviated (was it msg, mssge, or msge?).

Do not try to make your convention all-encompassing. Address the issues that can be easily formalized, but leave freedom for the unexpected.

Consider the following ideas as a starting point in creating a name convention:

- Consider using some kind of Hungarian notation. That is, use the first few characters to give information about the type, scope, etc., of your identifiers.
- Assign a standard meaning to often-used words. For example: "print" for printer, "display" for screen, "put" for direct file output, and "write" for stream.
- Abbreviate by taking the first letter and up to n subsequent consonants.
- Use typical one-character names for temporary variables. For example, use i, j, and k for indexes; p and q for pointers; c for characters; s for strings; x, y, and z for floats or doubles; l for longs; and n for ints.
- Use standard pairs of words for opposite functions: put/get, write/read, show/hide, etc.
- Use lowercase for macros that behave like functions (i.e., macros that evaluate each parameter exactly once), and uppercase for macros that do not.

6.5   Use short, descriptive names

■ Long names take more space, making expressions longer and more difficult to read.

■ Nondescriptive names make expressions cryptic.

■ Longer names are not necessarily more clear.

■ Strike a balance between length and descriptiveness.

■ Use standard short names.

```
Instead of:    ptr_to_data_key
               exclude_item_chain
               number
               typp          /* pointer to type */

Use:           pkey
               exc_chain
               num or n
               ptype
```

Good names make your program more readable. A good name should be short, descriptive, and precise. It should be short because long names make everything longer.   Simple expressions become long and complicated. Operators get lost between huge names. Thinking the program through or explaining it to somebody else gets slow and cumbersome. Dereferencing becomes a nightmare
 (e.g. `data->total_money_spent[type_of_expense][year_incurred]`).
True, individually each name becomes more clear, but is it worth it? You are writing code, not a book. It is difficult to establish a clear limit for name length, but every name of more than about twelve characters should earn the right to be that long.

A name should also be descriptive. Descriptive names do not have to be long. A variable named `t`, in the proper context, is not less clear than `time_from_event`.   There is always a compromise between length and descriptiveness. When you are about to create a long name, consider shrinking it by a few characters. You might be able to do it without losing much descriptiveness.

For temporary variables, use short names with standard meanings. You can use `i`, `j`, and `k` for index variables or to control loops; `c` for a character; `s` for a string; `p` and `q` for pointers; `x`, `y`, and `z` for variable real numbers; etc.

6.6   Use a consistent convention for uppercase and lowercase

- C distinguishes between uppercase and lowercase. Use case to carry information.

- Follow either the C tradition, a "Hungarian notation" standard, or some other convention.

- Be consistent.

```
Instead of:   #define    max_entries    50
              #define    Max_Files      10
              int   PREV_REC(void);
              int   Next_Rec(void);

Use:          #define    MAX_ENTRIES    50
              #define    MAX_FILES      10
              int   prev_rec(void);
              int   next_rec(void);
```

Because C is case-sensitive, case in names is usually used to convey additional information. It is common C practice to use uppercase for #defined constants; lowercase for variables, parameters, and functions; and a capital followed by lowercase for typedefs.

Case has special meaning in most variants of "Hungarian notation," and it is usually different from common C practice. Some programmers use their own conventions for case. For example, case can be used to separate words in names (SetCursorPos instead of set_cursor_pos).

If possible, follow common C practice. However, what convention you follow is not as important as following some convention. Be consistent and make sure that the case of your names carries some meaningful message.

6.7   Use a closing brace in front of `while` for `do ... while`

- The use of the same keyword (`while`) in two different control statements (`while` and `do ... while`) is one of the bad features of C.

- Upon seeing the keyword `while`, it is not immediately obvious whether the code being controlled is before or after the `while`.

- Always enclose the statement or statements within `do ... while` with braces.

- Use `}` `while` (a closing brace, space, and the keyword `while` all in one line as if they were just one token) for all your `do ... while` loops to allow for immediate differentiation.

Instead of:
```
do
{   if(tfiles<=++nfile)
    {   assert(tfiles<MAX_FILE);
        tfiles++;
        break;
    }
}
while(*a[nfile].name);
strcpy(a[nfile].name,pname);
```

Use:
```
do
{   if(tfiles<=++nfile)
    {   assert(tfiles<MAX_FILE);
        tfiles++;
        break;
    }
} while(*a[nfile].name);
strcpy(a[nfile].name,pname);
```

Ultimately, you can always tell whether a given while is part of a do ... while or not. If there is no semicolon right after the closing parenthesis of the while, then it is not a do ... while. But if there is, it can be either an empty while or a do ... while. You will have to look for the brace matching the one just before the while (which can be on a previous page), and see if it is immediately after a do.

C should provide a different keyword for these two different flow control statements, as Pascal does (while and repeat ... until). Since C does not, use "} while" for do ... while loops as if it were a single keyword. That way, your reader can tell immediately whether the while corresponds to a do ... while or not. Use braces even to enclose a single statement.

6.8   Do not write more than one statement per line

- Writing more than one statement per line makes your code confusing.

- A statement controlled by a flow control statement (if, switch, while, for, or do ... while) is considered part of the flow control statement. Therefore, it can appear on the same line as the flow control statement.

- Write more than one statement per line only when using break immediately after a single statement in a case.

Instead of: i=0; j=k=1; z=2;

Use: i=0;
                j=k=1;
                z=2;

                or

                i=0, j=k=1, z=2;

This advice might seem unnecessary since most C programmers probably follow it unconsciously. Still, it is useful to state this rule explicitly. If you put more than one statement on one line, you are likely to confuse the reader. When you want to pack a few actions onto one line, separate them with commas and make the whole line one statement. In general, writing compact code is good, but cramming as much code per line as possible is not.

Exercise

1. Assuming you are free to change all identifiers, rewrite:

```
void  PrevRec(void)
{   short DECRM;
    char  pnext = pbfnext;
    recno--;

    if(recno<0 || task_table[ntask].trecs-1<=recno)
    {   return;
    }

    if(pbuff=='|')
    {   n_opt--;
    }

    pbfnext = pbuff--;

    do
    {
        if(--pbuff<buffer)
        {
            DECRM = min(text_pos-TextOfs,
                        sizeof(buffer)+buffer-
                        pbfnext);

            if(DECRM<=0) {

                pbuff = buffer; return;

            }

            text_pos -= DECRM;
            pbuffer  += DECRM;
            pbfnext  += DECRM;

            err_seek(text_pos);
            err_read(buffer,
                     (unsigned)min(sizeof buffer,
                        text_len+TextOfs-text_pos));
        }
    }
    while(*pbuff!='\n');
    pbuff++;
}
```

C allows you to insert comments in your code. Text between /* and */ is ignored by the compiler, and can be used to provide explanatory comments. These comments are treated as white space by the compiler; a/* text */b=2 is not equivalent to ab=2. Also, comments do not nest.

Use comments to provide helpful notes or brief explanations to your reader. For long and detailed descriptions, a separate document might be better. However, if you want to provide long descriptions with the code, put them in blocks of text instead of interspersing them in the code. It is common practice to include a block of text at the beginning of every source file and before every function, providing detailed information.

Comments should complement the code. They should not be used to mirror it or overshadow it with their length.

7.1   Comment on what is being done instead of how

- Explain clearly *what* the code is doing. *How* it is done should be clear from the code.

- Provide information in your comments that is not easily obtainable from the code.

- Comment on what is being done when documenting complicated, unusual, or misleading code.

```
Instead of:    if(*msg || err)        /* if msg is not empty   */
                   show_errmsg();      /* or err is not zero    */
                                       /* show error or message */

Use:           if(*msg || err)        /* if there is a message */
                   show_errmsg();      /* or error, show it     */
```

Notes: The first form merely repeats what is obvious from the code.

When commenting code, do not comment on what can be easily seen from the code. A comment such as /* increment a */ is totally unnecessary after the statement a++;. Do not describe *how* every step of a process is done. This is usually obvious from the code. Instead, describe *what* is being done.

Instead of: Use:

```
/* increment p */         /* next free location */
/* search for ',' */      /* find end of term */
/* if count is not zero */ /* if there are elements left */
```

Provide information that cannot easily be gathered from the code.

7.2   Try to make your code readable without the comments

- Do not rely on the comments to make your code readable.

- Write code as if there were no comments.

- Make your variable names and function names self-documenting when possible.

Instead of: `cs();   /* clear screen to restart cycle */`

Use: `clear_screen();   /* restart cycle */`

Do not use comments as an excuse to write unclear or convoluted code. Do not force the reader to read the comments to understand the code. The code should be readable without the comments. To make your code more readable, use self-explanatory variable names and function names.

Use complicated techniques only when required, and document them clearly.

7.3   Use comments consistently

- Create and follow some standards for comments.

- Keep the comment density constant. Do not over-comment or under-comment areas of your code.

- Use a consistent verb tense for comments in the code.

- Decide on whether to write as if talking to the code or to the reader. Select one style, then be consistent.

- Assume a certain degree of knowledge on the part of the reader. Comment based on that assumption. Do not mix detailed explanations for inexperienced programmers with brief notes for experienced programmers.

```
Instead of:   memset(line,0,LINE_LEN);/* clear line          */
              color = cl++;            /* to use next color   */
              row   = 25;              /* sets maximum height */
              col   = 80;              /* and maximum width   */
              dflen = 15;
              restart_screen();        /* this displays screen */

Use:          memset(line,0,LINE_LEN);/* clear line          */
              color = cl++;            /* use next color      */
              rows  = 25;              /* set maximum height  */
              cols  = 80;              /* set maximum width   */
              dflen = 15;              /* set default length  */
              restart_screen();        /* display             */
```

Several decisions must be made when writing comments: what verb tense to use, whom to address, when to comment, how much detail to provide, etc. These decisions are usually made ad hoc, without much thought. As a result, comment style varies widely even within a single source module. To achieve consistency and to simplify comment writing, decide on a particular style and stick to it.

There are several possibilities for verbs. You can describe statements as if the action will occur in the future (e.g., `/* will clear line */`), as if it is occurring now (e.g., `/* clears line */`), or as if giving orders to the code (e.g., `/* clear line */`).

Even though you are always addressing the reader, you can write your comments as if addressing the reader or the code. You can also comment every single line, every few lines, every module, etc. You can assume that a brief comment will be enough, or you can provide a detailed and lengthy explanation.

Even though comments are not part of your executable code, they are part of your program. You can make your program easier to read by being consistent in the style of your comments.

7.4   Comment unobtrusively

■ Do not disrupt the code with too many comments.

■ When possible, insert comments after the code, on the same line. Comments occupying a full line distract the reader from the code.

■ When inserting full line comments, do not interrupt a statement or separate closely related statements.

■ If long descriptions are needed, insert them in the function headings or somewhere else. Consider writing a separate document.

Instead of:

```
char *memstr(char *bf,char *s,int len)
{  char *p,*q;

   /* examine each character in bf */
   for(; len; bf++,len--)

      /* if first character of pattern
         matches a character in source */
      if(*bf==*s)
      {
         /* compare the remaining characters
            in s with bf */
         for(p=bf,q=s;
              *p==*q && len;
              p++,q++,len--)

            /* if there are no more
               characters in s, return
               position of first character */
            if(!q[1]) return bf;

         /* if a character in s does not
            match bf, go back and look again
            for a character matching the first
            character in s */
         len += p-bf;  /* reset len */
      } /* for(; len; ... ) */

   /* if there are no more characters in bf
      matching the first character in s,
      return NULL (not found) */
   return NULL;
} /* memstr() */
```

Use:

```
/* memstr(): return the position of the
             first occurrence of the string s
             within the first len bytes of
             buffer bf.

   parameters:

      bf:    Buffer to be scanned.
      s:     String to be found
      len:   Length of buffer

   First look in bf for the first occurrence of the
   first character of s. If found, compare the rest
   of the characters in s against bf.  If the end
   of s is reached, return the position where the
   first character of s was found.  If there is a
   mismatch, go back and look for the next
   occurrence in bf of the first character of s.
   If there are no more occurrences or the end
   of bf is reached, return NULL.
*/

char *memstr(char *bf,char *s,int len)
{   char *p,*q;     /* temp, to traverse bf & s */
    for(; len; bf++,len--) /* loop through bf */
       if(*bf==*s)          /*  first char found */
       {  for(p=bf,q=st;
               *p==*q && len;
               p++,q++,len--)/* loop through s */
             if(!q[1]) return bf; /* end of s */
          len += p-bf;           /* restore len */
       }
    return NULL;                 /* return not found */
}
```

Do not forget that the primary objective of a source file is to contain C code (declarations, definitions, statements, etc.). Comments should aid, not distract, the reader. Too many comments make it difficult to read the code. Do not mix too much text with the code. Use file and function headings for long descriptions or write a separate document.

When mixing text with code, try to put the comments at the end of the line of code. If that is not feasible, use a full line. Try not to break statements or groups of closely related statements. It is very annoying to read a source file where each line of code is separated from the next line of code by blank lines and comments. It is even more annoying when comments break individual statements.

7.5   Make sure every comment is useful

- Include only necessary comments.

- If a comment does not provide useful information in addition to what can easily be seen from the code, remove it.

Instead of: `i++;    /* increment i */`

Use: `i++;`

Do not try to make your code look better documented by including unnecessary comments. Sheer comment volume will not make your code more readable. Include only comments that are truly informative.

7.6   Make sure every comment is true

- An inexact comment is worse than no comment.

- Make sure that comments are updated to reflect the code.

- Make sure that everything said in a comment is absolutely true. Consider all exceptional cases.

Instead of:
```
char *strncpy(char *s1, const char *s2, size_t n)
{  char *p;
   for(p=s1; *p && 0<n; --n)   /* Copy n chars */
       *p++ = *s2++;           /*   from s2    */
   for(; 0<n; --n)             /* Write nulls  */
       *p++ = 0;
   return s1;
}
```

Use:
```
char *strncpy(char *s1, const char *s2, size_t n)
{  char *p;
   for(p=s1; *p && 0<n; --n)   /* Copy up to n  */
       *p++ = *s2++;           /*   chars from s2 */
   for(; 0<n; --n)             /* Write zero or */
       *p++ = 0;               /*   more nulls   */
   return s1;
}
```

Notes: The comments in the first form are not totally correct.
`/* copy n chars from s2 */` is false when `strlen(s2)<n`.
`/* write nulls */` is false when `n<=strlen(s2)`.

When writing comments, take extra care to be accurate. Reread each comment and make sure that it is true for all situations, including special cases. Try to think of situations where your comment will not hold true. Do not settle for a comment that is mostly right. Keep in mind that the reader of your code will be relying on your comments. A comment that is not quite correct can greatly confuse the reader.

7.7   Insert a comment after every closing brace that is far from the corresponding opening brace

- Insert a short comment indicating what the closing brace is closing. Repeat part of the statement controlling the block, or the function name if the closing brace represents the end of the function.

- Without the comment, it is difficult to tell where exactly a long compound statement ends, especially if there are many levels of nesting.

Instead of:
```
int encode(char *dest,char *src)
{  ...
   while(*src)
   {  ...
      if(strchr("aeiou",*src))
      {  ...
         ...
      }
      ...
   }
}
```

Use:
```
int encode(char *dest,char *src)
{  ...
   while(*src)
   {  ...
      if(strchr("aeiou",*src))
      {  ...
         ...
      } /* end of if(strchr...) */
      ...
   } /* end of while(*src) */
} /* end of encode() */
```

Make it easy for the reader to associate every closing brace with its matching opening brace. When the closing brace is just a few lines from the opening brace, indentation is sufficient for this purpose. However, when the closing brace is far from its matching opening brace or when there are many levels of nesting, proper indentation is not enough. To aid the reader in finding the matching opening brace, include a brief comment immediately after the closing brace. If the closing brace marks the end of a function, include the function name within the comment. If the closing brace marks the end of a block controlled by a flow control statement, include part of that controlling statement within the comment.

Exercises

1. Rewrite:
```
int prime(int n)
{ int i;    /* temp.variable */

    /* loop up to sqrt(n) */
    for(i=2; i*i<=n; i++)

        /* if n modulo i is zero, return 0 */
        if(n%i==0) return 0;

    /* if end of the loop, return 1 */
    return 1;
}
```

2. Rewrite:
```
for(i=0; i<n; i++)    /* loop through m    */
    if(0<m[i])
        a[j++] = m[i]; /* store pos.number */
    else
        b[k++] = m[i]; /* store neg.number */
```

3. Rewrite:
```
int atoi(const char *s)
{ int sign=1;                /* set sign to 1    */
  int n;
  while(isspace(*s)) s++; /* skips blanks     */
  if(*s=='-')               /* if negative      */
  { sign = -1;              /* set sign to -1   */
    s++;                    /* skip sign        */
  }
  else
     if(*s=='+') s++;       /* if + skip sign   */
  for(n=0; isdigit(*s); s++) /* for every digit */
     n = n*10 + *s-'0';     /* subtract '0' and*/
                            /* add to n*10      */
  return s*n;               /* return n*s       */
}
```

Programs consist of two major parts: data and code. C provides the capability of defining many different types of simple and complex data objects. There are four basic data types in C: char, int, float, and double. Several qualifiers can be applied to some of them: short, long, signed, unsigned, volatile, and const. Two other simple types are available: void and enumerated types. More complex data objects can be created by defining pointers to, arrays of, structures of, or unions of other types. Pointers to functions can also be used.

Data objects can have different lifetimes and degrees of visibility. They can be visible to the whole program, to the current module, to one function, or to one block. They can exist throughout the program's execution or be dynamically created and destroyed. Some data objects can exist only within a given function and are destroyed on function termination. Other data objects are created and destroyed under program control. Four storage class specifiers define the scope and lifetime of data objects: auto, register, static, and extern.

Data objects are an important part of most programs. Learn how to use each basic type, qualifier, and storage class effectively.

8.1   Make your data initializations readable

■ Present the initialization data in an organized fashion. Format the data as a table whenever possible.

■ Do not use more than one line per array element, unless unavoidable.

■ Align related values.

■ Organize data so as to make proofreading easy.

```
Instead of:    char *month[12][4] = {"Jan","Feb","Mar","Apr",
                                     "May","Jun","Jul","Aug",
                                     "Sep","Oct","Nov","Dec"};
               int ndays[12] = {31,28,31,30,31,30,31,31,30,31,
                                30,31};

Use:           char *month[12][4] = {"Jan","Feb","Mar","Apr",
                                     "May","Jun","Jul","Aug",
                                     "Sep","Oct","Nov","Dec"};
               int ndays[12] =      { 31,    28,    31,    30,
                                      31,    30,    31,    31,
                                      30,    31,    30,    31 };
```

Notes: The second form makes it easier to associate the month name with the number of days in the month.

Initialize data objects in an organized manner. If you are initializing an array, try to structure the data as a table. Keep columns aligned. This will make it easier to read the data and to discover possible errors. Try not to use more than one line per array element, since this makes it more difficult to associate elements of the same type. (Elements spanning more than one line cause data within a column to alternate among several types.)

When initializing related data objects, present the data in such a way as to make the relationship obvious. Initialize the related data objects close to each other. Use the same column positions for all of them when possible.

8.2   Do not use too many temporary variables

- Do not break calculations into several steps using temporary variables unless the calculations are extremely complicated.

- Do not use temporary variables to hold return codes when there is no more to be done within the function. Do not hesitate to use several `return` statements for each function.

- Use temporary variables when doing so could significantly increase performance.

- Use function parameters as local variables (Rule 13.2).

Instead of:
```
tmp = ++st[i][0];
st[i][tmp] = ct;
```

Use:
```
st[i][ ++st[i][0] ] = ct;
```

Temporary variables are sometimes necessary. They can simplify for the reader code that would otherwise be too complicated. They can increase speed or reduce the quantity of code. Frequently, however, temporary variables are used unnecessarily.

Do not use temporary variables to hold a return value when you can return the value directly instead. That is, whenever possible, use `return` followed by the expression to be returned instead of assigning the result of that expression to a temporary variable, then returning that temporary variable. If necessary, use several `return` statements.

Do not use temporary variables for intermediate results of expressions unless you need the intermediate results (for debugging, etc.), the complete expression is very complicated, or the intermediate result has to be used several times. Most good optimizing compilers will not reevaluate the same expression several times. There might be no speed gain realized from using a temporary variable. Still, do use temporary variables when that could increase performance significantly. It is not good practice to rely on compiler optimizations.

8.3   Keep overhead in mind for small data objects

■ Mix fixed and variable techniques.

■ For small data objects, the memory and code overhead needed for manipulation might be bigger than the data object itself.

■ Sophisticated data structures and techniques designed for large data objects can be very inefficient for small data objects.

■ You might find it more efficient or easier to manipulate small data objects differently from large data objects.

■ malloc() requires a few extra bytes per allocated object.

Instead of:
```
char *table[1000],table_text[4000];
char *ptext = table_text;
...
table[i] = ptext; /* ptext points somewhere */
                  /* within table_text[].   */
```

or:
```
char *table[1000];
table[i] = malloc(len);   /* 1 <= len <= 4 */
```

Use:
```
char table[1000][7];
```

Notes: The three forms can be used to store up to 1000 identifiers, each up to 6 characters long (plus a terminating null).

Let us assume that each pointer takes 4 bytes, that the average identifier length is 3 characters (thus, 4 characters are needed including the terminating null), and that malloc() uses 2 extra bytes per allocated memory block.

The first form then requires 8000 bytes (4000 for pointers and 4000 for data). The second form requires 10,000 bytes (4000 for pointers, 2000 for malloc() overhead, and 4000 for data). The last form uses a simpler allocation scheme and requires only 7000 bytes.

Small data objects often can and should be manipulated differently from large data objects. When each element is just one byte or a few bytes long, the overhead introduced by some data schemes is bigger than the data themselves. For example, a tree where each node contains one character will probably require 5 or 9 bytes per node (depending on whether a pointer takes 2 or 4 bytes). (Each node should contain two pointers and a character.) Only 20% or 11% of the allocated space will be used for data. If the tree is used to search for characters and to add characters that are not already present, other techniques might be more effective. The tree can be replaced by a single string. To search for a character, use `strchr()`. To add a character, append it at the end of the string. This approach would be simpler and faster, and would require less memory.

Another possibility would be to use the character directly as an index into a small array. If the character is present, the corresponding element of the array should be 1. If the character is not present, the element should be 0.

You can use many techniques with small data objects that would be impractical for big data objects. If you have to allocate many small data objects and a few big ones in an array, used a mixed fixed/variable technique. That is, use a fixed size for most elements, and a variable size for the ones with an exceptional size. For example, to allocate several thousand words, most of them of no more than 3 characters, use something like

```
typedef struct   {  char     fixed;
                     char     *pdata;
                  }  Tvelem;

typedef union    {  char     fdata[4];
                     Tvelem   v;
                  }  Tdata;

Tdata a[MAX_ELEM];
```

If the word contains up to three characters, store it in `a[i].fdata`. If the word has more than three characters, allocate it somewhere else and make `a[i].v.pdata` point to it. `a[i].v.fixed` is used as a flag to differentiate fixed-size elements from variable-size elements. It should be non-zero for fixed length and zero for variable length. Notice that `fixed` and `fdata[0]` are guaranteed by the C standard to be at the same memory location. Therefore, whenever `fdata` contains a non-empty string, `fixed` will be true (non-zero), and whenever `fdata` contains an empty string, `fixed` will be false (zero).

8.4   Use simple data objects whenever possible

- Do not over-engineer; look for simple solutions.

- Do not nest data objects too deeply. Use several separate but related arrays or structures instead of one deeply-nested data object.

Instead of:
```
#define MAX_SYM 100
#define SYM_LEN 4
typedef struct {  int    left,right;
                  char   symbol[SYM_LEN];
                  int    code;
               } Tnode;
Tnode tree[MAX_SYM];

int getcode(char *sym)
{  int cmp,i=tree[0].right;
   while(i)
   {  cmp = strcmp(sym,tree[i].symbol))
      if(!cmp) return tree[i].code;
      if(cmp<0) i = tree[i].right;
      else      i = tree[i].left;
   }
   return 0;
}
```

Use:
```
#define MAX_SYM 100
#define SYM_LEN 4
char   list[MAX_SYM*SYM_LEN];
int    code[MAX_SYM];

int  getcode(char *sym)
{  char *p;
   p = strstr(list,sym);
   return p ? code[(p-list)/4] : 0;
}
```

Notes: The goal is to store a list of 100 three-letter symbols. These
                symbols will remain relatively constant. The list will be
                repeatedly searched to obtain the numeric codes associated
                with given symbols. Decent performance is required, but high
                speed is not necessary.

                The first form uses a binary tree to accomplish this. The `tree`
                data object is overkill in this context. It takes 10 bytes per
                element, of which only 6 bytes are needed to hold the symbol
                and code. Thus, 40% of it is overhead. (This is not too bad
                since the data object is small. Only 400 bytes will be wasted.)
                However, the functions to initialize and search the tree will be
                complicated. Only the search function is shown.

                The second form uses a string to store all the symbols. They
                are stored one after another separated with commas (e.g.,
                `"ADD,SUB,MUL,DIV"`). Initializing the list and finding an
                element are much easier.

                The second form works by using `strstr()` to find the position
                of the code within the character array `list`. If the code is
                found, `getcode()` divides the position of the code relative to
                the beginning of the list by four, then uses this number as an
                index into the array `code`.

                The first form will require up to 7 comparisons, the calls to
                `strcmp()`. The second form will do a linear search. Because
                `strstr()` is usually highly optimized, the second form will not
                be much slower than the first form, if at all.

                Since speed is not of the highest importance in this case, the
                second form is better. It is much simpler.

     Complicated data structures are useful for complicated problems. Simple
problems, however, can be solved without using complicated data structures.
Resist the temptation to over-engineer. Simple data structures can often be
used to solve problems with slight or no performance degradation. Simple data
structures are easier to maintain and access. Use trees, hashing schemes,
linked lists, etc., when the performance gained by using them is worth the
additional complexity.
     Also, avoid nesting data objects too deeply. Keep related elements in
structures when there is a clear advantage to it. Otherwise create parallel
(separate but related) data objects.

8.5   Do not overuse `malloc()` and `calloc()`

- Do not `malloc` many very small memory blocks when memory is at a premium. (`malloc()` takes a few extra bytes per allocated block.)

- Do not `malloc` what can be allocated in a static data structure. Static data objects are safer than `malloc()`.

Instead of:

```
char *store_word(char *word)
{  char *p;
   p = malloc(strlen(word)+1);
   assert(p);
   strcpy(p,word);
   return p;
}
```

Use:

```
#define BUFF_SIZE 2000

static char *last_block=NULL;

char *store_word(char *word)
{  static char *p=NULL;
   static int  len=0;
   int tl;
   tl = strlen(word)+1;
   if(len<tl)
   {  len = tl+sizeof p;
      if(len<BUFFSIZE) len = BUFFSIZE;
      p = malloc(len);
      assert(p);
      *(char **)p = last_block;
      last_block = p;
      p   += sizeof p;
      len -= sizeof p;
   }
   strcpy(p,word);
   p   += tl;
   len -= tl;
}
```

Notes:

Both forms accept a pointer to a string that contains a word, copy the word to dynamically allocated memory, and then return a pointer to the copy. The average word length is about five characters, and very few words exceed 20 characters (not counting the terminating null).

The first form wastes dynamic memory by repeatedly allocating very small memory blocks. Assuming an overhead of 2 bytes per allocation, it wastes about 25% of the total memory used (i.e. 2/(2+6), 2 overhead bytes in addition to each 6 usable bytes) .

The second form allocates memory in chunks of at least 2000 bytes. The allocated memory is almost fully utilized. (The last few characters are not used if the next word does not fit exactly, and the last block is only partially used.) This form wastes approximately (2n+10(n–1)+1000) bytes on average, where n is the number of memory blocks allocated. (2 bytes per allocated block + 10 bytes of space wasted at the end of each block + 1000 bytes wasted at the end of the last block, assuming 2 byte pointers.) For 10 allocated blocks, it wastes about 5% on average.

The second form is also faster ,since it calls `malloc()` only once per 400 calls.

(In this example we assume that all memory allocated for words will be freed simultaneously. Towards this purpose, the second form keeps a pointer, `last_block`, to the last allocated block, which in turn points to the previously allocated block, and so on.)

Dynamic memory allocation is a very useful feature. Dynamically allocated data objects occupy memory only until freed. Once freed, the memory formerly used by them is available for other data objects. Dynamic allocation is ideal for medium-size or big data objects whose size or number is not known in advance. It is also ideal for big data objects that need to exist only at limited times during program execution.

In C, `malloc()` and `calloc()` are used to dynamically allocate memory. Do not abuse these functions. Dynamic memory allocation has its drawbacks. Each call to `malloc()` or `calloc()` takes some time and wastes some memory (usually 2 or 4 bytes, needed to keep a linked list of allocated blocks). Bugs related to dynamic memory allocation are very difficult to find (see Rule 4.6). Dynamically allocated memory usually will need to be freed at some point. Freeing memory properly is trickier than allocating it.

Data objects of a clearly bounded size which have to exist throughout most of the program's execution should be static. Small data objects should be dynamically allocated in groups or should be allocated in static memory to avoid overhead (see Section 19.10).

8.6 Do not rely on the internal representation of data objects

■ The internal representation of data objects is implementation-dependent. Rely on it only when there is no alternative.

■ Do not assume that pointers are the same size as short, int, or long.

■ Do not assume that low-order and high-order bytes of integer numbers are in any particular order.

■ Do not assume that sizeof(char) < sizeof(short) < sizeof(long); they might all be equal.

■ Bit fields might be allocated from left to right or from right to left.

■ Do not assume that a pointer to a function has the same size as a pointer to data.

Instead of: `offset = *(short *)(message+14);`

Use: `offset = message[14] & message[15]<<8;`

Notes: The two bytes at message[14] and message[15] contain an offset. The low-order byte is at message[14] and the high-order byte at message[15]. The first form assumes that shorts are represented by two bytes, low-order byte first (which is true for many implementations). The second form makes no such assumptions; it is more portable.

Programmers working with only one implementation of C frequently make assumptions about how data objects are represented by the language. Often these assumptions are made almost unconsciously. The C language, however, specifies very little about internal representation. The C Standard does not specify byte ordering, representation of negative numbers, bit ordering within structures with bit fields, etc. Neither does it specify the size of char, short, int, or long. The Standard guarantees only that each of them will have at least a certain minimum size and that each of them will be at least as big as the previous one on the list. The actual ranges of integer types for a specific implementation are specified in limits.h. The ranges of floating-point types are specified in float.h. Also, pointers to functions do not necessarily have the same size as pointers to data. (For example, under the Intel architecture, both sizes could depend on the memory model used.)

Whenever possible, code without making any assumptions about the internal representation of data objects. There is very seldom any need for such assumptions. Avoid assumptions even if the code is not intended to be ported. Code independent of internal representations can usually be written without much complication. If you need to convert or manipulate values often, create a set of macros.

A common situation would be writing or reading files or messages. If you want to write or send an int, explicitly break it into two or more chars. In your file or message documentation, clearly specify byte ordering, sign, etc. Do not rely on your reader's knowledge of your C implementation.

8.7   Minimize repetition of data

■ Keep each data item in only one place.

■ Minimize copying of data from one variable to another.

■ Repetition of data introduces the possibility of synchronization problems.

■ Do copy data items when performing operations that might have to be backed out or when doing so could improve performance.

■ To avoid using long dereferenced names, use #define or pointers to create short replacements.

Instead of:
```
strcpy(sfield,field[nfld].text)
row = field[nfld].row;
col = field[nfld].col;

... /* several operations on sfield, */
... /* row and col, with no need     */
... /* for back-out.                 */

field[nfld].col = col;
field[nfld].row = row;
strcpy(field[nfld].text,sfield);
```

Use:
```
#define SFIELD field[nfld].text
#define ROW    field[nfld].row
#define COL    field[nfld].col

... /* several operations on SFIELD, */
... /* ROW and COL, with no need     */
... /* for back-out.                 */
```

In any program, there are often several repeated pieces of information. That is, two or more data objects might be holding the same piece of information. (Notice that this implies that they have the same value. However, data objects holding the same value do not necessarily hold the same piece of information. For example, one can be holding the number of rows and the other, the number of columns.) This is sometimes necessary. For example, a program-wide value might be passed as a parameter to a function. Often, however, the repetition is unnecessary. One data object usually suffices for each piece of information. Do not copy it to another data object unless you will be doing modifications that you might need to back out. Particularly, do not copy values just because the original data object is complicated to access (e.g., much dereferencing has to be done). Restructure that data object, or use a macro or pointer to simplify access.

Having more than one data object holding the same information introduces the need for synchronization. Bugs can easily be introduced by forgetting to update one data object. Avoid repetition whenever possible. Repetition is useful in very few cases (e.g., when it significantly improves performance).

8.8   Use const for unmodifiable data objects

- Use const in parameter lists and declarations of variables. It allows the compiler to detect some illegal attempts at modification.

- Although it is useful, const offers only weak protection. const data objects can still be modified indirectly.

- const can protect not only pointers, but also data objects pointed to by them.

- const in parameter lists serves to inform the user of the function that certain parameters will not be modified.

- Use const to create constants of a specific type, especially for complex data objects.

Instead of: `int avg(int a[], int n);`

Use: `int avg(const int a[], int n);`

A data object declared to be const is less likely to be modified. The compiler cannot assure that a const data object will not be modified indirectly. It should, however, warn you of any direct attempt to modify a const data object. const also provides a way of specifying complex constants. Constants defined with #define will simply be replaced by a sequence of characters before processing by the compiler. Constant arrays, structures, unions, etc., cannot be created with #define. A data object with the qualifier const is a step in this direction. Remember, however, that these "constants" could still be indirectly modified.

Use const whenever appropriate. It provides you an extra level of protection. In a parameter list, it protects data passed in arrays or data referenced through a pointer. A const declaration for a parameter tells the compiler and the user of the function that the argument should not be modified.

8.9   Use volatile for objects that can be modified externally to the code

- Use volatile to inform the compiler that a data object could be modified by events independent of the normal program flow.

- Use volatile to prevent the compiler from rearranging several reads of a data object with no intervening assignment.

Instead of:
```
/***** implementation dependent: MS-C & PS/2 *****/
#define ALT_BIT 0x80
static int *key_stat;
FP_SEG(key_stat) = 0x40;
FP_OFF(key_stat) = 0x17;
...
while(*key_stat & ALT_BIT) delay();
```

Use:
```
/***** implementation dependent: MS-C & PS/2 *****/
#define ALT_BIT 0x80
static volatile int *key_stat;
FP_SEG(key_stat) = 0x40;
FP_OFF(key_stat) = 0x17;
...
while(*key_stat & ALT_BIT) delay();
```

Notes: The only difference between the two forms is that the second includes the keyword volatile. This is an implementation-dependent example. It will work when compiled with the Microsoft C 6.0 compiler and run on any PC or PS/2. The pointer key_stat is made to point to the keyboard status byte. Bit 3 of this byte is 1 when one of the Alt keys is pressed, 0 otherwise.

The intended effect of both forms is to test the status of the Alt key and wait until it is released. However, since the first form does not define key_stat as volatile, an optimizing compiler might restructure the code so as to read *key_stat only once. If the Alt key is pressed when the program is entering the loop, the program will stay in an infinite loop.

Declare as volatile any data objects that can be modified by events external to the program. If you don't, an optimizing compiler will not realize that the value might change unexpectedly. The optimizing compiler might remove or rearrange repeated references to that value when there are no intervening assignments that it can see.

8.10   Declare a data object as global only if it has to be used by more than one function. Otherwise, make it local

- Global data objects (those declared outside of functions) can be modified by more than one function. Use them only when necessary.

- Do not declare data objects as global if they will be used only within main(); declare them within main().

- Declaring data objects used in main() within main() eliminates the possibility of modification of those data objects by other functions.

- Use the keyword static for those local data objects that you want not to be allocated on the stack (implementation-dependent).

Instead of:

```
/*** Fragment with bug ***/
int i,j;
...
int prime(int n)
{   for(i=2; i*i<n; i++)
        if(n%i==0) return 0;
    return 1;
}
...
int main()
{   ...
    for(i=2; i<100; i++)
        if(prime[i]) printf("%5i",i);
    ...
    exit(0);
}
```

Use:

```
/*** Fragment with bug ***/
int prime(int n)
{   for(i=2; i*i<n; i++)
        if(n%i==0) return 0;
    return 1;
}
...
int main()
{   int i,j;
    ...
    for(i=2; i<100; i++)
        if(prime[i]) printf("%5i",i);
    ...
    exit(0);
}
```

Notes: There is a bug in this program. The function `prime()` should have declared its own variable `i`. In the first form, the global variable `i` will be used. This will cause the program to loop forever. In the second form, the compiler will detect that `i` has not been declared but is used within `prime()`. This particular bug is relatively easy for the reader to catch. Similar bugs might be much more difficult to detect. If you don't make your variables unnecessarily global, it is more likely that the compiler will catch this type of error.

Data objects declared within a function are local to that function. Data objects declared outside of functions are global. They are accessible to all functions after the declaration. Declare as global only those data objects that need to be global.

A common practice is to declare data objects to be used only in `main()` as global. Don't do this. Global data objects can be used and modified by any function. By making the data objects global, you expose them to other functions, introducing the possibility of subtle bugs.

Local variables are usually allocated on the stack. If you don't declare big data objects as `static`, you might overflow the stack. To allocate them in static memory, declare them `static` rather than making them global.

8.11   Do not use fixed-size data objects when variable size is more appropriate

- Fixed-size data objects may waste too much space; variable-size data objects can be managed easily and efficiently in C.

- Use `malloc()` or allocate data within a static buffer.

- Use variable-size data objects when a few of the data items can be much bigger than average.

Instead of:
```
char s[100][300];
...
strcpy(s[i], buffer);
```

Use:
```
char *s[100],text[15000];
char *ptext = text;
...
s[i] = ptext;     /* ptext points to somewhere  */
                  /* within text[]              */
strcpy(s[i], buffer);         /* Copy text      */
ptext += strlen(buffer)+1     /* Point to next  */
                              /* free location  */
```

Notes: Both forms allow you to store up to 100 sentences with lengths of 1 to 300 characters (averaging less than 150 characters). The first form will take 30,000 bytes; the second will take only 15,400: 100*150 bytes for the data and 100*4 for the pointers (assuming 4 bytes for pointers). The first form will only allow sentences of up to 300 characters, the second will allow sentences of several thousand characters (see Rule 2.3). This technique is described in detail in Section 19.10.

Data objects of fixed size have obvious limitations. To store a thousand strings of lengths from 0 to 99 in an array, 100,000 bytes would be required. Each element of that array would use 100 bytes regardless of the length of the stored string. If only a few of the 1000 strings were close to 99 characters long, while the average length was 19, 80,000 bytes would be wasted. The ratio of used to allocated memory can be calculated by dividing the average size by the size of the biggest element. If this ratio is small, memory utilization can be greatly improved by managing variable-size elements.

Managing variable-size elements is more complicated than managing fixed-size elements. Fortunately, C makes it relatively easy. If you want to handle an array of variable-size elements, create an array of pointers. Allocate each element using `malloc()` or some other technique, then make the corresponding pointer within the array point to the allocated element. Do not use `malloc()` for very small elements (see Rule 8.5). If the elements are small, allocate them in a buffer of your own (see Section 19.10).

8.12   Do not use variable-size data objects when fixed size is more appropriate

- Variable-size data objects usually have some overhead. If the data are not too variable in size, fixed size might be more efficient.

- The savings in space from using variable-size data objects might be too small. A simpler, fixed-size approach might be better.

- Manipulation of fixed-size data objects is usually faster and easier.

- Use fixed size when maximum size is clearly bounded and close to average.

Instead of:
```
char *months[12] = { "January",   "February",
                     "March",     "April",
                     "May",       "June",
                     "July",      "August",
                     "September","October",
                     "November", "December"};
```

Use:
```
char months[12][10] = { "January",   "February",
                        "March",     "April",
                        "May",       "June",
                        "July",      "August",
                        "September","October",
                        "November", "December" };
```

Notes: The first form uses variable-size data objects. It allocates 12 pointers which are initialized to point to 12 string constants. The second form uses fixed-size data objects. It allocates 12 arrays of 10 characters each.

Assuming 4 bytes for pointers, the first form requires 134 bytes; the second, 120. In this case variable size does not offer any advantage over fixed size.

This example allocates only a few elements, making it somewhat unimportant which of the two forms is chosen. It demonstrates, however, that is easy to be misled into thinking that variable size saves space when it does not.

Data objects of variable size are useful, but have some drawbacks. They are more difficult to manipulate than fixed-size data objects, and they usually require more overhead. Do not use variable-size data objects unthinkingly just because the data size varies. In some situations fixed size is better, even though it appears to waste some space. If the total memory used by the data is small, the space saved by using variable size might be negligible. If the average size of each element is close to the maximum size, little space will be saved by using variable size. Sometimes the memory overhead needed to handle variable-size data objects is bigger that the space wasted by using fixed size. Also, the code to handle data objects of variable size will generally take more memory and run slower than equivalent code to handle fixed-size data objects.

In some situations, the degradation in performance and the additional complexity of variable size might be unacceptable. Even though variable-size data objects provide a space advantage, fixed-size data objects are easier and faster to manipulate.

Exercises

1. Rewrite:
    ```
    char *days[7] = { "Mon","Tue","Wed","Thu","Fri",
                      "Sat","Sun" };
    int  hours_day[7] = { 8,8,4,8,8,4,0 };
    ```

2. Write a program that reads text from standard input and prints the number of times that each character appears in the text.

3. Rewrite:
    ```
    int hash(char *code)
    { int h;
      for(h=0; *code; code++) h += *code;
      /* return low order byte of h */
      /* to force to range 0..255    */
      return *(char *)&h;
    }
    ```

CHAPTER 9: **Numbers**

C supports several numeric types. There are two basic groups: integer numbers and floating-point numbers.

There are four integer types: char, short int, int, and long int (the keyword int can be omitted after short or long). Each of them has a range that is at least as wide as the range of the previous one. Each of these types has two flavors: signed and unsigned. The C Standard only guarantees a minimum range for each of them. The actual ranges for a particular implementation are defined in limits.h.

There are also three floating-point types: float, double, and long double. Each of them has a precision and range greater than or equal to the precision and range of the previous one. The C Standard only guarantees a minimum range and precision for each of these types. The actual ranges and precisions for a particular implementation are defined in float.h.

How these numbers are represented internally is implementation-dependent. Negative integers are usually represented in two's complement. Floating-point numbers are usually represented in binary, although some implementations support BCD (Binary-Coded Decimal).

9.1   Beware of overflow on integer types

■ Make sure that operations on integer types will not overflow, or that the overflow can be easily detected.

■ unsigned integer types wrap around on overflow. They obey the laws of arithmetic modulo 2^n, where n is the number of bits used for the number representation.

■ signed integer types usually wrap around on overflow.

■ Most implementations do not signal integer overflow.

■ Beware of overflow in intermediate steps of expression evaluation.

■ Bugs introduced by integer overflow are difficult to detect.

Instead of:
```
int a,b,c,d;
...
a = b*c/d;
```

Use:
```
int a,b,c,d;
...
a = (long)b*c/d;
```

Notes: The second form should be used when the result of b*c might overflow the range of int, even if the result of b*c/d doesn't. The first form will return an incorrect result when b*c overflows. The value of b*c will be wrapped into the valid range for int, then divided by d. (The second form assumes that b*c will never overflow the range of long. If it might overflow, use float or double instead.)

The second form works by explicitly converting b to long. This causes c and d to be converted to long too, before the multiplication and the division. The results of both operations are longs. The long quotient is converted to an int before being assigned to a. Explicit typecasts for c and d are unnecessary and not recommended.

Overflow of integer values is handled very differently from overflow of `float` or `double`. Overflow of an unsigned value causes the value to wrap around into the valid range. (The result of a division by zero is undefined and is not considered an overflow in this section.) For example, in a system with two-byte ints, the sequence `unsigned int x; x = 0xffff; ++x;` will cause `x` to have the value 0. The sequence `unsigned int x; x = 0xffff; x *= 3;` will cause `x` to have the value `0xfffd`.

The result of overflow of `signed` values depends on how negative values are represented by an implementation. Usually, negative values are represented in two's complement. That is, negative numbers have their high-order bit set, and their negative value is equal to the complement of their unsigned value plus one. For example, in a system with two-byte ints, the sequence `signed int x; x = 0xfff3;` will cause `x` to have the value -13. This is because the complement of `0xfff3` is `0x000c` (12).

In a two's complement system, arithmetic operators perform the exact same action on the group of bytes representing signed and unsigned values. For example, in a system with two-byte ints, the sequence `signed int x; x = -13; x *= 2;` will cause `x` to have the value -26. `x=-13` stores `0xfff3` in the two bytes representing `x`. `x*=2` is equivalent to adding `0xfff3` to `0xfff3` or shifting `0xfff3` one position to the left. The result of this operation is `0x1ffe6`. The leading one is lost, since only two bytes are used, resulting in `0xffe6`, which represents -26. Therefore overflow of a positive `signed` value results in a negative value and vice versa. For example, in a system with two-byte ints, the sequence `signed int x; x=0x7fff; x+=5;` will cause `x` to have the value -32,764 (`0x8004` or `-0x7ffc`).

Overflow of unsigned values is never considered an error, and overflow of two's complement `signed` values is usually not considered an error. Some such overflows can be very difficult to detect, especially if the overflow occurs in an intermediate calculation but the end result is not too far off from the expected value.

A strange kind of overflow can also occur at the positive end of the range of two's complement signed values. In systems with two-byte ints, `signed ints` cover the range -32,768 to 32,767. Notice that +32,768 cannot be represented as an int. The sequence `signed int x; x = -32768; x *= -1;` will cause `x` to have the value -32,768. That is, `x *= -1` will have no effect whatsoever.

Make sure that no unexpected overflows occur.

9.2   Beware of number conversions

- Conversions can occur when mixing different types in an expression (including assignments), when calling a function, or when typecasting.

- Conversions can produce unexpected results.

- To force conversions, use typecasts.

Instead of:
```
int a,b;
double x;
...
x = a/b;
```

or:
```
int a,b;
double x;
...
x = (double)(a/b);
```

Use:
```
int a,b;
double x;
...
x = (double)a/b;
```

Notes: In the first and second forms the division will be performed on two ints, giving a result of type int. The fractional part of a/b will be lost. Only then will the result be converted to double.

The third form explicitly converts a to double causing b to be converted to double. Both conversions occur before the division. The division is then performed on two doubles yielding a double, which preserves the fractional part.

Type conversions can be made implicitly or explicitly. Explicit type conversion is caused by typecasts. Implicit type conversion can occur during parameter passing or expression evaluation. When a function with an ANSI style prototype is called, the arguments supplied are converted to the specified parameter types. When an expression is evaluated, the operands of most binary operators are converted to one common type. The right operand of any assignment operator is converted to the type of the left operand. Implicit type conversions within expressions occur as the values are evaluated. If you need a conversion to occur before the evaluation order would dictate it, use an explicit typecast.

Unexpected type conversions might introduce subtle bugs. Make sure that all type conversions occur as and when desired. However, we do not recommend using too many unnecessary casts.

9.3   Beware of **signed/unsigned** confusions

■ signed/unsigned confusions are a major cause of difficult bugs.

■ signed quantities might or might not be sign-extended when promoted to bigger types.

■ Negative signed quantities might test bigger than some unsigned quantities.

■ Assignment of a negative quantity to an unsigned variable is allowed and will not be flagged as an error by the compiler.

■ Assignment of a big unsigned quantity to a signed variable is allowed, and might result in a negative value.

■ unsigned variables cannot hold negative values. This obvious fact is often overlooked.

Instead of:
```
unsigned char a[5000], *p=a;
...
while((*p++=getchar())!=EOF)
{  ...
   ...
}
```

Use:
```
signed char a[5000], *p=a;
...
while((*p++=getchar())!=EOF)
{  ...
   ...
}
```

Notes: The first form will loop forever on many implementations. This is because EOF is usually represented as a negative value: -1. Assuming that the size of char is 1 byte, the size of int is 2 bytes, negative numbers are represented in two's complement form, and we are at the end of the file, the following takes place. getchar() return a negative int: -1. This value is stored in *p as 0xff (a positive value: 255). The value of *p is then promoted to int to compare it with the int constant EOF. The two int values, 255 and -1, are compared for inequality. The result is 1 (indicating inequality), and the loop will continue forever.

The first form would still fail in some implementations even if *p had been declared as just char. This is because whether plain char is signed or unsigned is implementation dependent.

The second form works correctly. The value returned by getchar() is stored as -1 in *p and promoted to int as -1. The two int values, -1 and -1, are compared for inequality and yield 0 (false).

Incorrect usage of signed and unsigned values is a common cause of subtle bugs in C. Sign extensions and type promotions can cause very baffling behavior. Learn the type promotion rules and be careful when mixing signed and unsigned values.

When the two operands of a binary operator are of different types, one of them is usually converted to the type of the other before the operation is performed. The type converted to is usually the larger of the two types. signed values can be converted to unsigned or to a larger signed type. unsigned values can be converted to a larger signed or unsigned type. This is called type promotion.

Unsigned integer types are converted to higher integer types by adding leading bits set to zero. Signed integer types, however, can be converted to higher integer types in two ways: by adding leading bits set to zero or by adding leading bits matching the highest order bit. Either way, positive numbers are always extended by adding leading zeros. Negative numbers can be extended, depending on the implementation, with either leading zeros or leading ones. The approach that extends a value by replicating the sign bit is called sign extension.

The combination of type promotion and sign extension can cause negative numbers to compare greater than large positive values. (For example, (signed char)-1 can be "promoted" to (unsigned short)65535.)

unsigned numbers cannot hold negative values, a fact that is sometimes easy to forget. For example, a data object of type unsigned char cannot hold 256 valid characters (0...255) *and* a distinct EOF character (-1). EOF will be represented as 0xff (255). This is why most character-oriented functions in the Standard C Library use int instead of char.

9.4   Beware of rounding errors

■ `float` and `double` values are usually represented internally in binary. (Some implementations support BCD. That is, they represent numbers in decimal.)

■ Most numbers that have an exact decimal representation do not have an exact binary representation. In particular, 96% of the numbers with up to two digits after the decimal point cannot be represented exactly. Only numbers terminating in .00, .25, .50, or .75 can be represented exactly.

■ In binary, only fractions whose denominator can be simplified to a power of two can be represented exactly. For `double` x or `float` x, the expression `(x=1.0/n, x*n)` will evaluate to exactly 1.0 only if n is an integer power of two.

■ Repeatedly adding .01 to x (when x starts at 0.0) will seldom cause x to be exactly 1.0.

Instead of:
```
int quad_roots(double a, double b, double c,
               double *r1, double *r2)
{   double d;
    d = b*b-4*a*c;
    if(d<0) return E_IMAG;
    d   = sqrt(d);
    *r1 = (-b+d)/(2*a);
    *r2 = (-b-d)/(2*a);
    return 0;
}
```

Use:
```
int quad_roots(double a, double b, double c,
               double *r1, double *r2)
{   double d;
    d = b*b-4*a*c;
    if(d<0) return E_IMAG;
    d   = sqrt(d);
    if(0<b) d = -d;
    *r1 = (-b+d)/(2*a);
    *r2 = *r1 ? c/(*r1 * a) : 0.0;
    return 0;
}
```

Notes: Both forms calculate the roots of a quadratic equation.
                    However, if the magnitude of one root is much smaller than
                    the magnitude of the other, the first form might give a very
                    incorrect value for the root with the smaller magnitude. This
                    is due to the limited precision of floating-point numbers. It
                    presents a problem in this case when the difference between
                    the magnitudes of d and b is calculated. When the magnitude
                    of these two values is almost equal, the difference will lose
                    precision and might even be incorrectly calculated as zero.

                    The second form uses a method that is mathematically
                    equivalent, but that avoids calculating the difference of two
                    numbers that may be almost equal. It does so by first
                    calculating the root that is greater in magnitude, then using its
                    value to calculate the second root. (A test is included to cover
                    the case when both roots are zero.) This method gives the
                    correct result even for those cases for which the first form
                    does not.

Floating-point numbers are usually represented in binary. In binary, as in
decimal, some fractions cannot be represented with a finite number of digits.
For example, 1/3 in decimal is 0.33333... (infinite repetition of 3). The base
of the decimal system, 10, has the two factors 2 and 5, which include all of the
factors of the base of the binary system. Therefore, any number that can be
represented with a finite number of binary digits can also be represented with
a finite number of decimal digits. The converse, however, is not true. This is
because the base of the decimal system has a factor, 5, which is not a factor
of the base of the binary system. Thus not only is 1/3 not exactly representable in binary, but so is, for example, 1/10, which is 0.00011001100110011...
(infinite repetition of 0011) in binary. Most non-integers that can be
represented exactly in decimal cannot be represented exactly in binary.
    While 2*0.5 will be equal to 1, 10*0.1 will be very close but not equal to
1.0, and 4*0.1 may not be exactly equal to 2*0.2.
    Some implementations support BCD floating point. Since BCD numbers
are stored as decimal digits, they can represent exactly any number that can be
represented exactly in decimal. However, even in BCD, (1/3)*3 will not be
exactly equal to 1.0.

9.5   Do not check `floats` or `doubles` for equality

■ Because of rounding and limited precision, floats and doubles seldom hold the exact intended value. Therefore, computed float and double values seldom compare equal.

■ Check for closeness. That is, check to see if the absolute value of the difference between two numbers is small compared to their magnitude.

■ Do not compare for greater than or smaller than when two values may be very close to each other.

Instead of:
```
double x,y;
...
if(x==y) return;
```

Use:
```
#include <float.h>
...
#define EPS   (DBL_EPSILON*100)
#define EQ(x,y) (fabs((x)-(y))<=fabs((x)+(y))*EPS)
...
double x,y;
...
if(EQ(x,y)) return;
```

Notes: Since x and y will very seldom compare exactly equal, the first form will almost never cause execution of return. The second form tests whether the difference between two numbers is smaller than or equal in magnitude to their sum multiplied by a very small number. For most practical purposes, this can be interpreted as the two numbers being equal. Notice that the macro EQ() also works correctly when both numbers are zero, only one number number is zero, or the numbers have opposite sign.

Two floats or doubles that hold computed values will very rarely hold the exact same value. Even if that were the intended objective, limited precision and rounding will most likely cause the two values to be slightly different (see Rule 9.4). Instead, two floats or doubles should be considered equal when their values are very close to each other. The degree of closeness should be measured as a fraction of their absolute value. This fraction should be clearly bigger than DBL_EPSILON. (DBL_EPSILON is defined in floats.h. It is the smallest number x such that 1.0+x is not equal to 1.0.) A macro such as the one in the example should be used to test for equality. Unfortunately, this and similar macros require some extra operations (a multiplication and two function calls in this case), making the comparison slower than ==.

For similar reasons, do not compare two floats or doubles with < or > unless you are sure that their values are not too close. If the values are close enough to be considered equal, < and > may yield meaningless results. Also, do not use <= or >= with floats or doubles, since they include a test for equality. For < <= > and >= use macros such as the following:

```
#define LE(x,y)  ((x)<(y) || EQ(x,y))
#define GE(x,y)  ((y)<(x) || EQ(x,y))
#define LT(x,y)  (!GE(x,y))
#define GT(x,y)  (!LE(x,y))
```

9.6   Use the most efficient numeric type for big arrays

- Do not use numeric types with bigger range or higher precision than necessary in big arrays.

- When choosing the most efficient numeric type, consider portability. Ranges and precision of numeric types can vary from implementation to implementation.

- Make sure that the chosen type will support all cases where it is used.

- For big arrays, use float instead of double, short or long instead of float, short instead of long, and char instead of short when possible.

- For separate integers and small arrays of integers, use int; int is usually the type naturally supported by the machine.

```
Instead of:    #define MAX_NUM           50000
               #define MAX_PRIMES          100
               #define MAX_FACTORS         100

               int     prime[MAX_PRIMES];
               int     factor_table[MAX_NUM][MAX_FACTORS];
               int     power_table[MAX_NUM][MAX_FACTORS];

Use:           #define MAX_NUM           50000
               #define MAX_PRIMES          100
               #define MAX_FACTORS         100

               unsigned char   prime[MAX_PRIMES];
               unsigned char   factor_table[MAX_NUM][MAX_FACTORS];
               unsigned char   power_table[MAX_NUM][MAX_FACTORS];
```

Notes: The arrays prime, factor_table, and power_table are used
                    to factor the numbers from 1 to 50,000. prime will hold all
                    necessary primes to factor these numbers. factor_table will
                    hold the prime numbers that are factors of a given number,
                    and power_table will hold the powers of those primes. (The
                    end of the list of factors for a given number n will be
                    represented by zero in both factor_table[n][i] and
                    power_table[n][i]. A prime number n will be represented
                    by a zero in both factor_table[n][0] and
                    power_table[n][0].)

                    unsigned char is used for the three arrays because no prime
                    or power bigger than 256 will be required.

Extra range and precision cost you in memory and speed. When you need
to store or process large quantities of numbers, make sure you are using the
most appropriate type. Integer types can frequently be used instead of float
or double for fixed point operations (e.g., dollar amounts can be stored as a
number of cents in an int or long). Also, larger types can often be replaced
by smaller, similar types (e.g., char instead of short).

There is at least one exception to the principle that smaller is better for
large arrays. In many implementations, operations on ints are faster and
more compact than operations on shorts or chars. If speed is essential, ints
might be the best choice.

When choosing an appropriate type, keep portability in mind. ints might
be four bytes long in your implementation, but only two bytes long in other
implementations. Use the macros in floats.h and limits.h to determine
the range and precision of numeric types, or rely on the minimum guaranteed
values. The C Standard guarantees the following minimum ranges and
precision for numeric types:

```
signed char        -127..127
signed short       -32767..32767
signed int         -32767..32767
signed long        -2147483647..2147483647
unsigned char      0..255
unsigned short     0..65535
unsigned int       0..65535
unsigned long      0..4294967295
float              -1e37..-1e-37, 1e-37..1e37 (6 digits)
double             -1e37..-1e-37, 1e-37..1e37 (10 digits)
```

Do not assume that int is bigger than short, long bigger than int, or
double bigger than float.

Exercises

1. Rewrite:

```
/* binomial(): calculate binomial coefficients
       for n<13 and any k.
*/

int binomial(int n,int k)
{   int a,b;
    if(k<0 || n<k) return 0;
    for(a=1,b=1; 0<k; n--,k--)
       a*=n,b*=k;
    return a/b;
}
```

2. Rewrite:

```
/* same_frac(): return true if the fraction
    represented by the numerator n1 and the
    denominator d1 is equivalent to the
    fraction represented by the numerator n2
    and the denominator d2.
*/

int same_frac(int n1,int d1,int n2,int d2)
{   return n1/d1==n2/d2;
}
```

3. Rewrite:

```
unsigned long t;
int i;

...
if(i<t) return;
```

CHAPTER 10

Input and Output

Most programs accept input, process it, and produce output. It is natural to concentrate most of the programming efforts on the middle part: processing. However, input and output are also very important. Do not neglect them. The user's perception of a program is very often shaped more by how the program handles its input and by how it presents the output than by the actual processing.

Many of the rules presented in this chapter assume that you have some control over the functional design. This is often true for small programs. In bigger projects, somebody else might dictate the functional design. If you do have any influence over the functional design, apply the rules presented here.

10.1   Test for incorrect input

- If there is an error in the input, provide an error message and attempt to recover.

- If possible, try to continue reading the input after an error. This will allow the user to discover several errors in one pass.

Instead of:

```
void value(void)
{  if(c=='(')
   {  c = getchar();   /* skip '('    */
      expression();    /* parse expr. */
      c = getchar();   /* skip ')'    */
   }
   else
   ...
}
```

Use:

```
void value(void)
{  if(c=='(')
   {  c = getchar();                /* skip '('    */
      expression();                 /* parse expr. */
      if(c==')') c = getchar(); /* skip ')'    */
      else       error(E_PAREN);
   }
   else
   ...
}
```

Notes:
The function value() is part of a program for parsing expressions. The program always maintains in c the next character to be processed. The fragment presented here attempts to parse an expression if the next character is an opening parenthesis.

The first form assumes that there is a closing parenthesis. The second form displays an error if the closing parenthesis is missing and attempts to continue parsing.

Test your input. If there are any errors, try to report them as accurately as possible. If you can recover and continue processing, do so. This will allow you to detect additional errors in one pass. Do not, however, let the errors pass unreported. Small syntactic errors, even if easily corrected by your program, might be symptoms of more serious errors. That is one of the reasons why compilers report missing semicolons and closing parentheses even when they could supply them.

10.2   Provide clear and correct error messages

■ Make sure your error messages are understandable.

■ Make sure your error messages are correct.

Instead of:
```
if(fin=fopen(fname,"r"))
    error("File %s not found",fname);
```

Use:
```
if(fin=fopen(fname,"r"))
    error("Can't open file %s",fname);
```

Notes: The function `fopen()` could fail for reasons other than file not found. The message of the first form is incorrect in those cases.

Don't be lazy when creating error messages. Error messages are usually not displayed very often. When displayed, however, they become very important. An unclear or incorrect message might antagonize users or send them searching in the wrong direction. Make sure that the error message is clear and provides as much information as might be applicable to the situation.

Take special care to avoid incorrect messages. This is much more difficult than it at first appears. There could be situations other than the anticipated ones for which the error message, correct for most situations, will be plainly incorrect. Try to report errors as accurately as possible, without trying to predict possible causes, unless the prediction is stated as such. Be particularly careful with error conditions that might have many different causes.

10.3   Make sure no input can break your program

- No input should produce unexpected behavior of your program.

- Make sure either that no input will overflow your buffers or that a buffer overflow will be detected and reported.

- Try to anticipate possible problems with the input and report them.

Instead of:
```
char s[MAXS];
...
gets(s);
```

Use:
```
#define     GETS(s)                    \
    ( s[sizeof(s)-1]=0, gets(s),       \
      (s[sizeof(s)-1] &&               \
         stop("line too long: ",s)),\
      s                                \
    )

char s[MAXS];
...
GETS(s);
```

Notes: The input might be longer than the array s. The first form does not test for this case. The input would be written into the memory immediately after s, overwriting whatever was stored there. The program would then behave unpredictably depending on what was destroyed. The second form aborts when the input is longer than the array s. It operates by storing a null character at the last position of s, and verifying that it is still there after the call to gets(). When the input is too long, this null character will be overwritten by some other character different from null. In that case an error message is printed and the program is terminated. No recovery is possible.

Parentheses are not used around s in the macro because the macro is designed to work only with array names.

The input to your program will not always be correct. Your program might be fed numbers that are too big or too small, sentences that are too long, values in incorrect sequence, plain garbage, or other types of incorrect input. Code defensively. Avoid misbehavior on incorrect input. Do not depend unnecessarily on input patterns. If you are expecting a number, make sure that you can also handle non-numeric text. If you expect a sequence of words (sequences of characters separated by white space), be ready to receive a 10,000-character word.

When possible, provide a clear error message. If providing a clear error message is too troublesome, use `assert()` or an equivalent to flag the error. The key thing is to inform the user that something went wrong. The program should not attempt to process input that it cannot handle.

10.4   Use consistent input and output formats

- Develop a convention for input and output and use it whenever possible.

- When possible, format your input and output so that one of your programs could accept as input the output produced by another.

When possible, require input and present output in a consistent format (consistent with each other and with other programs). This makes it easier for the user to learn to use a new program. It also reduces the possibility of user errors. By making the output of one program acceptable as the input to another, you make both programs more useful. The programs can then be combined to suit user needs. Programs that can operate in this fashion are called "filter programs" and are very popular in the UNIX community.

10.5   Accept order-independent, self-identifying input

- Do not impose unnecessary order requirements on the input.

- Accept input that identifies itself, regardless of position. This can be achieved by using short tags for each piece of data, by recognizing data by their patterns, and by other means.

- It is easier to discover errors and recover when reading order-independent, self-identifying input.

It is sometimes convenient to depend on a particular input order. Order dependence eliminates the need for data-identifying tags. Dependence on order is, however, very dangerous. A missing element can cause misinterpretation of all the remaining elements. If you depend on order to identify the input and output files, a shift or reversal of elements will have disastrous consequences. Order dependence is relatively safe when very few elements are required, or when they are all of the same type and have roughly the same function. In all other cases, order dependence is dangerous.

Whenever possible, do not rely on order. If tags for the data can be provided without adding too much overhead, use them. Also, it is often possible to recognize data by their patterns. For example, a compiler (with no linker) running under MS-DOS can safely assume that a name with extension ".c" is the input file and a name with extension ".obj" is the output file. A program that creates a cross-reference for words in a text can assume that a name with extension ".crf" specifies the output file. Using explicit tags or recognition by patterns increases the likelihood of detecting errors in input data.

10.6   Provide clear, self-explanatory, easy to look at output

- Present output so that it can be understood without additional explanations.

- Format output neatly. Use a tabular format when appropriate.

- Sort output when appropriate.

- Avoid mixing different types of data in the same column. That is, avoid rows that take more than one line.

- Do not provide unnecessary data.

- Do not provide unnecessary precision.

Instead of:
```
Binomial Coefficients:
1
1 1
1 2 1
1 3 3 1
1 4 6 4 1
1 5 10 10 5 1
1 6 15 20 15 6 1
1 7 21 35 35 21 7 1
```

Use:
```
Binomial coefficients ( n )
                      ( m )

n  m -> 0    1    2    3    4    5    6    7
0       1
1       1    1
2       1    2    1
3       1    3    3    1
4       1    4    6    4    1
5       1    5    10   10   5    1
6       1    6    15   20   15   6    1
7       1    7    21   35   35   21   7    1
```

Make your output as readable as possible. Provide brief descriptions if they add to the readability. Do not force the reader to read a separate document to understand the output when a little extra information on the spot would suffice.

Organize the information in a logical fashion. Use a table or any other device to add structure to the data. Data are easier to read and errors are easier to detect in well-organized output.

Do not drown the user with unnecessary detail. In particular, avoid unnecessary precision. In most cases, the user does not care whether the exact value is 15.735234% or 15.735237%. Usually 15.74% will do. Numbers displayed with excessive precision are harder to read. Also, the original data might not be precise enough to discriminate at the sixth decimal place.

10.7   When portability is essential, write only chars to a file

- char is the most stable type across platforms; most systems use the same internal representation (ASCII).

- All other types (short, int, long, float, double, struct, union, array, etc.) are more implementation-dependent. The system reading the file might have a different internal representation.

- Convert any type other than char either to human-readable text or to some other character-based representation.

- Write types other than char to a file only when the file will always be written to by the same system.

- If the file will be read in many different environments, either write only chars or clearly document the internal format of the other types used.

- Do write non-chars to a file if the file will always be written and read under the same environment.

Instead of: int x;
                 ...
                 fwrite(x,sizeof(int),1,fout);

Use: int x;
                 ...
                 putc(x & 0xff,fout);
                 putc(x>>8 & 0xff,fout);

Notes: Assuming that x is used to represent a value in the range -32,768 to 32,767, the second form will always write x in the same format, even under different implementations.

Standard C does not specify any particular internal format for data objects. Implementors of the C language are free to choose from many different internal formats. In most situations, the programmer need not worry about the internal representation of data objects. Writing to and reading from files are notable exceptions.

A data object is written to a file by writing the group of bytes holding its value. When this group of bytes is read back into a data object of the same type under the same implementation, the resulting value is the same as the value written to the file. If, however, this group of bytes is read into a data object of the same type under a different implementation, the resulting value might be different. The effect is equivalent to that of copying (`memcpy()`) the group of bytes representing the data object written to the data object read into. The same group of bytes can be interpreted differently by different implementations.

`chars` can also have different internal representations. However, most computers today use one of two standards for character representation: ASCII or EBCDIC. ASCII is used by most micros and minis, while EBCDIC is used by many mainframes. Most programs are not ported across these boundaries (micro to mainframe and vice versa). For most situations, you can assume that `chars` are internally represented in the same way.

If you are sure that a given file will be written and read under only one implementation, you can write any type of data objects directly to it. If the file may be written under one implementation and read under a different implementation, convert all data objects to `char` before writing and after reading. Values can be converted to human-readable text or to some internal code. If a file will be written under only one implementation but can be read under several implementations, a possible, but not recommended, alternative is to write non-`char` data objects directly to the file. In that case, clearly document their internal representation.

Exercises

1. Rewrite:
```
#define MAX_LEN   100
int nwords,wc[MAX_LEN];
...
void count_len(void)
{  int len;
   nwords = 0;
   do
   {  while(!isalpha(c=getchar()))
         if(c==EOF) return;
      nwords++;
      for(len = 0; isalpha(c=getchar()); len++);
      wc[len]++;
   } while(c!=EOF);
   return;
}
```

2. Rewrite:
```
int mdays[12] = { 31,29,31,30,31,30,
                  31,31,30,31,30,31 };
void check_date(int y, int m, int d)
{  if(y<0 || 99<y)        error("Bad year");
   if(m<1 || 12<m)        error("Bad month");
   if(d<0 || mdays[m]<d)  error("Bad day");
   if(m==2 && d==29 &&
      (y%4 || (y%100==0 && y%400)))
      error("Bad day");
}
```

3. Rewrite:
```
int n=0,s=1;
...
c = getchar();
if(c=='-')
{  s=-1;
   c = getchar();
}
while(isdigit(c))
{  n = n*10 + c-'0';
   c = getchar();
}
n *= s;
```

PART III: **C Usage**

C provides two types of statements: flow control statements and expression statements. An expression statement is simply an expression followed by a semicolon. Flow control statements transfer control to different parts of the program; they are treated in Chapter 12. Expression statements do the "actual work."

Most of C's fame as a difficult and somewhat arcane language is due to C's large set of operators. C allows programmers to express complicated operations in a clear and concise notation. Most experienced C programmers take advantage of C's expressive power. C expressions may seem cryptic at first, but once mastered they are fairly readable. This can be compared to mathematical notation. For the uninitiated, a complicated mathematical equation is a formidable puzzle. For the mathematician, however, the equation is easier to read than plain text. The concept that takes a few lines of clear and concise mathematical notation may take several pages of nearly unintelligible text.

Master the notation.

C experts do not create complicated expressions for the fun of it. Frequently the expression is complicated because the problem is complicated. Using terse expressions usually simplifies the code, reduces the probability of error, and makes maintenance easier. Do not create unnecessarily complicated expressions.

11.1   Do not use too many unnecessary parentheses

- Each operator has a level of precedence.

- There are a total of fifteen levels of precedence that, to a considerable extent, minimize the use of parentheses.

- The order of precedence can be summarized as follows (from higher to lower):   dereferencing and function call, unary, math, shift, relational, bitwise, logical, ?:, assignment, and comma.

- Operators at the same level of precedence have a well-defined direction of association. All unary operators, all assignment operators, and ?: associate from right to left; all others associate from left to right.

- Use parentheses when you want an "unnatural" order of evaluation.

- Emphasize order of evaluation with spaces.

- Use parentheses that are not strictly necessary only when there is great potential for confusion.

Instead of: `if( (0<x) && (0<y) ) return;`

Use: `if(0<x && 0<y) return;`

Notes: Since && has a lower precedence than <, parentheses are not needed around 0<x and 0<y.

Many programmers feel that using parentheses to emphasize precedence makes programs more readable. We think, however, that using too many unnecessary parentheses is bad style (when writing code for an audience of experienced C programmers). Use a few extra parentheses in complicated expressions only if you feel that they will increase clarity.

Many programmers use many unnecessary parentheses in C expressions for two basic reasons:

1. The programmer does not know or is unsure about the order of evaluation.

2. The programmer thinks that the reader might not know or might be unsure about the order of evaluation.

The first reason is no excuse. You should either learn the precedence level of all operators or have a table handy. Consult the operator precedence table as often as necessary in the same way that you routinely consult the documentation for the Standard C Library. Keep the precedence table in a visible place, unless you have fast electronic access to it. A copy of this table is included in Appendix B.

It is easy to dispose of the second reason as well. A C programmer should know the precedence level of most operators, and you are writing code for C programmers. In math, we write ax^2+by+c instead of $(a(x^2))+(by)+c$. This allows for clear and concise expression. We do not write 2+(3*4) instead of 2+3*4 to make it more clear for the reader. If the readers do not know that multiplication is performed before addition, they should not be reading anyway.

True, there are fifteen levels of precedence in C, and that makes things difficult. But in most expressions fewer levels are involved. The order of precedence is easy to remember if you consider ten basic levels (instead of fifteen). These levels (from higher to lower) are dereferencing and function call, unary, math, shift, relational, bitwise, logical, ?:, assignment, and comma. Also remember that ?: and all unary and assignment operators associate from right to left. The rest of the operators associate from left to right. These ten levels are easy to remember because they are arranged in a logical order (except bitwise operators). Note that not all the operators in each of these groups have the same precedence. For example, + is lower than *, and || is lower than &&. However, these precedence relationships are obvious and relatively easy to remember.

Not everybody has memorized the precedence levels of all operators. Even though in most cases precedence is obvious, sometimes it's not. Use extra parentheses sparingly to indicate precedence when you feel that there can be some confusion.

The first reaction of an experienced C programmer upon seeing an expression using unnecessary parentheses is to assume that those parentheses are actually needed. The programmer therefore assumes that some "unnatural" order of evaluation is intended and tries to figure out what those parentheses are used for. This leads to confusion. Is (ab)+(cd) more clear to you than ab+cd?

It is not a bad idea to emphasize the order of evaluation, and white space is the ideal tool for this purpose. Write a*b < c*d+e to emphasize that the comparison will be evaluated after the multiplications and the addition.

11.2   Use the values of relational and logical expressions

- Relational and logical expressions are just a class of expressions. They can be used wherever any other expressions can be used. There is no reason to limit their use to if, while, for, and do ... while.

- Relational and logical expressions evaluate to 0 for false and to 1 for true.

Instead of:

```
if(0<x) return 1;
else    return 0;
```

Use:

```
return 0<x;
```

Notes: The expression 0<x will evaluate to one if x is greater than zero, and to zero if x is less than or equal to zero.

Instead of:

```
if(*p && MAX_COUNT<count) too_long = TRUE;
else                      too_long = FALSE;
```

use:

```
too_long = *p && MAX_COUNT<count;
```

Notes: The flag too_long will be set to one if the pointer p is pointing to a non-zero element and count is greater than MAX_COUNT. The flag will be reset to zero otherwise.

Some programmers think that relational and logical expressions are a special class of expressions that can be used only within if, while, for, and do ... while statements. This is not so. A relational or logical expression is just an ordinary expression using ordinary operators. In fact, there is nothing in C that is formally defined as a relational or logical expression. These terms are used informally to refer to expressions using any of the operators ! < <= > >= == != && and | |. These operators return the int values 0 for false and 1 for true.

C has no boolean or logical type like some other languages. Logical and relational operators can be freely intermixed with any other operators (+, *, etc.). It is valid to write 8 + 4*(0<x) as a substitute for 0<x ? 12 : 8. If x is greater than zero, 8 + 4*(0<x) will be equivalent to 8 + 4*1, and if x is less than or equal to zero, it will be equivalent to 8 + 4*0.

Some programmers prefer to consider relational and logical expressions to be different from numerical expressions. They avoid mixing them. This point of view is typical of programmers who are used to strongly typed languages like Pascal. On the other hand, Assembler programmers frequently mix numerical and relational operations. For them, there is no essential difference between one and the other. The differentiation between numerical and relational or logical expressions in C is artificial. Whenever doing so is useful, treat results of relational or logical operators as numbers.

11.3   Use a instead of a!=0, a!=NULL, or a==TRUE; use !a instead of a==0, a==NULL, or a==FALSE

- In any context where a true/false value is required, zero is false and non-zero is true.

- In any context where a true/false value is required, a is equivalent to a!=0 and to a!=NULL. Both are true only when a is non-zero.

- Similarly, !a is equivalent to a==0, a==NULL, and a==FALSE. All of them are true only when a is zero.

- When a can only take a value of 0 or 1, a and a==TRUE are equivalent. Both are true only when a is true (1).

- Read statements like if(p) as "if p is not zero then" and statements like if(!p) as "if p is zero then."

- Use forms like a!=0 only when a value of 0 or 1 must be generated, as opposed to just true/false. Note that if a is 99, then a!=0 yields 1. Both are true, but they are not equivalent in a context where the numerical value is relevant.

- Do not use forms like !a when doing so requires an additional set of parentheses around a.

- The constant TRUE is usually defined as 1. Therefore, a==TRUE will evaluate to false if a is true (non-zero) but different from 1.

Instead of: `for(p=buffer; *p!='\0'; p++);`

Use: `for(p=buffer; *p; p++);`

Notes: Both expressions should be read "set p to buffer and increment p while the element pointed to by p is not zero." The second form eliminates six unnecessary characters, making the statement shorter and easier to read.

C differs from some other programming languages in that it does not have a logical or boolean type. Any expression can be used where a truth or falsehood is being evaluated. A non-zero value will be interpreted as true, and a zero value will be interpreted as false.

It is redundant to use a!=0 or similar forms instead of just a. Some programmers feel that by explicitly comparing against zero, the statement is made more clear. They argue that, for example, if(*p!=0) is more clear than if(*p). While it may be more clear for inexperienced readers, experienced programmers are used to the second form and might consider the first form to be unnecessarily long. To minimize confusion, read statements like if(x) as "if x is non-zero then" instead of "if x is true then." When a can take only the values 0 or 1, a==TRUE is equivalent to just a, but is longer and redundant.

Keep in mind, however, that a and a!=0 are equivalent only when a true/false result is required. For values of a different from 0 or 1, both expressions are true but have different numerical values. To generate a value of 0 or 1, use a!=0. Also keep in mind that TRUE and FALSE are usually #defined to 1 and 0, respectively. Therefore, a==TRUE yields false for any value of a different from 1, including values that are considered true (non-zero).

Use !a instead of a==0, a==NULL, or a==FALSE unless doing so requires an additional set of parentheses. The last three expressions yield false when a is true (non-zero) and true when a is false (zero); this is exactly what !a does. !a is exactly equivalent to a==0, a==NULL, and a==FALSE.

11.4   Use the values of assignment expressions

■ There is no assignment statement in C. Assignments are expressions.

■ There are eleven assignment operators. They are =   +=   −=   *=   /=
 %=   >>=   <<=   &= |=   ^=.

■ The value of an assignment expression is the value of the sub-expression on the right of the assignment operator.

■ Using the value of assignment expressions reduces the number of statements and frequently reduces repetition of statements.

■ The comma operator can be used to combine several assignments into a single expression.

Instead of:
```
c = getch()
while(c!=EOF)
{  process(c);
   c = getch();
}
```

or:
```
for(;;)
{  c = getch();
   if(c==EOF) break;
   process(c);
}
```

Use:
```
while((c = getch()) != EOF) process(c);
```

Notes: The first example repeats c = getch(). The second example uses a forever loop with **break** to avoid the repetition of c = getch(). Using a forever loop terminated by a **break** statement should, in general, be avoided. The last example reduces the code length and enhances readability.

In contrast with many other languages (Pascal, BASIC, etc.), C does not have an assignment statement. Instead, C provides many assignment operators (again in contrast with most other languages, which provide only one type of assignment). These operators are = += -= *= /= %= >>= <<= &= |= and ^=. These binary operators assign a value to the sub-expression on the left of the operator, which must be an lvalue. (Lvalues are expressions that designate memory locations.) The simplest assignment operator (=) assigns the value of the sub-expression on the right of the operator to the lvalue on the left. The remaining operators are shorthand for a = a <oper> b. The rest of this discussion will be limited to the = operator, although some of it applies to all assignment operators.

The result of evaluating a=b is the new value of a, and this value can be further used. For example, a=(b=c) is equivalent to b=c,a=b because the result of (b=c) is the new value of b. Since the parentheses are unnecessary (assignments associate from right to left), you can write a=b=c.

You can write if(a=b) instead of a=b; if(a). This form is extremely useful, not only in ifs as in this example, but also in whiles and fors.

There is, however, one big problem with C assignments. The expression a=a+1 appears to be an absurd equation. Programmers are taught to read it as "take the value of a, add one, and put the result back into a." This would be better supported by an assignment symbol such as <-. (Pascal provides :=, an excellent choice.)

The =, which should be used for comparisons, is used in C for assignments. To compare two values, == is used. (C uses a shorter symbol for assignment because assignments are used more often than comparisons. C was originally designed to minimize keystrokes.) Unfortunately, this choice of symbols makes it possible to think that if(a=b) compares the values of a and b. This mistake is very common among programmers new to C. If C had a different assignment operator (for example, :=), there would be less room for confusion. A statement like if(a:=b) is much clearer.

Forms such as while((c = getch()) != EOF) are extremely useful in spite of the potential for confusion. To minimize the danger of confusion, use a space on each side of the single equal sign. We do not recommend writing comments to warn the reader. (The reader is assumed to be a proficient C programmer and should not be reminded of standard features of the language.)

11.5   Minimize repetition of expressions and function calls

- Repetition of expressions increases the possibility of errors.

- Repetition of expressions makes reading and maintenance more difficult.

- Repetition of function calls can be computationally expensive.

- Repetition of function calls might be impossible because of side effects of the function. (The function might not return the same value twice.)

- C allows several ways of reducing repetition of expressions and function calls. The most important are a?b:c, a++, a--, a <oper>= b, temporary variables, and macros.

Instead of: `a[i][k+s] = a[i][k+s] * a[j][k+s]`

Use: `a[i][k+s] *= a[j][k+s]`

Notes: Future changes to `a[i][k+s]` will be easier on the second form. There will be no possibility of forgetting to modify the right side of the assignment.

Instead of:
```
if(x<MAX_X) ycalc = a*x*x + b*y*y + c*z*z;
else        ycalc = a*x*x + b*y*y + c*z*z -
                    xcr*(x-OFS_X);
```

Use:
```
ycalc = a*x*x + b*y*y + c*z*z -
        (x<MAX_X ? 0 : xcr*(x-OFS_X));
```

Notes: The second form emphasizes that the formula used for both cases is basically the same. An additional term is added if **x** is greater than or equal to MAX_X.

Whenever you see an expression repeated in a program, think: can this repetition be avoided? Repetition of expressions increases program length. It also makes the program more difficult to read and maintain, and increases the probability of errors.

When you repeat a complicated expression several times, you must make sure that it is indeed the same in all cases. In addition, readers of your program will have to double check that the expression is the same in all instances. They might even expect to find some difference justifying the repetition. Modifications to your code will require careful verification that changes are done to all instances of the expression. Repetition of function calls can be computationally expensive or, in some cases, nearly impossible if the function has significant side effects.

There are several ways to avoid repetition of expressions and function calls. When two expressions are very similar except for one or two additional terms, use the ternary operator, ?:. When performing a simple operation on a complicated lvalue, use ++, --, or <oper>=. When necessary, assign the result of a complicated expression to a temporary variable, then use the temporary variable. If you need to make it one expression, separate the assignment from the use of the temporary variable with a comma. Use temporary variables also when the result of a function with side effects needs to be used several times. Finally, if a long, computationally cheap expression is repeated too many times and you cannot find any other elegant way to eliminate the repetition, use a macro.

Exercises

1. Rewrite:
```
char *s;
int n,val,num;
...
n = 0;
s = get_term();
while((*s!='\0') && (MAX_OPS>n))
{  if(isdigit(*s)) num = atoi(s);
   else            num = value(s);
   op[n] = get_oper();
   switch(op[n])
   {  case '+': val += num; break;
      case '-': val -= num; break;
      case '*': val *= num; break;
      case '/': val /= num; break;
      case '%': val %= num; break;
      case '|': val |= num; break;
      case '&': val &= num; break;
   }
   n++;
   s = get_term();
}
```

2. Rewrite:
```
if((yterm_xst==FALSE) || (yterm>MAX_YTERM))
    return *(++p)+(a*x*x)+(b*x*y)+(c*y*y);
else
    return *(++p)+(a*x*x)+(b*x*y)+(c*y*y)+yterm;
```

3. Rewrite:
```
int find(int a[], int num_elem, int num)
{  int low=0,high=num_elem-1;
   int n = (high+low)/2;
   while((a[n]!=num) && (high>=low))
   {  if(a[n]<num)  low  = (n+1);
      else          high = (n-1);
      n = (high+low)/2;
   }
   if(a[n]==num) return TRUE;
   else          return FALSE;
}
```

C offers great flexibility in flow control. It supports all the basic flow control constructs: two-way (if) and multiway (switch) decisions, loops with a test before (while, for) and after (do ... while) the body of the loop, and goto. In addition, C provides the ability to exit a loop (break) or to start a new iteration (continue) from any point within the body of a loop, to exit a function from any point within the function (return), to use more than one control variable in a loop, to change a control variable within the body of a loop, and to fall through from one option to the next in multiway decisions. The Standard Library supports additional flow control capabilities: termination of the current program at any point (exit() and abort()) and inter-function jumps (setjmp() and longjmp()).

There are a few weak points, however. The keyword break is used both to exit a switch and to exit a loop, making it impossible to exit directly from within a switch to the outside of a loop. There is no direct way to exit from more than one level of loops, except by using goto. switch does not support the use of non-constant expressions to label the alternatives.

When coding in C, do not adhere fanatically to the structured programming ideal of "one entry point, one exit point, no goto." Exiting loops and functions at more than one point will frequently simplify your code and make it more readable. On the other hand, C provides no facility for entering functions at more than one point.

Even though for, while, and do ... while can replace each other, use the one among them that is the most appropriate for the task at hand. Structure your code to take maximum advantage of the power of C's flow control statements.

12.1   Write the short clause first in `if ... else`

- Bring the `else` as close as possible to the corresponding `if`. Write the shorter statement after the `if` and the longer statement after the `else`.

- Reverse the condition in the `if` whenever necessary, unless this increases the number of parentheses needed or makes the condition much less intuitive.

- Reverse the condition even if it requires an additional set of parentheses when one of the statements is short (one or a few lines long) and the other is long.

- Bringing the `else` closer to the `if` makes it easier to visualize both branches of the condition simultaneously.

Instead of:
```
if(in_user_code)
{  in_user_code == FALSE;
   r2 = r;
   reset_pharlap();
   send_sig_segv();
}
else revert();
```

Use:
```
if(!in_user_code) revert();
else
{  in_user_code == FALSE;
   r2 = r;
   reset_pharlap();
   send_sig_segv();
}
```

Notes: In the first form, we have to go back several lines to find out when the function `revert()` will be called. In the second form, `revert()` is right next to the `if` statement, while the rest of the code has been moved away from it just a little.

Whenever you write an `if` statement with an `else` clause, you have the option of writing it in two equivalent ways:

```
if(condition)      statement1;
else               statement2;   or


if(!condition)     statement2;
else               statement1;
```

The difference between them is that in the second form the condition has been inverted (here represented by *!condition*), as has the order of the two statements (either of which could be a compound statement).

Since both forms produce the same result, the decision as to which one to use is usually made somewhat randomly (for example, `if(n<10)` ... instead of `if(9<n)` ...). Often, however, the one with the simpler condition is used (for example, `if(n%10)` ... instead of `if(!(n%10))` ...). Sometimes one form of the condition is more intuitive than its inverse.

Whenever possible, bring the `else` as close as possible to the corresponding `if`. Rarely is there a good reason not to do this. Changing the condition to reverse the order of the statements requires at most three additional characters: a not operator (`!`) and an additional set of parentheses. Usually this maximum is needed in assignments and operations with modulo (`%`). When the required inversion would make the condition less readable, stay with the simpler condition if both statements are of similar length or are blocks of over ten lines.

Bringing the `else` closer to the corresponding `if` makes it easier to see both branches of the condition simultaneously. It also allows the reader to understand and dispose of the simpler case first and then concentrate on the more complicated one. If the simpler case is an exception, the reader can concentrate on the normal case knowing that the exception has already been handled. If the simpler case is the normal case, the reader can concentrate on the exception knowing how the normal case has been dealt with.

By the time the reader reaches an `else` that is far from its corresponding `if`, the condition might be long forgotten. The reader might have to backtrack to find the opening brace that matches the closing brace just before the `else`. This would be particularly annoying if a page boundary had been crossed.

12.2   Use braces to indicate else pairing for nested ifs

- Whenever you use else within nested ifs, there is a potential for misunderstanding.

- The compiler associates every else with the closest if not yet associated with an else.

- The use of braces that explicitly indicate which else is associated with which if makes your code more readable.

Instead of:
```
if(n<MAX)
        if(n) a[t++] = n;
        else  zeros++;
else
{  overflows++;
   for( ; n; n=reduce(n));
   {  backtrack(n);
      back++;
   }
}
```

Use:
```
if(n<MAX)
{  if(n) a[t++] = n;
   else  zeros++;
}
else
{  overflows++;
   for( ; n; n=reduce(n));
   {  backtrack(n);
      back++;
   }
}
```

Notes: If later on you decide to remove else zeros++; in the second form, the rest of the code will not be affected. However, if you remove else zeros++; in the first form, the meaning of the remaining else will be changed.

It may seem unnecessary to use braces to indicate else pairing. The compiler will always associate an else with the closest if not yet associated with an else. However, it is easy to make a simple mistake, especially if there are several statements between the else and the if. Such an error can be very difficult to catch, since usually the indentation will mislead the reader of the code into associating the else with the wrong if. For example, the following code fragment will not behave as expected because the compiler will associate the first else with if(isdigit(*s)) even though the indentation clearly shows that this was not the programmer's intention.

```
if(*s)          /* String is not empty */
    if(isdigit(*s))
    {   get_number();
        s++;
        ntokens++;
    }
else            /* String is empty     */
{   nerrors++;
    error(12);
    recover(p);
    if(*p) continue
    else
    {   fatal_error(9);
        return;
    }
}
```

Anybody reading this code fragment will have a hard time finding the error, since both the indentation and the comment conflict with the compiler's interpretation. To avoid the possibility of introducing an error of this type (which is so hard to find), use braces even if they are redundant.

12.3   Do not use **else** after **break, continue,** or **return**

- The three statements break, continue, and return, when used within an if, transfer control out of the function or loop that contains that if. Therefore, an else clause for that if is unnecessary.

- By eliminating the else you can indent the statements following the if that contains break, continue, or return at the same level as the if, reducing the number of indentation levels.

Instead of:
```
if(MAX<=n)
{   restore(n);
    return;
}
else
{   a[n]++;
    process(n);
    add_word(s[n]);
}
```

Use:
```
if(MAX<=n)
{   restore(n);
    return;
}
a[n]++;
process(n);
add_words(s[n]);
```

Using this rule, you can eliminate a level of indentation. It is not necessary to use an else clause immediately after (with or without a closing brace separating it from) break, continue, or return. If the condition controlling the if is true, the statements after break, continue, or return within the same block will not be reached, since control will be transferred out of that block.

The use of the else clause in this context does not add any clarity to the code. Not using else violates strict structured programming ideals, but the ideals are being broken anyway (break, continue, and return violate the "one exit" ideal). The else clause just adds unnecessary indentation.

12.4   Use **break, continue,** and **return**

- Use break, continue, and return to avoid duplicate testing of conditions or flags.

- Use break, continue, and return to minimize nesting of ifs.

- break, continue, and return violate the ideals of strict structured programming. Use them anyway.

Instead of:
```
int  isprime(int n)
{   int i;
    for(i=2;  i*i<=n && n%i;  i++);
    return n<i*i;
}
```

Use:
```
int  isprime(int n)
{   int i;
    for(i=2;  i*i<=n;  i++)
        if(n%i==0) return 0;
    return 1;
}
```

Notes: The second form tests i squared against n only once. This follows more closely the way this problem would be intuitively approached: to find out whether a certain number is prime, divide that number by every integer greater than one and smaller than or equal to the square root of the number being tested. As soon as one of these numbers divides the number with no remainder, return 0 (not prime); if none of them divides the number evenly, return 1 (is a prime).

The three statements break, continue, and return allow the writing of code that does not conform to the strict structured programming ideal of "one entry point, one exit point." That is probably why they are not included in some other structured languages. They are, however, extremely useful.

Using break, continue, and return, you can write code that reflects more closely the way the solution would be stated in words. You can also avoid duplication of statements, avoid re-evaluation of conditions, and minimize nesting of ifs. These benefits far outweigh the potential disadvantages of breaking strict structured programming rules. Having several exit points in loops and functions is usually more clear than creating extraneous flags, duplicating code, or double-checking conditions.

Sometimes a sequence of statements within a loop has to be performed in order to determine whether to continue or end the loop. There are at least two possible ways of handling this without using break or continue.

```
statement1;                 do
statement2;                 {   statement1;
while(condition)                statement2;
{   statement3;                 if(condition)
    statement4;                 {   statement3;
    statement1;                     statement4;
    statement2;                 }
}                           } while(condition)
```

In one of them you are forced to repeat some statements, and in the other you are forced to repeat the condition. Using break you can write

```
for(;;)
{   statement1;
    statement2;
    if(!condition) break;
    statement3;
    statement4;
}
```

You can often reduce the number of nested ifs by using return or continue. When the remaining statements within a function or a loop are to be executed only if a certain condition holds, it is usually better to invert the condition and return or continue.

Instead of:

```
void    function(void)              while(condition0)
{  statement1;                      {  statement1;
   statement2;                         statement2;
   statement3;                         statement3;
   if(condition1)                      if(condition1)
   {  statement4;                      {  statement4;
      statement5;                         statement5;
      if(condition2)                      if(condition2)
      {  statement6;                      {  statement6;
         statement7;                         statement7;
      }                                   }
   }                                   }
}                                   }
```

Use:

```
void    function(void)              while(condition0)
{  statement1;                      {  statement1;
   statement2;                         statement2;
   statement3;                         statement3;
   if(!condition1) return;             if(!condition1) continue;
   statement4;                         statement4;
   statement5;                         statement5;
   if(!condition2) return;             if(!condition2) continue;
   statement6;                         statement6;
   statement7;                         statement7;
}                                   }
```

12.5   Use **for** instead of **while** whenever reasonable

- **for** holds together three key pieces of a loop: the initialization, the controlling test, and the change of control variables. Having these pieces in one place makes your code more readable.

- **for** can be used with more than one control variable.

- The quantity by which each control variable is changed does not have to be constant as in some other languages.

- The terminating condition does not have to be directly related to the control variable. It can be any valid expression.

- Use **for** when one or two control variables are being changed within the loop, even if one of the three parts of the **for** is missing.

- Do not use **for** if only the middle section is used (condition testing); if the initialization, testing, and change sections are unrelated to each other; or if several control variables are used.

Instead of:
```
int i = 0;
while(letter[i].code!=E_CODE)
{ bline.x1 = p_x1 + letter[i].x*scale1;
  bline.y1 = p_y1 + letter[i].y*scale1;
  bline.x2 = p_x2 + letter[i].x*scale2;
  bline.y2 = p_y2 + letter[i].y*scale2;
  i++;
}
```

Use:
```
for(i=0; letter[i].code!=E_CODE; i++)
{ bline.x1 = p_x1 + letter[i].x*scale1;
  bline.y1 = p_y1 + letter[i].y*scale1;
  bline.x2 = p_x2 + letter[i].x*scale2;
  bline.y2 = p_y2 + letter[i].y*scale2;
}
```

Notes: The **for** statement makes it clear that the variable controlling the loop is i, that its starting value is 0, and that it is incremented by one on each iteration, as well as that the loop will end when letter[i].code becomes equal to E_CODE.

Most programmers use `for` when the situation obviously requires it. Few programmers would write

```
i=0;
while(i<count)
{   ...
    i++;
}
```

instead of

```
for(i=0;  i<count;  i++)
{   ...
}
```

However, many programmers do not realize that the `for` statement in C is much more flexible than `for` in most other languages (e.g., Pascal and BASIC). In most other languages, `for` controls only one variable and that variable has to be changed by a constant amount in each iteration. Also, many languages do not allow the control variable to be altered within the loop, and most require the terminating condition to be an upper or lower limit on the control variable.   None of these limitations apply to C.   Several variables can be modified, each can be altered by any amount in each iteration, each can be modified within the `for` body, and the terminating condition can be any valid expression.

Many programmers, especially those coming from Pascal or BASIC, do not realize that

```
i = 1;
e = 1.0;
t = 1.0;
while(i<=n)
{   e += t;
    t /= ++i;
}
```

can be rewritten as

```
for(i=1, e=t=1.0; i<=n; t/=++i) e += t;
```

Use `for` whenever it reasonably applies. Using `for` makes your code shorter and clearer. You could always use `while`, but that will leave the initialization, check, and change of the key variables in the loop dispersed about the code. One glance at a `for` statement will tell your readers what variable is controlling the loop, what its starting value is, how it changes, and when the loop will end.

12.6   Use `for(;;)` instead of `while(TRUE)` to loop forever

- `for(;;)` is the standard way of expressing an "infinite" loop.

- `for(;;)` can be read as `for(ever)`.

- `while(1)` or `while(TRUE)` are longer and somewhat confusing. `while` implies that the loop terminates.

Instead of:
```
while(TRUE)
{  get_command();
   reset_status();
   process_command();
}
```

Use:
```
for(;;)
{  get_command();
   reset_status();
   process_command();
}
```

Even though both `for(;;)` and `while(TRUE)` are equivalent, use the former. The word `while` implies that the loop terminates and is not used in everyday language for things that do not terminate. Nobody says: "This [thing] will last while true is true." The word `for` does not imply that the loop terminates and can be very conveniently read as "forever" in this context.

12.7   Do not use an empty `default` clause in `switch` statements

■ If no case is matched within the `switch` statement, control is transferred to the statement after the `switch`. An empty `default` clause is unnecessary.

Instead of:
```
switch(*p)
{  case 'B':  base =  2;   break;
   case 'D':  base = 10;   break;
   case 'H':  base = 16;   break;
   case 'O':
   case 'Q':  base =  8;   break;
   default:   ;
}
```

Use:
```
switch(*p)
{  case 'B':  base =  2;   break;
   case 'D':  base = 10;   break;
   case 'H':  base = 16;   break;
   case 'O':
   case 'Q':  base =  8;   break;
}
```

C guarantees that control will be transferred to the statement after the `switch` if no match is found. Many programmers feel compelled to add an empty `default` clause to any `switch` statement to "ensure" that their programs will behave properly if no `case` is matched. This is unnecessary.

12.8   Minimize fall-through in `switch` statements

- If you do not explicitly alter the program flow (usually with `break`) at the end of a `case` clause, program execution will continue at the next `case` clause. This is called "falling through."

- Falling through is very useful in some special circumstances, but it diminishes program clarity and makes it more likely for subtle errors to occur. Use it only when there is no elegant alternative.

- The reader usually expects each `case` clause to be independent of the others. If you fall through, include a comment to that effect.

Instead of:
```
switch(c)
{   case '\n':  nlines++;
    case '\t':
    case ' ':   nwhspaces++;     break;
    case '.':   nsentences++;    break;
}
```

Use:
```
switch(c)
{   case '\n':  nlines++;
                nwhspaces++;     break;
    case '\t':
    case ' ':   nwhspaces++;     break;
    case '.':   nsentences++;    break;
}
```

Notes: In the first form, the reader might miss the fact that newline characters are also counted in `nwhspaces`. Furthermore, without a comment it is unclear whether the omission of a `break` after `nlines++` is intentional or accidental. The second form is clearer at the cost of only two additional statements.

The switch statement is not a strictly structured statement; it is a multiway branch. If a given case is matched, control is transferred to the first statement after that label, as if a goto to that label had been executed. To avoid execution from continuing at the next case clause, a statement such as break or return has to be included at the end of each clause. When there is no such statement, execution "falls through" to the next case clause.

When several cases cause the same exact action, it is customary to list all the cases, each on one line, and then the corresponding code. Whenever control is transferred to any of these cases, the same code will be executed. This is not considered "falling through" in this book.

```
switch(expression)
{   case constant1:
    case constant2:         statement1;
                            statement2;   break;
    case constant3:
    case constant4:         statement3;   break;
}
```

Sometimes, two different cases differ only in a few initial statements. The unique initial statements can be written after the first case label and the common code after the second case label, allowing execution to fall through from the first case to the second.

```
switch(expression)
{   case constant1:         statement1;  /* fall through */
    case constant2:         statement2;
                            statement3;   break;
    case constant3:         statement4;   break;
}
```

This is a powerful but dangerous feature of C. Falling through makes your code dependent on the exact order of some of the case clauses, diminishes clarity, and increases the likelihood of errors. In general, avoid falling through. Repeat the common statements if they are few. Separate them into a function and call the function from both cases, if possible, or redesign your code.

If you do use fall-through, add a comment to warn the reader.

12.9   Use goto when necessary (very seldom)

- Use goto very seldom.

- Do not hesitate to use goto when necessary.

- Use goto to jump out of several levels of nested loops.

- Use goto only when there is no good alternative. First try to restructure your code.

- Use goto only to jump to the current or the next statement at some lexical level, or for exception handling.

Instead of:
```
stop = 0;
for(i=0; i<t && !stop; i++)
{  sum_j=0;
   for(j=0; j<t && !stop; j++)
   {  sum_k = 0;
      for(k=0; k<t && !stop; k++)
      {  sum_k+=a[i][j][k];
         if(sum_k*MARGIN<num*k)
         if(a[i][j][k]==num) stop = 1;
      }
      sum_j+=sum_k;
      if(sum_j*MARGIN<num*j*t) stop = 1;
   }
}
...
...
```

```
Use:           for(i=0;  i<t;  i++)
               {  sum_j=0;
                  for(j=0;  j<t;  j++,)
                  {  sum_k = 0;
                     for(k=0;  k<t;  k++)
                     {  sum_k+=a[i][j][k];
                        if(sum_k*MARGIN<num*k)
                        if(a[i][j][k]==num) goto next;
                     }
                     sum_j+=sum_k;
                     if(sum_j*MARGIN<num*j*t) goto next;
                  }
               }
       next:   ...
               ...
```

Notes: The second form eliminates a flag (stop) and three additional tests, and is clearer.

goto is probably the most criticized among the statements in any language that supports it. Many C programmers never use it; many college professors reject any C program that uses it. goto interrupts the normal execution flow, and allows the creation of totally unreadable code.

Many well-meaning programmers go to incredible lengths to avoid the "unstructured" goto. In their blind pursuit of "structured programming", they are willing to use flags and awkward constructions, complicating, slowing down, and obscuring several levels of nested loops.

The sad truth is that in some cases there is no simpler or more elegant solution than to use goto. Fanatically avoiding it will not make your code better or more readable. Remember, the objective is to make your code efficient and readable. Of course, do not use goto if there is an elegant alternative. First try to use other constructs (such as break or return) or restructure your code.

Do not use goto to jump indiscriminately to any part of your code, however. Jump to the beginning of the next or the current statement at some lexical level; in other words, use goto as a multilevel break or continue. Any other use of goto is not recommended except for very extreme situations or for exception handling.

12.10 Start from one for cardinals, from zero for ordinals

- When denoting a number of elements, start from one: refer to one element as 1.

- When denoting order, start from zero: refer to the first element as 0.

- When counting up to a cardinal n, count 0, 1, 2, ..., n-1.

- The first element of an array in C is element zero.

- Counting from zero simplifies pointer and other indexing arithmetic.

- Be consistent: *always* count from zero.

- When counting from zero, use < instead of <= to check for loop end.

Instead of:
```
for(line=1; line<=tlines; line++)
    process_line(global_text,line);
```

Use:
```
for(line=0; line<tlines; line++)
    process_line(global_text,line);
```

Have you ever wondered, when reading a program, if something numbered 1 is the first or the second something? It can be difficult to find out. Subtle off-by-one bugs can be introduced or overlooked because of this possible ambiguity.

To avoid this problem, be consistent. If your first element is *always* number zero, *always* one, or *always* another fixed number, there will be no confusion. Obviously, calling your first element anything other than zero or one is very confusing except in a few special cases. Therefore, there are two basic options: to start from zero or to start from one.

Often you will be referring to the first, second, etc. element of an array. In C, the first element of an array is element number 0. This is different in other languages: in BASIC the first element is element number 1; in Pascal the first element's number can be defined by the programmer. Remember that in C `a[i]` is equivalent to `*(a+i)`. `a[0]` is therefore equivalent to `*(a+0)` or `*a`. Since the name of an array is equivalent to a constant pointer to the first element, the first element must be 0. If you start from one, either you will have to leave element number 0 of each array unused or you will have to subtract one from your index. Start from zero.

Using zero for the first element has other advantages in addition to being the only option compatible with array addressing, If you have to multiply or divide your index to obtain a new index, using zero as the first element makes it easier. For example, if you have a string like `"mov add sub inc dec jmp"` and `i` contains the position of the first character of one of these three-letter terms within the string, `i/4` will give you the number of the term. If you use one as the first element of both the string and the terms, you must use `(i-1)/4+1` to get the number of the term. If you want to restrict your index to the first `k` elements, the modulo operator can be used as follows: `i%k`.

However, when you are representing a quantity, use 1 to represent one object, 2 for two objects, etc. (E.g., if you have three objects, you would use 3 to represent the number of objects. However, the objects would be referred to as object 0, object 1, and object 2.)

A number representing quantity is called *cardinal*; a number representing order is called *ordinal*. In some situations a given number might be used both as a cardinal and as an ordinal; or it might be unclear whether it is a cardinal or an ordinal. In such a case, use your best judgment, although a useful suggestion is to use it as an ordinal (zero start) unless you know that you are dealing with a cardinal.

12.11 Minimize repetition of statements

■ Repetition of statements makes the program more difficult to maintain and increases the likelihood of errors.

■ Avoid repetition of statements in loops by using break, continue, and return (Rule 12.4); and by using the values of assignments (Rule 11.4).

■ When necessary, create functions or macros to avoid repeating groups of statements.

Instead of:
```
get_token();
if(tkn==T_END) return;
if(tkn==T_START) start_proc();
while(ntokens<T_LIMIT)
{   process_token();
    add_entry();
    get_token();
    if(tkn==T_END) return;
    if(tkn==T_START) start_proc();
}
```

Use:
```
for(;;)
{   get_token();
    if(tkn==T_END) return;
    if(tkn==T_START) start_proc();
    if(T_LIMIT<=ntokens) break;
    process_token();
    add_entry();
}
```

Notes: This code fragment has been rearranged to avoid the repetition of three statements (the first three statements in the first form).

Whenever there is a repeated statement or group of statements, there is probably a way of avoiding such repetition. Sometimes, the most reasonable way of writing the code is to repeat a few statements. However, in most cases repetitions can be avoided, thus enhancing program readability. When statements are repeated, the code becomes longer and an additional source of errors emerges: modifications made to one group of statements have to be faithfully replicated onto the other.

12.12 Minimize nesting

- Too many levels of nesting make your program less readable.

- Use break, continue, and return (Rules 12.3 and 12.4).

- Use the values of relational and logical expressions (Rule 11.2).

- If necessary, restructure your code.

Instead of:
```
if(*text=='@')
{   if(text[1]==LINK_MARKER)
    {   g->levels[++level] = get_data(text+2);
        g->previous        = NULL;
    }
    else return rcode;
}
else return rcode;
```

Use:
```
if(*text!='@')                      return rcode;
if(text[1]!=LINK_MARKER) return rcode;
g->levels[++level] = get_data(text+2);
g->previous        = NULL;
```

When the left half of your program listing is blank, something is probably wrong. There is seldom any need to indent to more than about five levels. Occasionally, it might be necessary to indent a few statements a little deeper. But there is hardly ever a good reason to have many lines of code beyond the fifth or sixth level. Use Rules 11.2, 12.3, and 12.4 to reduce nesting. If your code still has too many levels of indentation, restructure it.

12.13 Minimize use of flags

- Flags diminish readability.

- Flags add complexity to your code and make debugging more difficult.

- Do not use loop controlling flags to adhere to strict structured programming. Use flow control statements: break, continue, and return, and even consider using goto.

- Make your code as modeless as possible. Make it possible for the reader to read your code with as little knowledge of variable contents as possible.

- Minimize flag parameters to functions enabling additional functionality. If possible, code additional functionality as a separate function.

Instead of:
```
err = 0;
for(i=1; i<t && !err; i++)
    for(j=1; j<t && !err; j++)
    { if(a[i][j]==NAN) err=12;
      else
      { a[i][0] += tk_root(a[i][j]);
        a[0][j] += tk_root(a[j][i]);
      }
    }
return err;
```

Use:
```
for(i=1; i<t; i++)
    for(j=1; j<t; j++)
    { if(a[i][j]==NAN) return 12;
      a[i][0] += tk_root(a[i][j]);
      a[0][j] += tk_root(a[j][i]);
    }
return 0;
```

Notes: The second form eliminates the variable err and simplifies the loops by eliminating one test from each for.

Always try to make your code as modeless as possible. The reader of your code should be able to understand as much as possible without knowing the contents of any variable. The use of flags breaks this basic rule.

Flags can be used to control loops. They are often used when `break`, `continue`, `return`, or `goto` could be used instead (see Rules 12.4 and 12.9). Do not use flags to control loops unless there is absolutely no alternative.

Flags can also be used as parameters to functions. Sometimes this usage is very appropriate. Often, however, flags are used to turn additional functionality within a function on or off. This latter use should be avoided when possible. If you can, split such a function in two. One function will perform the basic functionality; the other will perform the additional functionality.

Another use of flags is to reuse code. Sometimes you might need code that is almost the same as previously written code except for one or two statements. One option is to reuse that code with a flag controlling whether those one or two statements get executed or not. This is a fine alternative when used in moderation, but one that makes your code unreadable when used excessively. Consider redesigning your code, moving the common code to a separate function, or even duplicating the common code.

12.14 Use `longjmp()` when necessary (very very seldom)

- Use `longjmp()` very very seldom.

- Do not hesitate to use `longjmp()` when necessary.

- Use `longjmp()` mainly for exception handling (see Rule 18.7).

Instead of:

```
int   func_a(void)
{  ...
   if(ERROR) return EXIT;
   ...
}

int   func_b(void)
{  ...
   if(func_a()==EXIT) return EXIT;
   ...
}

int   func_c(void)
{  ...
   if(func_b()==EXIT) return EXIT;
   ...
}

int   func_d(void)
{  while(c!=EOF)
   {  if(func_c()==EXIT)
      {  recover();
         continue;
      }
      ...
   }
   ...
}
```

Use:

```
int   func_a(void)
{  ...
   if(ERROR) longjmp(jbuf,1);
   ...
}

int   func_b(void)
{  ...
   fcnt_a();
   ...
}

int   func_c(void)
{  ...
   func_b();
   ...
}

int   func_d(void)
{  while(c!=EOF)
   {  if(setjmp(jbuf))
      {  recover();
         continue;
      }
      func_c();
      ...
   }
   ...
}
```

Most of what has been said about goto applies to longjmp(). The main use of longjmp() is to exit from several levels of function calls, usually for exception handling. It does for functions what goto does for loops. If you have to exit from several levels of functions, one alternative is to use an "exit" return value in each of them, then to check for that return value whenever any of them is called and, if it is encountered, return to the next higher level. In this fashion, several returns are executed in succession. This way of handling multiple-level function exit is inefficient and cumbersome. The setjmp()/longjmp() combination is a simple and efficient alternative.

The need to exit from several levels of function calls does not arise too frequently. Most often it appears in exception handling. Whenever you are about to use longjmp(), review your code to see if it can be restructured. Use longjmp() only when no elegant alternative is found.

longjmp() is described in detail in Rule 17.7. Additional suggestions can be found in Rule 18.7.

Exercises

1. Rewrite:
```
x = 0;
while(!x)
{  panel_move(message,get_key());
   if(*message==0)
   {   error("Selection error");
       return 0;
   }
   else
      if(strcmp("OK",message)==0)
      {  if(key==K_ESC) x=1;
         continue;
      }
}
```

2. Rewrite:
```
rtn = DoForm(initp,nfields);
if(rtn==FR_IO)
{  if(err_code)
   {  error(err_msg);
      return;
   }
   else
   {  if(scr_num==S_DEF || scr_num==S_DEF2)
      {  if(npass=3) verify();
         if(*c=='@')
         {  aflag = 0;
            npass++;
         }
      }
   }
}
return;
```

3. Rewrite:
```
if(group!=NULL)
{  i = NGROUPS;
   cptr = sfind(group,fl);
   if(cptr==NULL) return NOT_FOUND;
}
else return NOT_FOUND;
```

4.   Rewrite:

```
len = strlen(s);
stop = 0;
i    = 0;
while(len!=0 && !stop)
{   if(0<a[len])
    {   data[i++] = s[len];
        t = s[len]*a[len];
        if(t<MIN_T) nmin++;
        if(MAX_T<t) nmax++;
        if(s[len]==a[len])
        {   len--;
            stop = 1;
        }
    }
    len++;
}
```

5.   Rewrite:

```
t = 1;
x = 1;
while(TRUE)
{   if(limit<t) break;
    x *= 3;
    t += x;
}
```

6.   Rewrite:

```
get_data(s);
process_data(s,a,&len);
stop = 0;
while(!err && !stop)
{   nodd = i = 0;
    while(i<len) nodd += a[i++]%2;
    if(nodd<MAX_ODD)
    {   get_data(s);
        process_data(s,a,&len);
    }
    else stop = 1;
}
```

CHAPTER 13: **Functions, Parameters, and Variables**

The C language offers a powerful but sparse framework. Most of the functionality is provided by functions, to such extent that a part of the library usually supplied with the language has been included in the Standard. Interestingly, most of the library functions can be, and usually are, written in C. This stands in contrast to other languages, such as Pascal, that include functions that are clearly not implementable in the language itself.

13.1   Include parameter type within function parentheses

- The new format for function declaration was introduced in ANSI C.

- Old style function declarations are supported for compatibility with existing code but should not be used for new code.

- The new format allows for parameter checking and conversion.

- The new format is more compact.

Instead of:
```
int convert(dest, src, count)
char *dest;
char *src;
int  count;
```

Use:
```
int convert(char *dest, char *src, int count)
```

Notes: The second form takes only one line (compared to four for the first form) and allows parameter checking and conversion.

The new format for function declaration is one of the biggest changes introduced by the ANSI committee. The original definition of C did not include parameter checking and supported only the format shown in the first form of the example on this page. The old format is still supported in Standard C to allow existing programs to compile with no changes; using the old format for new programs is not recommended.

The new format allows the compiler to detect parameter mismatches. If you call the function with fewer or more parameters than required, or if the type of any parameter does not match the type specified in the declaration, the compiler may generate an error or warning. The compiler will also generate type conversions as if the supplied arguments had been typecast to the type of the parameters in the declaration.

Even though the old style makes it easier to comment each parameter by using one line per parameter, parameter checking and conformance to the new style are stronger advantages which justify the use of the new format.

13.2   Use parameters as local variables

- Parameters are *copies* of what is passed to the function.

- Consider the parameters to be initialized local variables.

- Using parameters as local variables saves stack space and makes the program a little shorter.

Instead of:
```
char *strchr(char *bf, char c)
{  char *p;
   for(p=bf; *p; p++)
      if(*p==c) return p;
   return NULL;
}
```

Use:
```
char *strchr(char *bf, char c)
{  for( ; *bf; bf++)
      if(*bf==c) return bf;
   return NULL;
}
```

Do not be afraid to change the value of a function's parameters. They are just copies of the original values supplied. They are equivalent to local variables that have been initialized to the values supplied to the function.

If you need to preserve those values throughout the execution of your function, create additional local variables. (The function strcpy(), for example, needs to preserve the destination address.) However, if you do not need to preserve the original values of the parameters, feel free to use them as you would use any other local variables. Do not use extra stack space for unnecessary local variables.

13.3   Do not use recursion unless it is necessary

- Recursion is less efficient than a loop; use a loop instead of recursion whenever you can.

- Consider using recursion when some instances need to call more than one new instance.

- Recursion is usually clearer; use recursion when efficiency is not as important as clarity.

Instead of:
```
unsigned int fibonacci(unsigned int n)
{  if(n<2) return n;
   return fibonacci(n-1)+fibonacci(n-2);
}
```

Use:
```
unsigned int fibonacci(unsigned int n)
{  int a=0,b=1,c;
   if(n<2) return n;
   while(2<=n--)
   {  c = a+b;
      a = b;
      b = c;
   }
   return c;
}
```

Notes: The first form is more elegant, shorter, and clearer. It is also terribly inefficient. To calculate the Fibonacci number n the function will call itself `2*(fibonacci(n+1)-1)` times. For example, to calculate `fibonacci(20)` the function will call itself 21,890 times.

The second form is less elegant, longer, and less clear, but it takes only n-1 iterations to calculate `fibonacci(n)`. To calculate `fibonacci(20)` it will go through the loop 19 times. Compare that to 21,890 function calls!

By the way, `fibonacci(n)` can be calculated directly without loops or recursion as

$$\frac{\phi^n-(-\phi)^{-n}}{\sqrt{5}} \quad \text{where} \quad \phi=\frac{1+\sqrt{5}}{2} \quad \text{(the golden ratio)}$$

Recursion is a very powerful technique. Unfortunately, it is often overused. In many cases, recursion is a very inefficient way of solving the problem at hand. Because of its power and beauty, recursion is often emphasized as the solution of choice, especially in college courses. One typical example of recursion is the definition of n factorial: `0! = 1, n! = n*(n-1)!`. While this is a very elegant way of defining factorial, it is an inefficient way of computing it. Factorial should be implemented as a simple loop. A function call requires more work than one iteration through a loop. Usually, the arguments and the return address have to be pushed on the stack and some register and stack housekeeping has to be performed. Upon return, the arguments have to be removed from the stack.

In some cases, the use of recursion is fully justified. Quicksort and tree-traversing, for example, lend themselves to recursive implementations. Non-recursive implementations would require the use of a stack to emulate recursion.

A recursive function that calls itself only once per instance (for example, factorial) can usually be replaced by a loop. Recursive functions that call themselves more than once in at least some instances (for example, quicksort) are usually much more difficult to replace with a loop. Sometimes, however, there are straightforward non-recursive equivalents (for example, `fibonacci()`). Use recursion only when it substantially simplifies your code or when clarity is much more important than efficiency.

13.4 Use global (or static) variables instead of function parameters when appropriate

- Do not use parameters for values that have to be used by many functions.

- Use parameters only when they truly add flexibility.

- Do not hesitate to access and modify variables global to a file, module, or system.   While this is not good practice in a library function, it is reasonable in a function that will be used only within one program.

- Make your global variables visible only to the modules that need to use them.

Instead of:
```
int next_char(FILE *fl)
{   int c;
    c = getc(fl);
    return tolower(c);
}

void next_word(FILE *fl, char *word)
{   int c;
    while((c=next_char(fl))!=EOF &&
          !isalnum(c));
    for(; isalnum(c); word++,c=next_char(fl))
        *word=c;
    *word = 0;
}
```

Use:
```
static char    c,word[MAX_WORD];
static FILE    *fl;

int next_char(void)
{   c = getc(fl);
    return c=tolower(c);
}

void next_word(void)
{   char *p;
    while(next_char()!=EOF && !isalnum(c));
    for(p=word; isalnum(c); p++,next_char())
        *p=c;
    *p = 0;
}
```

Notes: Several functions, of which `next_char()` and `next_word` are two, read data from one file at a time; `fl` stays the same throughout most of the program. At any given time there is only one current character (`c`) and one current word (`word`). Several functions need to operate on these values. These three variables should be `static` as shown in the second form. If you pass them as parameters, you will have to pass them to many functions, making your code longer and more complicated. Using them as parameters will not give you any additional flexibility, but will cause several unnecessary copies of these values (`fl`, `c`, and `word`) to be allocated on and deallocated from the stack.

C, like most modern languages, allows you to create functions that accept parameters and return values. Usually, you can use a function without knowing how it works. You can treat it as a black box that takes the supplied arguments and returns a value.

This is a very powerful feature, but it is often overused. Not everything should be passed as a parameter. Functions should take some values as parameters and other values directly from the environment (as predefined constants and global variables). For example, I/O is greatly simplified by using standard input and standard output as defaults in some functions.

Many programmers and too many professors abuse parameter passing. It is nice to have a function that is as flexible as possible, but you should not carry it to ridiculous extremes. After all, a truly flexible function would be one that takes one parameter, a pointer to a buffer containing machine language code, and executes that code. Such a function will be able to do anything you will ever want, but it will be difficult to use and will not save you much work.

There is a trade-off between how easy a function is to use and how much functionality it provides. Passing everything as parameters is absurd. Do not pass something as a parameter if the same value has to be used by many different functions, especially if that value is relatively stable. It is better to use one global variable than to have ten copies of the same value on the stack and make the function calls more complicated.

When you are writing functions for a library, try to depend on global variables as little as possible. However, when you are writing functions that will be used in only one program for a very specific purpose, use global variables freely. Of course, do not carry this to ridiculous extremes either. Do not create, for example, a function that will look for the first occurrence of the character in the global variable `c` within the null-terminated string contained in the global variable `buffer`.

We use the term "global variables" here to refer to variables visible to more than one function. They do not have to be visible to all modules. Rather, make them visible only to the module in which they are used (by using the keyword `static`) whenever possible.

13.5   If a function takes destination and source, put destination first

- Be consistent with the Standard C Library convention (as used in `strcpy()`, `memcpy()`, etc.).

Instead of:
```
char *unpack_number(char *src, char *dest)
{ char *d;
  for(d=dest; *src; src++)
  {  *d++ = *src&0x0f + '0';
     *d++ = *src>>4   + '0';
  }
  *d = 0;
  return dest;
}
```

Use:
```
char *unpack_number(char *dest, char *src)
{ char *d;
  for(d=dest; *src; src++)
  {  *d++ = *src&0x0f + '0';
     *d++ = *src>>4   + '0';
  }
  *d = 0;
  return dest;
}
```

When a function takes source and destination you have two options. You can put source first, or you can put destination first. At first sight, both options seem equally reasonable. However, you should use destination first to be consistent with the Standard C Library. Consistently using destination first saves the reader from wondering, for every function, which parameter is destination and which parameter is source. Consistently using source first would also be useful, but would conflict with the Standard C Library usage and would force the reader to remember two conflicting conventions.

13.6   Return zero for OK, non-zero for error

- Non-zero can have several values; use different codes for different errors.

- This rule applies only when the returned value is purely for reporting errors. Use other mechanisms when you also have to return a result (as `getc()` does, for example).

Instead of:
```
#define OK2(n,p) (isdigit((p)[0]) && \
                      isdigit((p)[1]) && atoi(p)<(n))
int good_time(char *time)
{   if(time[2]!=':' || time[5]!=':') return 0;
    if(time[8])           return 0;
    if(!OK2(24,time))     return 0;
    if(!OK2(60,time+3))   return 0;
    if(!OK2(60,time+6))   return 0;
    return 1;
}
```

Use:
```
#define OK2(n,p) (isdigit((p)[0]) && \
                      isdigit((p)[1]) && atoi(p)<(n))
int bad_time(char *time)
{   if(time[2]!=':' || time[5]!=':') return E_COLON;
    if(time[8])           return E_LENGTH;
    if(!OK2(24,time))     return E_HOURS;
    if(!OK2(60,time+3))   return E_MINUTES;
    if(!OK2(60,time+6))   return E_SECONDS;
    return 0;
}
```

Notes: The second form is more complete and equally easy to use. You can use `bad_time()` to determine if the time is incorrect. If the time is incorrect, you can use the error code to determine what is wrong with it. (In OK2, `(p)[0]` is used instead of `*(p)` to parallel `(p)[1]`.)

There are two possible ways of returning error/OK signals for functions returning an acknowledgement. You can return non-zero for OK, or you can return zero for OK. As usual, it is more important to be consistent than to choose one option or the other. Returning zero for OK has the advantage that it allows you to report different error codes. When something is OK, it is enough to just indicate that fact, but when something is wrong, it is usually useful to indicate what is wrong. There is only one distinct zero value, but there are several distinct non-zero values. It is therefore natural to use zero to indicate OK and non-zero to indicate errors.

13.7   Use **void** for functions not returning a value or not accepting parameters

- Use void for return values and parameters when appropriate. This allows the compiler to verify that the function is being used properly.

- Functions with no declared value are int by default.

Instead of:
```
init()
{  calc_primes();
   calc_factorials();
}
```

Use:
```
void init(void)
{  calc_primes();
   calc_factorials();
}
```

The type void was not originally included in the language, but has become popular and has been incorporated into the Standard. One of the main additions of the Standard is the ability to verify that a function is called with the right type and number of parameters. Using void when appropriate allows the compiler to make sure that your function is used correctly. It also provides the reader with more information about the function and follows the new convention of explicitly specifying return and parameter types.

13.8   Use a variable number of arguments when necessary

■ A variable number of arguments is a very powerful feature of C. Do not be afraid to use it.

■ Always use the macros contained in `stdarg.h`.

■ Optional parameters are not type checked or converted.

Example:
```
double a,b,c;
...
double poly(int dgr, double x, ...)
{  double s=0.0, xp=1.0;
   va_list p;
   va_start(p, x);
   while(0<=dgr--)
   {  s  += xp*va_arg(p, double);
      xp *= x;
   }
   return s;
}
...
y1 = poly(2,x,c,b,a);      /* OK    */
y2 = poly(2,5,1,2,3);      /* Wrong! */
```

Notes: The function `poly` evaluates a polynomial of any degree. Notice that the second call to `poly()` will not behave properly because the third, fourth, and fifth arguments (1, 2, and 3) will not be converted to `double`.

C supports functions with a variable number of arguments. (That is the reason why most implementations of C push the first argument last on the stack and require the caller to remove the arguments from the stack.) C functions like `printf` can be implemented in C, in contrast to many other languages. For example, Pascal procedures like `write` and `read` cannot be implemented in Pascal.

Do not hesitate to use a variable number of arguments when required. You do not have to know machine language or C implementation internals. Instead, just use a few simple macros. In some implementations, there are macros to traverse variable-length argument lists in two headers: `stdarg.h` and `varargs.h`. Always use `stdarg.h`. This header is part of the Standard and will work with any implementation of Standard C. Do not use `varargs.h`, the older, UNIX-compatible set of macros; it is not included in the Standard. Do not try to access the parameters directly based on your knowledge of the C implementation you are working with: your code will not be portable.

13.9   In general, keep the length of your functions to one printed page

- Use fewer than about 60 lines per function (not including introductory comments).

- Functions that are too long are difficult to read, understand, and debug.

- Use lengthy functions only in a few very special cases.

- Do not limit your functions to just one screen (usually 24 lines).

Limit your functions to a reasonable fixed length. Although a few exceptional cases justify using very lengthy functions, in most cases lengthy functions should be broken down into smaller ones. Smaller functions are easier to understand and maintain.

Do not make your functions too short either. If you set yourself a maximum length that is too short, you will often have to break functions that should not be broken. Some programmers use a screenful as the maximum size of a function. That is too short. Limit your functions to one printed page (usually about 60 lines).

Some programmers provide a detailed description in a long comment for some functions. Do not include this description or any other introductory comments when counting function lines.

Exercises

1. Rewrite:
```
double  factorial(n)
int n;
{  return 1<n ? n*factorial(n-1) : 1;
}
```

2. Rewrite:
```
int  pack(char *src, int *dest)
{  int d,u;
   u = src[0]-'0';
   d = src[1]-'0';
   if(u<0 || 9<u || d<0 || 9<d) return 0;
   *dest = u+10*d;
   return 1;
}
```

3. Rewrite:
```
print_val(f, n)
FILE *f;
int n;
{  fprintf(f," %i ",n);
}

print_oper(f, n)
FILE *f;
int n;
{  fputs(oper[n],f);
}

print_expr(FILE f, Tnode *nd)
{  if(nd->left)  print_expr(f, nd->left);
   else          print_val(f, nd->value);
   print_oper(f, nd->value);
   if(nd->right) print_expr(f, nd->right);
   else          print_val(f, nd->value);
}

main()
{  FILE *fileout;
   Tnode *root;
   ...
   fileout = fopen(filename, "w");
   print_expr(fileout, root);
   ...
}
```

CHAPTER 14: **Pointers and Arrays**

A key feature of the C language is that pointers and arrays are treated similarly. An array name is treated as a constant pointer to the first element of the array. The difference between an array and a pointer is that the definition of a pointer allocates storage for the pointer (usually 2 or 4 bytes), which can then point to another memory location. The definition of an array allocates storage for the elements of the array and creates a symbol (the array name) for the location of the first element. It does not allocate any storage for this symbol. An array name can be used as a pointer but not as an lvalue.

Indexing and pointer arithmetic are also closely related in C. Adding an integer n to a pointer causes the pointer to point n elements after the location previously pointed to. In other words, the pointer will be incremented to point n*sizeof(*element pointed to*) bytes after the location previously pointed to. For example, *(p+1) will return the contents of the element right after the one pointed to by p.

Indexing combines the operations of adding to the pointer and dereferencing the result. We could have used p[1] in our previous example to achieve the same result. a[i] is equivalent to *(a+i) (and therefore, surprisingly, to i[a]). Also, &a[i] is equivalent to &*(a+i) and therefore to a+i. Any of these forms can be used for both arrays and pointers. In general, from among the equivalent forms to access a given element, use the shortest one.

14.1   Use a[b] instead of *(a+b)

- a[b] is equivalent to *(a+b); a[b] is shorter.

- In a[b], a can be any pointer expression and b can be any integer expression (including negative values).

- Use a[b] instead of *(a+b) to dereference both pointers and arrays (unless b is the constant 0).

```
Instead of:     start_row = *(p+10);
                start_col = *(p+11);
                num_rows  = *(p+12);
                num_cols  = *(p+13);

Use:            start_row = p[10];
                start_col = p[11];
                num_rows  = p[12];
                num_cols  = p[13];
```

Most programmers use brackets to access a given element of an array. However, many do not use brackets to refer to a given element of a buffer pointed to by a pointer. As explained in the introduction to this chapter, what can be used with array names can be used with pointers and vice versa (except that an array name cannot be used as an lvalue). Use a[b] for both pointers and arrays; it is shorter and clearer.

14.2   In general, use *a instead of a[0]

- *a is equivalent to a[0]; *a is shorter.

- In *a, a can be any pointer expression.

- Use *a to refer to the first element for both pointers and arrays.

- Use a[0] instead of *a when parallelism with other statements is desired.

Instead of:
```
if(buffer[0]) return 1;
else if(buffer[0]==0xe0) return 4;
else buffer[0] |= code | 0xe0;
```

Use:
```
if(*buffer) return 1;
else if(*buffer==0xe0) return 4;
else *buffer |= code | 0xe0;
```

Most programmers refer to the element pointed to by a pointer p as *p. However, many programmers refer to the first element of an array a as a[0]. As explained in the introduction to this chapter, the first element of an array is the element pointed to by the array name. (It can be used as if it were a constant pointer.) When referring to the first element of an array, use * to dereference the array name. It is shorter and clearer.

However, when a[b] is used in a parallel construction, do use a[0]. That is:

Instead of:
```
*coord   = x;
coord[1] = y;
coord[2] = z;
```

Use:
```
coord[0] = x;
coord[1] = y;
coord[2] = z;
```

14.3   In general, use a+b instead of &a[b]

- a+b is equivalent to &a[b]; a+b is shorter.

- In a+b, a can be any pointer expression and b can be any integer expression (including negative values).

- Use a+b for both pointers and arrays.

Instead of: memmove(&a[p], &a[q], len);

Use: memmove(a+p, a+q, len);

Most programmers use a+b to add an offset to a pointer. However, many programmers use the construct &a[b] when referring to the address of element b in the array a. As explained in the introduction to this chapter, &a[b] is equivalent to a+b since the address of element b is just the array name a plus the offset b (where the special pointer arithmetic rules of the C language govern the meaning of "plus"). Use a+b for both pointers and arrays. It is shorter and usually clearer.

14.4   Whenever possible, use pointers instead of indexes in loops

- Accessing elements in a loop through a pointer requires fewer calculations and is faster than using an index (when no optimization is performed).

- Use indexes when additional clarity is important, but speed is not.

Instead of:
```
for(i=0; s[i]; i++);   /* Find end of string */
s[i++] = c;
s[i] = 0;
```

Use:
```
for(p=s; *p; p++);   /* Find end of string */
*p++ = c;
*p   = 0;
```

When you refer to an element by its index (a[i]), you are using an indirect way of specifying its location. The compiler has to generate code to multiply the index by the number of bytes in one element, then add the result to the base address of the array, and then use the resulting address to access the element. In a loop, using a pointer (*p) is a more direct way to specify the element's location and is usually faster and shorter. When you increment the index and reference the next element (a[++i]), the generated code has to increment the index and multiply it again by the size of one element. It then has to add it again to the base address and use the resulting address to access the element. If, instead, you increment a pointer to achieve the same result (*++p), the generated code will just have to add the size of one element to the pointer. It will then be able to use the resulting address to access the element. Accessing an element through a pointer requires fewer operations and no multiplication.

Most modern optimizing compilers will rewrite a loop using indexes (such as the one in the example on this page) to use pointers. In other words, the code produced by a good optimizing compiler for the two forms presented as an example might be exactly the same. Nevertheless, it is good practice to use pointers instead of indexes. In general, it is not a good idea to rely on the compiler for this type of optimization. Use indexes only when they significantly increase the clarity of your code.

14.5   Use a->b instead of (*a).b

- a->b is equivalent to (*a).b.

- a->b is shorter and does not require parentheses.

- a can be any pointer expression and b can be any structure or union member.

Instead of:
```
for(p=recs; *(*p).key; p++)
    if((*p).key==new_key) return p;
return NULL;
```

Use:
```
for(p=recs; *p->key; p++)
    if(p->key==new_key) return p;
return NULL;
```

Notes:
Both forms traverse an array of pointers to structures, searching for a given key. If the structure containing the key is found, a pointer to it is returned. Otherwise, NULL is returned. In the second form, *p->key is used instead of *(*p).key to test whether the key of the structure pointed to by p is an empty string.

Pointers to structures are very common in C. One way to refer to a member b of a structure pointed to by a pointer a is (*a).b (the parentheses are necessary because the precedence of the operator . is higher than the precedence of *). That is, you have to first dereference the pointer and then select the desired member. Fortunately, C offers a shortcut, the operator ->. a->b is equivalent to (*a).b. Use ->; it is shorter and does not require an additional set of parentheses.

Exercises

1. Rewrite:
```
void ascii_ebcdic(char *dest, char *src)
{   int i;
    for(i=0; src[i]; i++)
        dest[i] = tbl_ascii_ebcdic[src[i]];
}
```

2. Rewrite: `if((*context).field[nfld].text[0]) return;`

3. Rewrite: `*(buffer + *p++)`

CHAPTER 15: **The Preprocessor**

The C preprocessor is a powerful facility. The preprocessor operates as a logically independent step. As its name implies, it manipulates the text before the compiler. The preprocessor allows you, among other things, to include other source files into the compilation, to create names for constants and common operations, and to conditionally compile or skip portions of the code. The preprocessor is underused by most programmers.

15.1   Surround macro parameters and result with parentheses

- Use parentheses around parameters and result to avoid conflicts of precedence.

- Macros should, whenever possible, accept any expression as a parameter.

- Leave parentheses out only in a few special situations.

Instead of: `#define SCALE(x)   (x*size+ofs)`

Use: `#define SCALE(x)   ((x)*size+ofs)`

Notes: The first form will expand `SCALE(a+b)` incorrectly to `(a+b*size+ofs)`.

The parameters are replaced by the values supplied to the macro. For example, a+b, supplied for the parameter x, will replace x.

If x is not surrounded by parentheses, a+b will not act as one unit. Instead, it will be integrated into the surrounding text. The resulting expression will then be evaluated according to the C precedence rules. If one of the operators surrounding x has a higher precedence than the plus operator within a+b, the resulting expression will be incorrect. To avoid this, surround every parameter with parentheses.

When the result of the macro expansion is an expression, it should also be surrounded by parentheses. When you use a macro, you assume that the resulting expansion will work as one unit. If the expanded expression is not surrounded by parentheses, it may not be evaluated correctly when used as part of a larger expression.

In some macros, parentheses around some parameters are not needed. This happens when a parameter is supplied as an argument to a function or to another macro. In that case, a conflict of precedence cannot occur (see, for example, the macros `LE()`, `GE()`, `LT()`, and `GT()` in Rule 9.5).

In some other macros, parentheses around parameters not only are unnecessary, but would generate an error (e.g., macro `EXPR()` in Rule 4.5).

15.2   Whenever possible, make macros expand to expressions, not statements

- Macros that can be used wherever an expression can be used, are more generally useful. Whenever possible, make macros work like functions.

- Coding a macro as a statement precludes its use within an expression. This practice makes the macro unusable as a parameter to a function and makes it difficult to use within another macro.

- Coding some macros as statements and some as expressions is inconsistent. This practice leaves room for doubt on whether to put a ; after the macro.

Instead of: `#define SWAP(a,b,t)  {(t)=(a); (a)=(b); (b)=(t);}`

Use: `#define SWAP(a,b,t)  ((t)=(a), (a)=(b), (b)=(t))`

Notes: This version of `SWAP()` requires a temporary variable. It can be used to swap values between two data objects of the same type. The data objects can be of any non-composite type. (Compare to the other `SWAP()` macros in Rules 15.6 and 16.6.)

Most macros can be made to expand to an expression. Whenever possible, code your macros that way. It is natural to treat macros as functions (keeping in mind possible multiple evaluations of parameters). Macros that expand to statements cannot be used in some situations and might be confusing to use.

A sequence of expression statements can always be replaced by several expressions joined with commas. A macro needs to be expanded to one or more statements only when a for, while, do ... while, switch, continue, break, or return has to be embedded into it. This is because these statements cannot be replaced by expressions.

15.3   Do not replace C keywords or idioms with macros

■ Do not customize the language. Share a common language with other programmers.

■ Do not force the C language to look like a different language.

■ Do not replace idioms with macros.

■ Do not create replacements for C keywords.

Instead of:
```
#define forever  for(;;)
...
forever
{  ...
   ...
}
```

Use:
```
for(;;)
{  ...
   ...
}
```

Notes: Most C programmers know the idiom `for(;;)`. A reader of the first form is forced to read the definition of the macro **forever**. Even though the meaning is clearly suggested by its name, no experienced programmer will rely on the suggestion without looking at the definition. The reader of the first form is thus forced to look up the definition of a replacement for an idiom that he or she probably already knows. A level of indirection is introduced with no clear benefit.

The preprocessor gives you the ability to create your own terms. You might be tempted to make corrections to the C language. You might want to replace do ... while with something like repeat ... until to avoid the need to use the same keyword, while, for two different purposes. Or you might want to make the language similar to some other language. You could, for example, #define begin as { and #define end as }. Yet another possibility is to create terms for C idioms. Why not #define STRING_EMPTY(q) as (!*(q))? Or #define PUSH(x) as (*stk++ = (x))?

Don't do any of this. Do not customize the C language. The C language, like the English language, has some shortcomings. Yet it is a powerful and beautiful language. It offers you the big advantage of being understood by many people. In English, do you frequently coin new words or refuse to use existing idioms because they are inelegant? Do you refuse to use capital letters for proper names or at the beginning of sentences because you have a better convention? When writing in English, you compromise by following some stupid rules. As a result, what you write is readable by many people. On some occasions you might need to create a word. This usually happens when there is no existing word that matches the concept, or when several words or even sentences would be required.

Do in C as you would in English. Use the language, even with its shortcomings. When you replace a keyword or idiom, you force the reader to look for the corresponding #define (no conscientious programmer would accept your new terms without looking at the corresponding #define). The reader will wonder, with good reason, why you didn't use the keyword or idiom directly. To read your code, the reader will have to remember some extra words. When reading somebody else's code, new ones will need to be remembered. Little is gained in clarity (forever is not any more clear to us than for(;;)), but much is lost in general readability.

More sophisticated idioms should not be replaced either. Even though !*p might seem cryptic at first, it is soon accepted as what it is, an idiom. Idioms are easily learned and remembered as a unit. To an experienced C programmer, if(!*p) means "if p is pointing to an empty string." The less experienced programmer will run into idioms like this very often and should, therefore, learn them.

Do create new macros. Create macros for functionality not provided by the language or by existing idioms. Create macros that expand to constants, complicated expressions, and useful constructs not provided by the language.

15.4   Whenever possible, evaluate each macro parameter exactly once.

- Repeated evaluation of some parameters increases the probability of errors due to side effects.

- Macros that sometimes evaluate some of their parameters more than once or not at all are not as generally useful as macros that evaluate all of their parameters exactly once.

- Clearly document any parameters not evaluated exactly once.

- We suggest using lowercase for macros that behave like functions (i.e., each parameter is evaluated exactly once) and all uppercase for macros that do not evaluate all parameters exactly once.

Instead of:
```
#define ISNUMERIC(c) \
    (isdigit(c) || c=='+' || c=='-' || c='.')
```

Use:
```
#define isnumeric(c) (strchr("01234567890+-.",c))
```

Notes: Both forms expand to a non-zero value if c is a digit, '+', '-', or '.'. The second form, however, will always evaluate c exactly once. (The second form could be a little slower, since it introduces a function call.)

Programmers using macros should be prepared for some ill effects. They should know that a parameter may be evaluated more than once or not at all. Some macros, however, work as cleanly as a function. They always evaluate each of their parameters exactly once, and expand to a parenthesized expression. We suggest using lowercase names for such function-like macros. Whenever possible, make your macros behave in this way.

For those macros that do not always evaluate each parameter exactly once, we suggest using uppercase names (conforming to common C practice) and documenting which parameters are not well-behaved.

15.5   Use # to convert arguments to strings

- The # converts a parameter into a string.

- # inserts an extra \ before every \ or ".

- Parameters are not replaced within strings. For example, you can use "string1, " #param ", string2" to achieve the same effect as "string1, param, string2".

Example: #define printexp(fmt,q) \
                     (printf("\n %s = " fmt,#q,q));

Notes: This macro will print an expression and its value. For example, printexp("%3i",a[i]+b[j]) will expand to (printf("\n %s " "%3i","a[i]+b[j]",a[i]+b[j])). Note that # is not used for fmt because it is natural to supply the format as a string.

is a useful macro operator. Its effect is to convert the parameter after it to a string constant. This feature, together with the fact that adjacent string constants are automatically concatenated, allows you to perform the equivalent of a macro expansion within a string. A text such as "expression: " #p will expand to "expression: " "a+b" if a+b is passed as the parameter p. These two adjacent strings will then be concatenated to produce the string "expression: a+b". The same effect can be achieved by surrounding a+b with quotes when using the macro and removing the # operator just before p. The # operator, however, is extremely useful when you want both to evaluate an expression and to use its text representation.

15.6   Use ## to concatenate parameters and text

■   After parameter substitution, all **##** operators and surrounding white space characters are removed

Example:
```
#define SWAP(a,b,t)  ( zz ## t = (a),  \
                       (a)      = (b),  \
                       (b)      = zz ## t)
```

Notes: This macro interchanges the values of two variables of type t. It uses one of a set of global variables whose names start with zz. These variables should be declared elsewhere.

For example, SWAP(a[i],a[j],int) expands to (zzint=(a[i]), (a[i])=(b[i]), (b[i]) = zzint), (Compare to the other SWAP() macros in Rules 15.2 and 16.6.)

The **##** macro operator concatenates tokens. The preprocessor simply removes any **##** together with the surrounding white space. The resulting text is re-scanned.

15.7   Use #if !defined in headers to avoid duplicate inclusion

■ Create your headers so as to allow multiple inclusion.

■ To avoid redefinitions, surround the text inside header files with
  #if !defined *FILENAME_H* and #endif.   Within the text, use
  #define *FILENAME_H*. (*FILENAME_H* should be based on the name of
  the include file, e.g., stdio_h.)

Examples: #if !defined PROJ01_H
                 #define PROJ01_H
                 ...
                 #endif

Each header should be written so as to allow multiple inclusion. This
allows headers to include other required headers without danger of
duplications. Use the macro directive #if !defined for this.

#if !defined name will ignore the text up to the matching #endif when
name is defined. Within the text controlled by #if !defined, #define a
name unique to the header. We suggest using the filename and extension
separated by an underscore.

15.8   Use #if 0 to comment out large sections of code

- Comments do not nest. Comments cannot be used to comment out sections of code containing other comments.

- #if 0 ... #endif turns off compilation of a section of code. This construct does nest, and can be used to turn off compilation of code containing comments and other #ifs.

Example:

```
#if 0
... /* code possibly containing          */
... /* comments, #if 0's, and other #ifs */
#endif
```

In C, comments do not nest. A fragment such as /* a /* b */ c */ will not be considered just one comment by the compiler. Instead, a and b will be inside the comment, c will be outside, and the */ after c will be an invalid token. This is because the /* between a and b will be ignored and the */ between b and c will be treated as marking the end of the comment.

As a result, code that includes comments cannot be "commented out" by surrounding it with /* and */. Instead, you must use #if 0 ... #endif. The #if macro directive does nest. Therefore, code containing other #ifs will be processed correctly.

15.9   Use ?: or && instead of if within macros

- if( ) is a statement. It cannot be used within expressions.

- Use a ? b : c instead of if(a) b; else c; in macros.

- Use a && b instead of if(a) b; when the value of b is not important.

Example 1:   #define PUTC_ALL(c,f) \
        (isprint($\bar{c}$) ? putc(c,f) : fprintf(f,"\%2x",c))

Example 2:   #define PUTC_PRINT(c,f) (isprint(c) && putc(c,f))

    It is often necessary to use conditionals within macros. if, however, is a statement and cannot be used inside expressions. If you want the macro to expand to an expression, use either ?: or &&. Use (a ? b : c) when one of b or c has to be evaluated based on the condition a.

    Use (a && b) when there is only one expression to be conditionally evaluated (similar to if with no else) and its value is not used. && evaluates its left operand first. If the left operand is not zero, && evaluates the right operand. The result of the operation is 0 or 1. && does not yield the value of its right-hand operand even if that operand is evaluated. If that value is needed, use (a ? b : 0). && is better than ?: in this context because it does not force you to add the equivalent of an empty else clause.

15.10 Do not use "magic numbers" in your code; #define instead

- Do not use constants that are not self-explanatory directly in your code. Instead, #define them and use the macro.

- Do not replace self-explanatory constants that are not subject to change with macros. Use values such as 0, 1, -1, and string literals directly in your code.

- #defined values are easier to modify and maintain.

Instead of: ```
                 #define SPACE ' '
                 char buffer[100];
                 ...
                 memset(buffer,SPACE,100);
                 ```

Use:             ```
                 #define BF_SIZE 100;
                 char buffer[BF_SIZE];
                 ...
                 memset(buffer,' ',BF_SIZE);
                 ```


Do not insert unnamed constants ("magic numbers") directly in your code, unless they are self-explanatory. The reader will not know how those values were derived and what they represent. For example, do not use a number such as 24, representing the number of rows on the screen, directly in the code. Instead, #define NUM_ROWS 24 and use NUM_ROWS in the code. This will not only make your code more readable, it will also make modifications easier. To change the number of rows to 20, all you will have to do is #define NUM_ROWS 20. Without the macro, you will have to replace most 24s by 20s. You will incur the risk of changing a 24 that represents something other than the number of rows.

Do not, however, #define everything. Using ONE in your code, after a #define ONE 1, is not more clear than using 1. It is probably confusing. Do not #define values that are self-explanatory and are not subject to change.

15.11 Use the predefined identifiers __LINE__, __FILE__, __DATE__, __TIME__, and __STDC__

- __LINE__ and __FILE__ expand to the current file and line number. Use them in debugging macros.

- __DATE__ and __TIME__ expand to the date and time of compilation. Use them for version control, for debugging, and to inform users of compilation date and time.

- __STDC__ expands to 1 in Standard C environments. Use it to detect potential portability problems.

Example: #define HERE \
                        (printf("\n%s(%d)", __FILE__, __LINE__)

Notes: This macro prints the current filename and line number. It can be used in debugging to verify that a certain point in the program has been reached. For example, the statement HERE; in line 237 of the file main.c will print main.c(237) when executed.

Example: puts("\nCompiled " __DATE__ " " __TIME__);

Example: #if __STDC__ != 1
                 #error "Error: not a Standard C environment"
             #endif

The predefined constants __LINE__ and __FILE__ are very useful for debugging purposes. They expand to the current line number and filename. The predefined constants __DATE__ and __TIME__ expand to the date and time of compilation. They can be used to show the user what version of the software is running, or to print the date and time of compilation to a debugging file. The predefined constant __STDC__ expands to 1 in Standard C conforming environments. Use it within portable code to generate a compile time error when compiling in environments that do not conform to the ANSI C Standard.

Exercises

1. Rewrite: `#define MIN(a,b)  a<b ? a : b`

2. Rewrite: `#define SORT2(a,b,t) { if(b<a) SWAP(a,b,t); }`

3. Write a macro (let's name it `CALL`) that can be used to surround a function call. The macro should print the filename, the line number, and the complete function call to the file `fdbg` before calling the function. The macro should return the value returned by the function. For example, `p=CALL(strstr(s,w))` on line 373 of `main.c` should print `"main.c(373) strstr(s,w)"` and `p` should be assigned the value of `strstr(s,w)`.

PART IV: **C Review**

C has many operators. There are 45 of them including unary + and −. Learn to use all of them correctly. Learn their precedence levels and whether they associate from left to right or right to left. For example, ¦¦ associates from left to right. This means that the expression (a ¦¦ b ¦¦ c ¦¦ d) will be evaluated as (((a ¦¦ b) ¦¦ c) ¦¦ d). The precedence levels of the operators are fairly intuitive, and it is not difficult to remember all of them. Only three operators (& ¦ and ^) have somewhat unexpected precedence levels.

Unfortunately, because the standard character set is somewhat limited, some characters stand for more than one operator. Which operator they designate within a given expression is determined by context. The following characters represent more than one operator: + − & * and ( ).

Two key technical terms will be used in this chapter: *lvalue* and *sequence point*. An *lvalue* is an expression that denotes an object. It is so called because it can be used as the left value of an assignment. a, a[3], and *p are valid lvalues. x+3, sqrt(x), and 10 are not.

A *sequence point* is a point in the execution sequence at which all side effects of previous evaluations have been completed and no side effects of subsequent evaluations have taken place yet. The sequence points are: the call to a function after the arguments have been evaluated; the end of the first operand of any of these four operators: && ¦¦ , and ?, and the end of a full expression. A full expression is an initializer, the expression in an expression statement, the controlling expression for a flow control statement, any of the three expressions of a for statement, or the expression in a return statement.

Notice that, except for sequence points, the evaluation order is not defined. Thus, in the expression a && b, a will be evaluated first. However, in the expressions a & b and strcpy(a,b), either a or b might be evaluated first. Furthermore, expressions that modify an lvalue more than once with no intervening sequence points (e.g., a[i++] − a[i++]) are undefined. They can return different values from implementation to implementation or within the same implementation. The Standard allows any action as a result of such statements, including program termination.

16.1   Use function call, array dereference, and structure dereference operators effectively

- `()` `[]` `->` and `.` have the same precedence level (the highest level, level 1) and associate from left to right.

- `a(b,c,...)` evaluates the expressions `b`, `c`, etc. and delivers the results (usually by pushing them on the stack) to a function at the address indicated by the expression `a`. Note that `a` can be any valid expression that evaluates to the address of a function. The order of evaluation of `a`, `b`, `c`, etc. is not defined.

- `a[i]` is equivalent to `*(a+i)` and to `i[a]`. (Do not use `i[a]`.)

- `a->b` is equivalent to `(*a).b`.

Example: `a.b[c](d, e, f)->g`

Notes: The element number `c` will be selected from the member `b` of the structure `a`. This element should be a pointer to a function, which will be called with the arguments `d`, `e`, and `f`. The function should return a pointer to a structure whose member `g` will be selected.

Example: `(*p)(a, b)`

Notes: The function pointed to by the pointer `p` will be called with the arguments `a` and `b`. The parentheses around `*p` are necessary because `*` has a lower precedence than `()` (function call).

Example: `fctn[i](a, b)`

Notes: The function pointed to by `fctn[i]` will be called with the arguments `a` and `b`. Parentheses around `fctn[i]` are not necessary because `[]` and `()` (function call) have the same precedence and both associate from left to right.

Notice that in C, function calls and array dereferencing are done by using operators. Any expression of the correct type can be used instead of just a function name (i.e., `(*p->func)()`) or an array name (i.e., `strchr(s,c)[2]`). This flexibility has its price. The C compiler cannot detect errors that compilers for more rigid languages can (for example, Pascal). Still, the functionality offered is so useful that we gladly accept that price.

The function call operator, `()`, evaluates the expressions within the parentheses (the arguments to the function) and copies their values to some area accessible to the function to be called. Usually the values are pushed onto the stack, from last to first (some implementations might pass parameters in registers or by some other method). Then, the function call operator executes a call to the address specified by the expression just before `()`. The value returned by the function is used as the result of the operation. Notice that the order of evaluation of the expressions within parentheses (arguments) and the expression before the parentheses is not defined.

Usually, a function name is used just before the function call operator. This name is a constant set by the compiler or linker to the address of the beginning of the function. Any other expression returning the address of executable code can be used instead of the function name. For example, the following non-portable technique can be used in some implementations to call a machine language subroutine. Fill a character array `s` with valid machine language instructions (including a return instruction), then use the expression `((void (*)(void))s)()`, or some variation of it (in some Intel-based implementations `far *` may have to be used instead of `*`), to execute the machine language function. There is actually little trickery involved. The expression typecasts the array name `s` to a pointer to function (accepting no parameters and returning `void` in this particular example, i.e., `(void (*)(void))`). It then uses that pointer to call the function.

The operators `[]` `->` and `.` work in a similar fashion. That is, they operate on two valid expressions of the appropriate type. The array dereferencing operator `[]`, for example, requires an expression before the brackets and an expression within the brackets. One of these expressions should be of a pointer type and the other of an integer type. The result is equal to the sum of the two expressions, dereferenced.

Any valid expression can be used as either operand of `()` `[]` `->` and `.`, including a function call. For example, `(a(b))(c).d->e` is valid.

16.2   Use unary operators effectively

- ! ~ ++ -- + - * & (type) and sizeof have the same precedence level (level 2) and associate from right to left.

- ! converts 0 to 1 and non-zero to 0; ~ flips each bit in its operand.

- Use a++ instead of a=a+1 and a-- instead of a=a-1.

- (++a) is equivalent to (a++ + 1); (--a) is equivalent to (a-- - 1).

- ++ and -- can be used only on lvalues.

- Do not use an lvalue that has been used with ++ or -- again in the same expression, unless you use && || ?: or ,.

- Typecast only when necessary; do not typecast to void * to satisfy function prototypes. The type void * is assignment compatible with all other pointer types.

- Typecast the operands of an expression, not the result, if you want the expression to be evaluated using the type you are typecasting to.

- sizeof is an operator, not a function; it does not require parentheses, except when used on a type (e.g., sizeof(int)).

Example: *a.b[c]->d

Notes: This expression evaluates to the contents of the member d of the structure pointed to by a.b[c]. This is accomplished without the need of parentheses around a.b[c]->d because the precedence of the operator * is lower than the precedence of any dereference operator.

Example: sizeof a /sizeof *a

Notes: This expression evaluates to number of elements in the array a. This is a useful idiom.

Example: `*strchr(s, c)`

Notes: The function `strchr` will be called with the arguments `s` and
                `c`. The expression evaluates to the value pointed to by the
                result of the function. (Function call has a higher precedence
                than pointer dereference.)

Example: `while(a[i--]);`

Notes: After the loop, the variable `i` will contain the index of the
                element just before the first element with the value zero
                encountered working backward from the `i`-th element. This
                statement will misbehave if there are no elements with zero
                value in `a` in that portion of `a`, or if `i` does not have a proper
                value upon entering the loop.

Example: `while(!*++p);`

Notes: This loop will stop at the first non-zero value pointed to by `p`.
                Parentheses are not necessary within `!*++p` because `!` `*` and
                `++` have the same precedence level and associate from right to
                left.

Example: ```
                i   = 10;
                a[i++] = i;
                ```

Notes:          The result of the second statement is undefined. If you are
                lucky, `a[10]` will be set to either 10 or 11. The C Standard
                allows implementations to take any action for statements like
                this one, including program termination.
                ```

C provides a large set of unary operators. Among them are ++ and --. These two operators are a very nice feature of the C language. They allow you to express the common operation of incrementing or decrementing an lvalue in a compact and clear manner. They also provide the ability to obtain the value before incrementing or decrementing in the same expression that specifies the increment or decrement. For example, i=t++; will assign the previous value of t to i, then increment t. Without ++ we would have to use comma or write two statements: i=t; t=t+1;. Since ++ and -- affect the value of their operand, beware of evaluation order dependencies. The result of the statement a[i] = i++; is undefined; it might produce different results even in the same implementation. (It might also cause program termination.) In general, do not use an lvalue that has been operated upon by ++ or -- in the same expression, unless the use of the lvalue is separated by a sequence point.

Typecasting is another useful unary operation. Typecasts allow you to convert variables from one type to another. Typecasting a value of type z to a type y is equivalent to assigning the value of type z to a type y, then using the result of the assignment. In some cases, an actual conversion might be performed. For example, typecasting a positive value x of type double to int causes the fractional part of x to be discarded and the internal representation of x to be changed to represent the corresponding integer value. In other cases, however, the internal representation of the value is not changed. Rather, the internal representation is reinterpreted as being of the new type. For example, typecasting a pointer to int to the new type pointer to char leaves the pointer pointing to the same place. However, subsequent increment, decrement, dereference, etc. operations on that new pointer will assume elements of the size of char. Do not typecast unnecessarily. Remember that assignments and function calls (to functions with prototypes) automatically convert the result to the destination type.

Notice that the typecast operator (type) converts the value of the expression to its right to the new type, not the type of each element within the expression. For example, if a and b are of type short, the expression (long)(a*b) might overflow if the result of a*b is not representable in the type short. Only after the multiplication will the result be converted to long. Use (long)a * b or (long)a * (long)b instead.

All the unary operators have a precedence level of 2, one below dereferencing and function call operators. Therefore parentheses are not needed in the following expressions if the unary operator is to be applied last: *a(b, c), ++a[b].c, !a[b](c, d).

16.3   Use arithmetic operators effectively

- `*` `/` and `%` have the same precedence level (level 3) and associate from left to right.

- `+` and `-` have the same precedence level (level 4) and associate from left to right.

- `/` used with integer types truncates the result.

- The direction of truncation of `/` and the sign of the result of `%` are implementation-dependent for negative operands.

- Do not use `%` or `/` with powers of two to extract bits. Use bitwise operators instead.

- Use `a%n` to determine whether `a` is divisible by `n`. For example, use `a%10` to determine whether `a` is divisible by ten or not.

- Use `!(i%n)` to do something every `n` iterations (when `i` is incremented by one on each iteration).

- `%` works only with integer types. Use `fmod()` for `float` or `double`.

Example:
```
for(i=0; i<100; i++)
    printf("%c%5i", i%10 ? ' ' : '\n', prime[i]);
```

Notes: This loop will print 100 prime numbers. Whenever `i` is divisible by 10, a newline character will be printed before the number. Thus, there will be 10 prime numbers per line.

Keep in mind that the result of an arithmetic operation is of the same type as the larger type of the two operands. That is, if you add, multiply, divide, etc., a `short` and an `int`, the result will be `int`. Division of integer types results in loss of the fractional part of the quotient (which can be truncated toward or away from zero for negative values). Overflows might occur for any numerical type. Integer arithmetic overflow usually does not result in any signal to the user. The details are described in Rule 9.1.

16.4   Use bitwise binary operators effectively

- << and >> have the same precedence level (level 5) and associate from left to right.

- & (level 8) has a higher precedence than ^ (level 9), which has a higher precedence than | (level 10). The three of them associate from left to right.

- Remember that & ^ and | have a relatively low precedence level. You must use parentheses if you want them to be evaluated before relational operators.

- >> might fill vacated bits of signed quantities with ones or with zeros (implementation-dependent).

- Use | to set bits, & to reset bits, and ^ to flip bits.

- Use & with >> to extract groups of bits.

- Use ˜0 to generate implementation-independent quantities where all bits are 1.

- Use ^ to determine which bits are different between two quantities.

- Use ^ with two relational expressions to check whether one and only one of them is true.

Example: `x ^ 1<<n`

Notes: This expression will evaluate to the value of x with bit n flipped (the rightmost bit is considered to be bit 0).

Example: `x>>4 & 0x0f`

Notes: If x holds eight bits, this expression will evaluate to its left nibble (bits 7 through 4 shifted to positions 3 through 0, where 0 is the rightmost bit).

Example: `x & ˜(1<<n)`

Notes: This expression will evaluate to the value of x with bit n set to zero (the rightmost bit is considered to be bit 0).

There are six operators for bit manipulation, five binary operators (& | ^ << and >>) and one unary operator (~, mentioned in Rule 16.2). These operators can only be applied to integer types. They all have different precedence levels except for << and >>. The precedence levels of & | and ^ are lower than the precedence level of the relational operators, because they could be used to join relational expressions. They are very seldom used for that purpose, however, since the operators && and || are better suited for it. & | and ^ are the only operators whose precedence level is somewhat counter-intuitive.

These operators are used mostly to manipulate bits. Typical examples are:

x | 0x03   Evaluates to x with the rightmost two bits set.
x & 0x0f   Evaluates to the rightmost four bits of x.
x & ~0x03   Evaluates to x with the rightmost two bits reset.
x ^ 0x01   Evaluates to x with the rightmost bit flipped.
x >> 4   Evaluates to x shifted four bits to the right.

When manipulating bits, keep two things in mind. First, signed quantities might behave differently from unsigned quantities for the right shift (>>) operator. Second, if you want your code to be portable, do not assume any particular size for integer types. Try to make your expressions size-independent. For example, the expression (x & ~3) is better than (x & 0xfffc) since it does not depend on the size of the operand x.

& and | can also be used to join relational expressions. This is seldom done, but it might be useful under some circumstances. You can use & and | instead of && and || if you want to make sure that all the operands are evaluated (&& and || evaluate sequentially and stop evaluation as soon as they can return a correct value). Use & and | in this way only when you are sure that the operands will have a 0 or 1 value (relational operations yield only 0 or 1).

You can also use ^ to join to relational expressions. This is very useful, since there is no corresponding ^^ operator. ^ returns 1 if only one of the two operands is 1 and the other is zero. It returns 0 if both operands are equal. Note that when used with operands that can have only the values 0 or 1, ^ is equivalent to !=.

16.5 Use relational and logical operators effectively

- < <= > and >= have the same precedence level (level 6) and associate from left to right.

- == and != have the same precedence level (level 7) and associate from left to right.

- && (level 11) has a higher precedence than ¦¦ (level 12). Both associate from left to right.

- Relational and logical operators return a value of 0 or 1.

- Use double equal to test for equality; a single equal is assignment.

- We suggest not using > and >=; < and <= can always be used instead.

- Choose between < and <= to avoid adding or subtracting one.

- && and ¦¦ guarantee left to right evaluation and stop as soon as truth or falsehood has been established.

- Combine chains of ifs into one if by using && whenever possible.

Instead of:
```
if(i<MAX_ARRAY)
    if(a[i]==z) return;
```

Use:
```
if(i<MAX_ARRAY && a[i]==z) return;
```

Instead of:
```
if(x<0.0 ¦¦ x>10.0) return E_RANGE;
```

Use:
```
if(x<0.0 ¦¦ 10.0<x) return E_RANGE;
```

Notes: The second form shows immediately that E_RANGE will be returned if x is outside the range [0.0, 10.0]. x can be seen to be outside (to the left and to the right) of that range.

The relational operators compare two operands and give a result of type int; 0 for false, 1 for true. Note that there is no boolean or logical type in C. The result of a relational operation is just a number and can be used as such.

A bad feature of the C language is the use of double equal (==) to check for equality. A single equal (=) is the assignment operator, which returns the result of the expression to its right. It is very easy to use a single equal by mistake when intending to compare for equality. This error is very common (especially among Pascal programmers) and is difficult to detect. The program will compile correctly, and the intended condition will usually evaluate to true. Unfortunately, there is no general solution to this problem. Assignments in control clauses of fors, whiles, dos, and ifs are powerful tools, and therefore we do not advise against using them. If you are prone to commit this type of error, use a general expression search utility (e.g., grep) to find all single equal signs within fors, whiles, dos, and ifs. Some compilers can warn you of assignments used in this context.

We suggest not using > and >=. They can always be replaced by < and <= by reversing the operands. By using only < and <=, you can immediately visualize which quantity should be bigger. Smaller quantities will appear to the left of larger quantities, as on the x axis of a graph. Select between < and <= so as to eliminate a +1 or -1. For example, use (n<t) instead of (n<=t-1).

C offers two very useful logical operators: && and ||. These operators guarantee left to right evaluation. (&& || ?: and , are the only operators that guarantee evaluation order.) && and || stop evaluation as soon as a correct result can be ascertained. That is, && will not evaluate its right operand if the left operand is 0 (false), and || will not evaluate its right operand if the left operand is non-zero (true).

Instead of:
```
while(0<=i)
{  if(!a[i].data) break;
   i--;
}
```

Use:
```
while(0<=i && a[i].data) i--;
```

Notes: These two forms are exactly equivalent. The && in the second form guarantees that for negative values of i, a[i] (possibly an illegal element) will not be accessed. The first form is longer and clumsier.

&& can also be used to simplify chains of ifs and instead of an if in situations where if cannot be used (for example, in macros) (see Rule 15.9).

16.6   Use conditional, assignment, and comma operators effectively

- The ?: operator (level 13) associates from right to left.

- = += −+ *= /= %= &= ^= |= <<= and >>= have the same precedence level (level 14) and associate from right to left.

- The , operator (level 15) associates from left to right.

- The , and ?: operators guarantee left to right evaluation order.

- In a?b:c the expression a will be evaluated first and then only one of b or c.

- Use ?: in macros as a replacement for if.

- Use ?: when two long, similar expressions differ only by one term.

- There is an assignment of the form <oper>= for every binary arithmetic and binary bitwise operator.

- Use a <oper>= b instead of a = a <oper> b. It is shorter, and it avoids repetition of a.

- Use the comma operator to evaluate two expressions as if they were syntactically one. The comma operator is especially handy in for expressions, macros, and function calls, and to avoid using braces around groups of very short expression statements.

Example: #define MAX(a, b) ((a)<(b) ? (b) : (a))

Notes: This macro evaluates to the greater of a and b. Either a or b will be evaluated twice.

Instead of: `scr->width[nfld] = scr->width[nfld]+10;`

Use: `scr->width[nfld] += 10;`

Notes: The second form avoids repetition of a long expression.

Example: `#define SWAP(a, b)   ((a)^=(b),(b)^=(a),(a)^=(b))`

Notes: This macro swaps the values of two integer data objects a and
                   b without using a temporary variable. It relies on a nice trick
                   using exclusive or. a and b should be lvalues. Both will be
                   evaluated three times. The macro evaluates to the new value
                   of a.

Example: `if(a[i]==a[j]) i++,j--;`

Notes: A comma between i++ and j-- creates a compact statement.

`?:` is the only ternary operator in C. In an expression such as a ? b : c,
a is evaluated first, and then only one of b or c. It is the expression equivalent
of the `if() else` statement. Use it in situations where you want an
expression instead of a few statements (for example, in macros) and to avoid
writing a long expression twice, where one term depends on some condition.

In C, assignment is not a statement but an operation. This means that an
assignment is a sub-expression and can be further used within a bigger
expression.

Besides the usual assignment operator (=), C offers ten assignment
operators of the form <oper>=. These operators combine a binary arithmetic
or bitwise operator with assignment. a <oper>= b is equivalent to
a = a <oper> b. Use them instead of the longer form a = a <oper> b.
They result in shorter and clearer code, and avoid duplication. This is
especially handy when a in a <oper>= b is a long expression. Using an
<oper>= operator reduces the possibility of errors and saves the reader from
having to verify that the duplicate expression is indeed the same.

The comma operator has the lowest precedence level of all operators. It
simply evaluates its left and right operands and returns the value of the right
operand. Use it when you have to evaluate more than one expression, but you
want to do this within one bigger expression. The comma operator is
particularly useful in fors and macros. Comma can also be used to combine
several expression statements into one, to avoid using braces. Use comma in
this fashion only when the statements being combined are simple and related.

Exercises

1. Given the following definition of `ftable`, call the function pointed to by
    `ftable[2]`.

    ```
    int (*ftable)(void) = { fadd, fsub, fmul, fdiv };
    ```

2. Given the following declaration of the array `tree`, increment the member
    count of the element `tree[n]`.

    ```
    typedef struct {  char *data;
                      int  left,right,count;
                   } Tnode;

    Tnode tree[1000];
    ```

3. Rewrite:
    ```
    int gcd(int a, int b)
    {   int c;
        if(a<b) c=a,a=b,b=c;
        do
        {   c = a/b;
            c = a-b*c;
            a = b;
            b = c;
        } while(c);
        return a;
    }
    ```

4. Rewrite:
    ```
    if(age1<18)
    {   if(18<=age2) study_case();
    }
    else
    {   if(age2<18)  study_case();
    }
    ```

5. Rewrite:
    ```
    int a[MAX_ELEM];

    for(i=0; i<MAX_ELEM; i++)
    {   if(a[i]) break;
        ...
    }
    ```

CHAPTER 17: **The Standard C Library**

The C Library is almost a part of the language. The C language, by design, provides only a bare minimum. There is no I/O support, string support, or memory allocation support in the language itself. The C Library provides support for these areas and many others.

The C Library is a collection of functions catering to several different needs. It evolved haphazardly out of the separate efforts of early users and implementors of the language. The C Library is, however, such an integral part of any complete C implementation that the ANSI Standard C committee decided to define a Standard C Library. The result is a compromise between the existing functions and the ideals of the C Standard: consistency, environment independence, etc. Some major function groups were left out. UNIX style I/O (open(), close(), read(), write(), etc.) is one of them. New functions were added. Existing practice was unified and regulated when possible.

The Standard C Library defines the following fifteen headers:

```
assert.h   ctype.h   errno.h    float.h    limits.h
locale.h   math.h    setjmp.h   signal.h   stdarg.h
stddef.h   stdio.h   stdlib.h   string.h   time.h
```

Any *hosted* C environment should support the full Standard C Library. A *freestanding* environment needs to support only four headers: float.h, limits.h, stdarg.h, and stddef.h.

In this chapter, we will cover only the Standard C Library. Most full implementations provide additional functions. When possible, use Standard C Library functions; this makes your code more portable. Always include the headers for the functions you use.

Some functions are also implemented as macros. To call a function func masked by a macro, either use #undef func or use (func)(). All Library macros evaluate their arguments exactly once, except, possibly, getc() and put().

17.1   Use **assert.h** effectively

- **assert.h** provides the ability to verify whether a certain condition holds.

- **assert.h** defines only one macro, **assert()**, and it uses another macro (not defined by **assert.h**), NDEBUG.

- Use the macro **assert()** as often as possible in your code; it will help you to detect and document "impossible" situations.

- Assertions can be turned on or off at any point in your code by #undefining or #defineing the macro NDEBUG and including **assert.h**.

- Write your own equivalent of **assert()** if you need a different reaction on assertion failure.

- Use **assert()** only during testing; use a more sophisticated equivalent of **assert()** or #define NDEBUG to disable **assert()** in production systems.

- Do not put expressions with side effects within **assert()**; they will not be evaluated if assertions are turned off.

Example: assert(pform);
                 assert(!strncmp(pform->id, "FX", 2));
                 assert(pform->nrows<20);
                 assert(pform->ncols<72);

Notes: pform is a pointer to a structure containing data for a screen
                 form. Most likely, at least one of these assertions will fail if
                 pform is not pointing to a valid form.

The header `assert.h` defines the macro `assert()`. This macro has two different behaviors depending on whether or not the macro NDEBUG was defined when the header was last included. If NDEBUG was defined before including the header, `assert()` does nothing. If NDEBUG was undefined at the most recent inclusion of `assert.h`, `assert(x)` evaluates the expression x. If the expression x evaluates to non-zero, the macro does nothing else. If the expression x evaluates to zero (false), the macro prints the filename, line number, and the expression x, and calls `abort()` to terminate the program.

Use `assert()` to make assertions about your program. If you know that at a certain point in your program a condition must hold, use `assert()` to verify that indeed it does. Most of the time `assert()` will do nothing, but it may surprise you by aborting your program. This can save you a lot of debugging time. When you are no longer debugging the program, leave your assertions in: you can turn debugging off by defining NDEBUG before including `assert.h`. This will suppress evaluation of the assertion expression. `assert.h` can be included several times to turn debugging on or off for specific sections of code.

Since assertions can be disabled, causing the expressions supplied to them not to be evaluated, do not include expressions that should be evaluated (for the sake of their side effects) within `assert()`.

17.2   Use `ctype.h` effectively

- `ctype.h` provides the ability to test characters to determine whether they belong to a certain class (letters, digits, etc.). It also supports translation of uppercase to lowercase and vice versa.

- `ctype.h` declares many functions: `isalnum()`, `isalpha()`, `iscntrl()`, `isdigit()`, `isgraph()`, `islower()`, `isprint()`, `ispunct()`, `isspace()`, `isupper()`, `isxdigit()`, `tolower()`, and `toupper()`.

- Use `isdigit(c)`, `isalpha(c)`, etc., instead of the similar expressions (`'0'<=c && c<='9'`), (`'A'<=c && c<='Z' || 'a'<=c && c<='z'`), etc.; they are faster and more portable.

- Use `tolower(c)` and `toupper(c)` to convert to lowercase and uppercase instead of the similar expressions (`c-'A'+'a'`) and (`c-'a'+'A'`); they are more portable.

- The functions declared in `ctype.h` will work correctly with different character sets.

- Make as few assumptions as possible about the underlying character set.

- In some character sets, some lowercase letters might not have uppercase counterparts and vice versa, some letters might be neither lowercase nor uppercase, and some might be both.

- In some character sets, letters that are adjacent in the alphabet might not have adjacent numerical codes. The numerical difference between the uppercase and the lowercase values might vary from letter to letter.

- `isdigit()` and `isxdigit()` are locale-independent; all the remaining functions accept characters based on the locale.

- All the functions in `ctype.h` accept `int` arguments and return an `int` value. However, the arguments either should be representable as `unsigned char` or should have the value of the macro `EOF`.

Example:
```
int c,tsymbol;
char symbol[MAX_SYM_LEN];
...
int next_token(void)
{ char *p=symbol;
  while(isspace(c)) c = getchar();
  if(isalpha(c))
  { do
    { assert(p<symbol+MAX_SYM_LEN);
      *p++ = tolower(c);
      c = getchar();
    } while(isalnum(c);
    *p = 0;
    tsymbol = T_NAME;
    return 0;
  }
  if(isdigit(c) || c=='-' || c=='+')
  { do
    { assert(p<symbol+MAX_SYM_LEN);
      *p++= c;
      c = getchar();
    } while(isdigit(c) || c=='.')
    *p=0;
    tsymbol = T_NUMBER;
    return 0;
  }
  if(!ispunct(c)) return c;
  do
  { assert(p<symbol+MAX_SYM_LEN);
    *p++ = c;
    c = getchar();
  } while(ispunct(c));
  *p = 0;
  tsymbol = T_PUNCT
  return 0
}
```

Notes: The function next_token() returns one token on every call.
            The token is returned in the global variable symbol, and its
            type is returned in tsymbol. next_token() returns 0 if it
            could parse a token. Otherwise, it returns the character that
            could not be parsed. (This functions assumes that c always
            contains the next character to be processed.)

            Since next_token() uses the ctype.h functions, it is highly
            portable.

The functions declared in `ctype.h` offer several advantages over expressions for the same purpose, such as (`'a'<=c && c<='z'`). They are faster, shorter, clearer, more portable, and evaluate c only once. Use the `ctype.h` functions instead of similar expressions whenever possible.

Portability is the key advantage. If you want to write a portable program, make as few assumptions as possible about the underlying character set. It may be ASCII, EBCDIC, a local extension of ASCII, or something else. These functions will work with any character set.

These functions and their macro equivalents evaluate their argument just once. They are usually faster than similar expressions. To achieve these two objectives, one common approach is to code them using a character classification table. This table contains an entry for each valid character. Each entry is a collection of bits. Each function just ands the entry for its parameter with a specific mask. Thus, it returns non-zero if any of the corresponding bits is set, zero otherwise.

The C Standard guarantees that the character classification will return non-zero for the following characters or conditions under the "C" locale:

```
isdigit():   0 1 2 3 4 5 6 7 8 9
isxdigit():  isdigit() || a b c d e f A B C D E F
islower():   a b c d e f g h i j k l m n o p q r s t u v w x y z
isupper():   A B C D E F G H I J K L M N O P Q R S T U V W X Y Z
isalpha():   islower() || isupper()
isalnum():   isalpha() || isdigit()
ispunct():   ! " # % & ' ( ) ; < = > ? [ \ ] * + , - . / : ^
isgraph():   isalnum() || ispunct()
isprint():   isgraph() || <space>
isspace():   <space> \f \n \r \t \v
iscntrl():   \a \b \f \n \r \t \v
```

An implementation can add characters that will return non-zero for `ispunct()` and `iscntrl()` under the "C" locale. Other locales can add characters that will return non-zero for the following functions: `isupper()`, `islower()`, `isalpha()`, `isspace()`, `ispunct()`, and `iscntrl()`. Notice that some locales can have lowercase characters with no uppercase counterpart and vice versa. Some locales might also have characters that are neither uppercase nor lowercase, but for which `isalpha()` returns true.

`ctype.h` also includes the functions `toupper()` and `tolower()`. These functions convert characters to uppercase or lowercase when possible. They are clearer and more portable than expressions like (`c+'A'-'a'`). In some character sets the difference between the lowercase code and the uppercase code might vary from character to character. There may even be characters for which `islower()` and `isupper()` are both true.

17.3   Use **errno.h** effectively

- errno.h supports reporting of errors.

- errno.h defines two constants, EDOM and ERANGE, and the macro errno, which expands to a modifiable lvalue.

- errno is set to zero at program startup and can be set to non-zero by any Library function. However, it is never set to zero by any Library function.

- The C Standard specifies a few conditions (largely for math functions) under which errno must be set. Only two values, EDOM and ERANGE, are required by the C Standard to be defined in errno.h, but other values can be used.

- errno might not always evaluate to the same memory location.

- To use errno, set it to zero before calling a Library function and test it before the next call to a Library function.

Example:
```
errno = 0;
z = pow(x,y);
if(errno) return E_POWER;
```

Notes: This fragment returns E_POWER if there is a diagnosed range or domain error when attempting to calculate x to the power y.

The macro errno expands to a modifiable lvalue. It is usually used by setting it to zero before calling a Library function, and then testing for non-zero. The C Standard specifies some functions that must set errno to either EDOM or ERANGE. Other Library functions can set errno to EDOM, ERANGE, or other values, but no Library function sets errno to 0.

errno does not necessarily always evaluate to the same address. Its contents need not necessarily be defined until the macro is used. errno could, for example, expand to (*errf()). The function errf() would perform certain testing, store a value at some location, and then return a pointer to that location.

17.4   Use `float.h` and `limits.h` effectively

- `float.h` defines several macros that expand to floating-point limits and parameters.

- `limits.h` defines maximum and minimum values for the `signed` and `unsigned` types `char`, `int`, `short`, and `long`.

- Use these headers to determine sizes and limits of different types.

Example:
```
#define VMAX  100000L
#if VMAX<=UCHAR_MAX
    typedef Vtype unsigned char;
#elif VMAX<=USHRT_MAX
    typedef Vtype unsigned short;
#elif VMAX<=UINT_MAX
    typedef Vtype unsigned int;
#elif VMAX<=ULONG_MAX
    typedef Vtype unsigned long;
#else
    #error Vtype out of range
#endif

Vtype  i,j,k;
Vtype  a[100];
```

Notes: This group of macro directives defines the type `Vtype` as the smallest unsigned type that can hold values between 0 and `VMAX`. Changing `VMAX` will cause the size of the underlying type to be selected automatically. This fragment will work in many Standard C environments. It may fail in some environments because the preprocessor does not necessarily support the same numeric types as the compiler. Therefore, some of the constants might overflow.

The constants defined in `limits.h` and `float.h` provide information about sizes and limits of the numerical types. When using these values, remember that expressions such as `(INT_MAX<x)` where x is of type `int` are useless. Even if x overflowed as a result of some operation, it could not be bigger than `INT_MAX`, since `INT_MAX` is, by definition, the largest value representable in an `int`. Use expressions such as `(INT_MAX<x)` only when x is of a type bigger than `int`.

The following list shows all the macros defined in `limits.h` and `float.h`, with their permissible limits. (Some of them are not contrained by the C Standard.)

`<limits.h>`

```
CHAR_BIT              8  MB_LEN_MAX          1
SCHAR_MIN          -127  SCHAR_MAX        +127  UCHAR_MAX        +255
CHAR_MIN      see text   CHAR_MAX    see text
SHRT_MIN         -32767  SHRT_MAX       +32767  USHRT_MAX       65535
INT_MIN          -32767  INT_MAX        +32767  UINT_MAX        65535
LONG_MIN -2147483467     LONG_MAX +2147483467   ULONG_MAX 4294967295
```

`<float.h>`

```
FLT_RADIX             2
FLT_MANT_DIG             DBL_MANT_DIG             LDBL_MANT_DIG
FLT_DIG               6  DBL_DIG            10  LDBL_DIG            10
FLT_MIN_EXP             DBL_MIN_EXP             LDBL_MIN_EXP
FLT_MIN_10_EXP      -37  DBL_MIN_10_EXP    -37  LDBL_MIN_10_EXP  -37
FLT_MAX_EXP             DBL_MAX_EXP             LDBL_MAX_EXP
FLT_MAX_10_EXP      +37  DBL_MAX_10_EXP    +37  LDBL_MAX_10_EXP  +37
FLT_MAX          1E+37   DBL_MAX         1E+37  LDBL_MAX         1E+37
FLT_EPSILON      1E-05   DBL_EPSILON     1E-09  LDBL_EPSILON     1E-09
FLT_MIN          1E-37   DBL_MIN         1E-37  LDBL_MIN         1E-37
```

In a Standard C implementation, the values for these macros can have an absolute value equal to or greater than those shown, except for the macros on the last two lines. For these macros, the values can have an absolute value equal to or smaller than those shown.

`CHAR_MIN` can have the value `SCHAR_MIN` or 0, and `CHAR_MAX` can have the value `SCHAR_MAX` or `UCHAR_MAX`, depending on whether plain `char`s are signed or unsigned.

17.5   Use `locale.h` effectively

- `locale.h` provides some capabilities to allow the C language to be used internationally. It provides macros to control formatting of numbers (including monetary amounts and time), collating sequence for strings, and character classification.

- `locale.h` declares two functions, `setlocale()` and `localeconv()`; declares one type, `struct lconv`; and defines several macros, `LC_ALL`, `LC_COLLATE`, `LC_CTYPE`, `LC_MONETARY`, `LC_NUMERIC`, `LC_TIME`, and `NULL`.

- `LC_ALL` affects the program's entire locale.

- `LC_COLLATE` affects the behavior of `strcoll()` and `strxfrm()`.

- `LC_CTYPE` affects the behavior of all the functions in `ctype.h` except `isdigit()` and `isxdigit()`.

- `LC_MONETARY` affects the monetary formatting information returned by `localeconv()`.

- `LC_NUMERIC` affects the decimal point character used by the string conversion functions (`atof()`, `strtod()`, etc.) and by the formatted I/O functions (`printf()`, `scanf()`, etc.). It also affects the non-monetary information returned by `localeconv()`.

- `LC_TIME` affects the behavior of the `strftime()` function.

- The C Standard defines only two locale names: `"C"` and `""`. All Standard C programs start in the `"C"` locale. The locale name `""` specifies a native locale. Your program will behave as usual, in any country, in the `"C"` locale. In the `""` locale, it might change to some implementation-defined local behavior.

- You can change part or all of the locale to the `"C"` or to the `""` locale by calling the `setlocale()` function.

- Call the function `localeconv()` to obtain values for the formatting of numeric quantities (both monetary and non-monetary).

Example: `setlocale(LC_ALL, "");`
                       `setlocale(LC_CTYPE, "C");`

Notes: This code fragment sets the complete locale to the native
                       environment, then sets part of the locale (the character
                       classification and conversion functions) to the C locale.

Locales allow your program to adapt to different country standards.
Locales are subdivided into five categories:

LC_COLLATE	Controls the collating sequence
LC_CTYPE	Controls the character classification functions
LC_MONETARY	Controls the formatting of monetary amounts
LC_NUMERIC	Controls the formatting of non-monetary quantities
LC_TIME	Controls the formatting of time and date

All these categories except LC_MONETARY affect the behavior of Standard C
Library functions. Standard C defines only two locale names, "C" and "", but
implementations are free to add additional names. All programs start in the
"C" locale. Your program is then free to change all or part of the locale to
another locale (typically a native locale). Except for monetary amounts, that
is all you have to do. Standard C Library functions will modify their behavior
to suit the current locale. Functions like `islower()` may evaluate to non-zero
for additional characters, functions like `printf()` may start using a character
different from . as the decimal point, and so forth.

There are no Standard C Library functions dealing with monetary amounts.
Therefore, a change to the LC_MONETARY part of the locale does not affect the
behavior of any Library functions. You can, however, write a function to
format monetary amounts based on the information returned by
`localeconv()`. Your function can then change behavior based on the locale
in use.

17.6 Use `math.h` effectively

- `math.h` provides general mathematical functions. Most of them take arguments of type `double` and return `double`.

- `math.h` defines the macro `HUGE_VAL`, and declares many functions: `acos()`, `asin()`, `atan()`, `atan2()`, `ceil()`, `cos()`, `cosh()`, `exp()`, `fabs()`, `floor()`, `fmod()`, `frexp()`, `ldexp()`, `log()`, `log10()`, `modf()`, `pow()`, `sin()`, `sinh()`, `sqrt()`, `tan()`, and `tanh()`.

- Use the appropriate function rather than an equivalent expression. The math functions usually maximize speed and accuracy.

- If a domain error occurs, `math.h` functions set `errno` to `EDOM` and return an implementation-defined value.

- If the result overflows, `math.h` functions set `errno` to `ERANGE` and return `+HUGE_VAL` or `-HUGE_VAL`.

- If the result underflows, `math.h` functions return 0 and may set `errno` to `ERANGE` (implementation-dependent).

- Use `atan2()` to obtain angles in any of the four quadrants.

- Use `floor()` or `ceil()` to obtain an integer-valued double.

- Use `fmod()` to obtain the fractional portion of a value.

- Use `sqrt(x)` instead of `pow(x, 0.5)`; it is usually much faster.

- Use `x*x` instead of `pow(x, 2.0)`; it is usually much faster.

- Use `y=frexp(x, &n)` to separate a number into a fraction and a power of 2.

- Use `x = ldexp(y, n)` to reconstruct a number from a fraction and a power of 2.

Instead of: `atan(y/x)`

Use: `atan2(y, x)`

Notes: The first form will return values corresponding only to the
                     first and fourth quadrants (i.e., values in the range $-\pi/2$ to
                     $\pi/2$). The second form will return values corresponding to
                     any of the four quadrants.

Instead of: `exp(n*log(phi))`

Use: `pow(phi, n)`

All `math.h` functions, except `frexp()` and `ldexp()`, accept doubles and
return doubles or pointers to double. The C Standard guarantees that a
double has precision of at least 10 digits. It also guarantees a minimum range
of 10^{-37} to 10^{37}. Many implementations can represent more digits and a wider
range. A double can also represent the value 0 and, in some implementations,
a few additional special codes such as $-$Inf (negative infinity), +Inf (positive
infinity), and NAN (not a number).

The range of `double` values is usually not very wide, and their precision is
usually not very high. Overflow, underflow, and loss of precision must all be
considered when using `math.h` functions. Valid domains and ranges are
important considerations as well. The domain of a function is the set of values
for which the function is defined. For example, the domain of the square root
function is 0 and all positive reals. The range of a function is the set of valid
values returned by the function. A range error occurs when the result of the
function cannot be represented as a double. `math.h` functions set the value
of `errno` to EDOM or ERANGE whenever a domain or range error occurs
(implementation-dependent for range underflows). `math.h` functions return
zero for underflow, and $-$HUGE_VAL or +HUGE_VAL for overflow. HUGE_VAL is
a macro defined in `math.h` that evaluates to a very large double value.

Evaluating an expression might require intermediate results; loss of
precision there might cause the precision of the result to be lower than the
maximum possible precision. `math.h` functions are usually optimized to return
the maximum possible precision. In general, use the `math.h` functions instead
of equivalent expressions. For example, use `sinh(x)` instead of
`(exp(x)-exp(-x))/2`. `sinh(x)` not only is shorter and clearer, but also will
usually yield a higher precision.

17.7   Use `setjmp.h` effectively

- `setjmp.h` provides inter-function `goto` functionality. (See Rule 12.14.)

- `setjmp.h` defines the macro `setjmp()`, declares the function `longjmp()`, and declares a type: `jmp_buf`. The three of them are used together to perform inter-function `goto`.

- The values of any automatic variables that have been changed between the calls to `setjmp()` and `longjmp()` are undefined unless the variables are declared `volatile`.

- The value of `setjmp()` cannot be reliably assigned to a variable. `setjmp()` can be used only in a few limited contexts. It can be used as the entire expression of an expression statement, or as the entire controlling expression of a selection or iteration statement. In the second case, it can also be negated or compared with a constant integer expression.

- Do not use `longjmp()` from within a nested signal handler; its behavior is undefined in that context. (A nested signal handler is a function processing a signal which has been raised during the processing of another signal.)

- Do not call `longjmp()` when the function that called the corresponding `setjmp()` has terminated; the behavior of `longjmp()` is undefined in that context.

- `jmp_buf` is an array type. Therefore it is passed by reference, even though it appears to be passed by value.

In C, goto can only be used to transfer control within a function. The C language does not provide a mechanism to transfer control out of a function other than the return statement. The Library function longjmp(), in conjunction with setjmp(), provides such a mechanism. longjmp() can be used to jump out of a function, as long as the target function (the function that called setjmp()) is still active. That is, the target function must either be the same as the function using longjmp() or have (directly or indirectly) called the function using longjmp().

setjmp() and longjmp() work together. setjmp() saves the calling environment in a variable of type jmp_buf (usually by copying a portion of the stack). longjmp() restores that calling environment and transfers control back to the point at which setjmp() was called.

Global variables will retain the value they had when longjmp() was called. The values of data objects local to the target function that have been modified between the calls to setjmp() and longjmp() are undefined. Declare them volatile if you want them to retain their last values. This is necessary because otherwise some local data objects might be stored in registers, and be restored to the values they had before the call to setjmp().

In the absence of volatile declarations, it is not defined which data objects will be restored to previous values and which will retain their last values. The qualifier volatile provides a safeguard against this behavior. The C Standard guarantees that a volatile data object will not be altered by longjmp().

17.8 Use `signal.h` effectively

- `signal.h` provides the capability to generate and handle events that interrupt the normal execution flow.

- `signal.h` declares two functions, `signal()` and `raise()`; declares one type, `sig_atomic_t`; and defines several macros.

- A signal can terminate execution, cause a signal handler function to be called, or be ignored.

- By default, at program startup some signals are defined to be ignored (implementation-dependent) and the rest are defined to terminate execution.

- The Library functions behave as if they never called `signal()`.

- A signal handler that does not cause termination of the program should, if necessary, reestablish itself by calling `signal()` as part of the signal processing. Two actions occur whenever a signal is raised. First, the signal's handling is redefined to default handling (program termination). Then the function associated with that signal is called.

- An asynchronous signal handler may store values in static variables of the `volatile` type `sig_atomic_t`. It should do nothing else that could have side effects visible to the executing functions.

Example:
```
sig_atomic_t  att_flag = 0;

void int_handler(int sig)
{  signal(SIGINT,int_handler);
   att_flag = 1;
   return;
}

signal(SIGINT,int_handler);
```

Notes: This fragment defines and installs a signal handler for the interactive attention signal (Ctrl-C on most PCs). A program can then test `att_flag` periodically to determine whether an attention signal has been generated.

A signal is an indication of an event that occurs independently of the normal program flow. There are two types of events: synchronous and asynchronous. Synchronous signals are caused by your code (for example, overflow). Asynchronous signals are caused by events external to your code (for example, a user hitting the attention key).

A signal can cause program termination, signal handler invocation, or no action. You can create signal handlers to be called when a signal is raised for any event. A signal handler can terminate your program by using abort() or exit(), or it can perform some action and return. In the last case, execution resumes where it was when the signal was raised. When a signal handler is called, a second thread of execution is started. Asynchronous signals can interrupt Library functions, possibly in the middle of an I/O operation. Asynchronous signal handlers may neither call Library functions nor perform any I/O operations. They should, in general, modify the execution environment as little as possible. Note that modifying a global variable may be unsafe. Optimizing compilers will not consider the possibility of a variable being modified by a second execution thread unless it is declared volatile. If a signal is asynchronous, most global variables will not be safe, even if they are volatile. This is because the signal can occur in the middle of an update or read cycle. signal.h declares the type sig_atomic_t, which is always accessed in an atomic operation. That is, a signal will never interrupt a read or write cycle to a sig_atomic_t variable.

The functionality provided in signal.h has some serious limitations. A program could terminate because of an asynchronous signal, even if the program was attempting to manage all signals. This is because there is an unavoidable time window during which a signal is reset to default handling. An asynchronous signal might be raised after an earlier signal has started the signal handler, but before the signal handler has reestablished handling of the signal. This will cause the program to terminate.

Another problem is that after a signal handler sets a global variable and before the variable is tested, that information may be lost. (If a second signal is processed during that time, the global variable will have the value assigned by the second signal. The value assigned by the first signal will be lost.)

17.9   Use **stdarg.h** effectively

- stdarg.h provides support to handle a variable number of arguments.

- stdarg.h declares the type va_list and defines three macros: va_arg(), va_end(), and va_start().

- Use stdarg.h instead of the older header varargs.h. varargs.h is not part of the Standard C Library.

- Explicitly declare the function as having a variable argument list. That is, end the argument list with ellipsis (, ...).

- You must execute va_start() before using va_arg(), and va_end() after using va_arg().

- Do not supply to va_arg() a type that expands when passed as an argument. Use double instead of float, and int (signed or unsigned) instead of char or short (signed or unsigned).

- Do not supply to va_arg() a type that cannot be converted to a pointer type by appending *.

Example:
```
char *strcatz(char *dest, ...)
{ char *s;
  va_list v;
  va_start(v, dest);
  while(s = va_arg(v, char *)) strcat(dest, s);
  va_end(v);
  return dest;
}

strcatz(a," these "," will be appended ",
        " to string a",NULL);
```

Notes: strcatz() allows you to concatenate any number of strings to a destination string. The last argument should be a NULL pointer.

C functions can handle variable argument lists. The Standard C Library header `stdarg.h` provides the necessary tools. The macros `va_start()`, `va_arg()`, and `va_end()` allow you to retrieve the arguments. These functions usually work by moving a pointer through the stack. `va_start()` sets this pointer just after the last named variable. After that, each call to `va_arg()` returns the value at that location and moves the pointer to the next location. `va_end()` often does nothing, but is provided for implementations that need to do some housekeeping.

Do not try to retrieve the arguments by navigating through the stack directly. Doing so is unnecessary and non-portable. Although the functions in `stdarg.h` behave generally in the way just described, there could be many variations. For example, there may be holes of variable size between the arguments because of alignment or for other reasons. Let the macros in `stdarg.h` do the work for you. They will work in any Standard C implementation. Do not use the header `varargs.h` included in many implementations. It is a different, older implementation of variable argument list handling, not included in the Standard C Library.

The macros `va_start()` and `va_arg()` rely on the size of the supplied type. Do not use types that expand when passed as arguments (`char`, `short`, or `float`). These types may cause the argument pointer to be advanced incorrectly. For example, an argument of type `char` will be converted to `int` before being passed to the function.

The macros `va_start()` and `va_arg()` need to convert the supplied types to pointers. Many implementations do that by appending a `*` after the type. Do not use types that cannot be converted to pointers in this fashion. `int *` is safe, but `int []` is not. Beware of types with brackets or parentheses.

17.10 Use **stddef.h** effectively

- stddef.h defines several types and macros. Some of them (size_t, wchar_t, and NULL) are also defined in other headers.

- stddef.h declares three types, ptrdiff_t, size_t, and wchar_t, and defines two macros, NULL and offsetof().

- The difference of two pointers always yields a result of type ptrdiff_t. However, ptrdiff_t has little, if any, practical use. It suffers from the serious weakness that it is not guaranteed to be big enough to hold the result of all pointer subtractions.

- The type size_t can hold the result of a sizeof operation on any data object. Use size_t for array indexes and pointer arithmetic results unless you are certain that they can be represented by a smaller type.

- The type wchar_t is an integer type that can hold any possible value of any character set of any supported locale. It is used to hold wide (multibyte) character values. Several functions in stdlib.h use wchar_t.

- NULL is usually one of 0, 0L, or (void *)0. It is always equivalent to false. In a statement such as if(NULL) statement1;, statement1; will never be evaluated.

- The macro offsetof() provides the only portable way of obtaining the offset of a member within a structure.

The header stddef.h provides a place for standard definitions. Curiously, of the five types and macros defined in this header, three are also defined elsewhere. Only ptrdiff_t and offsetof() are unique to stddef.h. One may well wonder why stddef.h is necessary at all. One of the few reasons for its existence is that stddef.h is one of the four headers required in a *freestanding* environment (the other headers are float.h, limits.h, and stdarg.h). A freestanding environment is an environment that supports the Standard C language itself, but not necessarily the entire Standard C Library.

stddef.h defines three types: ptrdiff_t, wchar_t, and size_t. Any pointer difference is of the type ptrdiff_t. This type, however, is of very limited use. It is not guaranteed to be big enough to hold any possible pointer difference. wchar_t is an integer type that can hold valid codes for even the largest character set. Wide character constants (e.g., L'a') have a type wchar_t. wchar_t is also defined in stdlib.h.

The type size_t is the most useful of these three types. size_t is also defined in stdlib.h and in several other headers. size_t is an integer type that can represent the size of any data object. The result of sizeof is of type size_t. Use size_t for indexes and pointer arithmetic whenever possible. Your code will then work even under implementations with peculiar char, int, and long sizes. size_t is an unsigned type. If you need to represent negative values, use a signed type (e.g., long).

stddef.h also defines two macros: NULL and offsetof(). NULL is an implementation-defined null pointer constant. A very common definition is (void *)0, but some implementations use 0 or 0L. Some implementations use different representations for different pointers. NULL can be assigned to most pointer types except function pointers, but it cannot be safely used as an argument (in some cases, no type conversion will be performed). Use NULL whenever possible, but remember to typecast to the appropriate type for null function pointer constants and for arguments to variable argument list functions. A possible alternative is never to use NULL. Instead, you could write all null pointers as 0, possibly with a typecast.

The macro offsetof() is the only portable mechanism for obtaining the offset of a member within a structure. Some implementations may not accept an expression such as (char *)&s.m - (char *)&s.

17.11 Use **stdio.h** effectively

- stdio.h supports input and output.

- stdio.h declares three types: size_t, FILE, and fpos_t; defines many macros: BUFSIZ, EOF, FILENAME_MAX, FOPEN_MAX, _IOFBF, _IOLBF, _IONBF, L_tmpnam, SEEK_CUR, SEEK_END, SEEK_SET, stderr, stdin, stdout, and TMP_MAX; and declares many functions: clearerr(), fclose(), feof(), ferror(), fflush(), fgetc(), fgetpos(), fgets(), fopen(), fprintf(), fputc(), fputs(), fread(), freopen(), fscanf(), fseek(), ftell(), fwrite(), getc(), getchar(), perror(), printf(), putc(), putchar(), puts(), remove(), rename(), rewind(), scanf(), setbuf(), setvbuf(), sprintf(), sscanf(), tmpfile(), tmpnam(), ungetc(), vfprintf(), vprintf(), and vsprintf().

- Use the EOF macro; EOF might be different from -1.

- Use FILENAME_MAX as the length of buffers holding filenames.

- Standard C incorporates only stream I/O functions (fopen(), fclose(), etc.). UNIX style I/O functions (open(), close(), read(), write(), etc.) are not part of the Standard C Library.

- Open the file in the appropriate mode: text or binary.

- Use fclose() to ensure that all data are written to the output device. fflush() does not always cause data to be written to the output device.

- Use getc() and putc() instead of fgetc() and fputc(); they are faster.

- getc() and putc() are the only two functions in the Standard C Library whose corresponding macros may evaluate a parameter more than once.

- fputs() does not insert a newline after the string as puts() does.

- Field width and precision for the printf() family can be specified at run-time by using *.

- Avoid scanf(); read input into a string, then use sscanf(). This allows you to recover from incorrect input.

- Use sprintf() and sscanf() to encode and decode text representations.

- Use `vprintf()`, `vfprint()`, and `vsprintf()` with functions of variable number of arguments.

- Use `ungetch()` to simplify parsing algorithms. You can push back a character that is different from the one you read.

- Use `tmpfile()` to create a temporary file to be deleted at program termination.

- Use `tmpnam()` to generate temporary filenames that are guaranteed not to conflict with existing filenames.

- Check for errors; among the Standard C Library functions, the I/O functions are the most likely to fail, even under normal conditions.

- Do not read after you write or vice versa without an intervening call to `fflush()`, `fseek()`, `fsetpos()`, or `rewind()`. You can, however, write after a read at end of file.

- Do not use text files if you are planning to read or write non-printable characters other than horizontal tab and newline.

- Do not assume that you will be able to read back trailing spaces from text files.

- Do not assume that you will be able to read back a partial last line (not terminated by newline) in a text file.

- Do not assume that you can differentiate between an empty and a nonexistent file.

- Do not assume that you will be able to read exactly as many bytes as you wrote unless you take special precautions (you might get extra nulls at the end of the file).

- Do not assume that it is possible to determine the exact length of a binary file.

- Use `sprintf()` to convert numbers to text.

Instead of:
```
#define DTSEG(p,n) ( (p)[0]=(n)/10+'0',  \
                      (p)[1]=(n)%10+'0',  \
                      (p)[2]='/'          )
```

```
char *cdate(char *buffer, unsigned int ndate)
{ DTSEG(buffer, ndate>>5 & 0x0f);
  DTSEG(buffer+3, ndate & 0x10f);
  DTSEG(buffer+6, ndate>>9);
  buffer[8] = 0;
  return buffer;
}
```

Use:
```
char *cdate(char *buffer, unsigned int ndate)
{ sprintf(buffer,"%02i/%02i/%02i",
          ndate>>5 & 0x0f, ndate&0x1f, ndate>>9);
  return buffer;
}
```

Notes: The function cdate() converts a date from a numeric format to a string. The date is encoded as a number of form yyyyyyymmmmddddd. That is, the year takes the first 7 bits, the month the next 4 bits, and the day the last 5 bits. The resulting string has a format of the form "mm/dd/yy".

The second form of the function is much simpler. We did not use itoa() in the first form, because it is not part of the Standard C Library.

Instead of:
```
printf("\n%3i", a);
for(i=0; i<t; i++) putchar(' ');
printf("%3i", b);
```

Use:
```
printf("\n%3i%*s%3i", a, t, "", b);
```

Notes: Both forms will print t spaces between the 3-character fields containing a and b. The second form is shorter, requires only one statement, and does not require an additional variable.

Example:
```
putc(*p++, fl);
```

Notes: This is correct when using the Standard C Library, even if putc() is a macro. Only the second argument might be evaluated twice. (*p++ will be evaluated exactly once.)

Example:
```
void  dbg_printf(char *fmt, ...)
{ time_t  t;
  va_list args;
  if(!dbg) return;
  va_start(args, fmt);
  time(&t);
  fprintf(dbg_file, "\n%8.8s ", ctime(&t)+11);
  vfprintf(dbg_file, fmt, args);
  fclose(dbg_file);
  dbg_file = fopen(dbg_file_name,"a");
  assert(dbg_file);
  va_end(args);
}
```

Notes: dbg_printf() is a debugging version of printf(). It prints
            to a debugging file if the flag dbg is set. It time-stamps every
            line and closes and reopens the file to flush the file buffer.
            This enhances the probability of a line being written to the
            output file, even if the program crashes thereafter.

Example:
```
int readchar(void)
{ static char tri[] = "=/'()!<>-";
  static char sym[] = "#\^[]|{}~";
  int c,d;
  char *p;
  if((c = getc(fl) != '?') return c;
  if((d = getc(fl) != '?')
  { ungetc(d, fl);
    return c;
  }
  d = getc(fl);
  return p = strchr(tri, d) ? sym[p-tri] :
                          ungetch(d, fl), 0xff;
}
```

Notes: This function reads a character from a file. If the character
            is '?', readchar() reads one more character to determine if
            the sequence may be a valid trigraph. Trigraphs are
            sequences of three characters equivalent to a single character.
            They were introduced with Standard C to support terminals
            that cannot represent the symbols # \ ^ [ ] | { } and ~.
            They are, respectively, ??= ??/ ??' ??(??) ??! ??< ??>
            and ??-. If the second character is not '?', readchar()
            pushes it back to be retrieved with the next getc(). If the
            third character does not complete a valid trigraph,
            readchar() makes no use of the three characters and returns
            0xff. (Only the third character is pushed back.)

stdio.h is probably the most frequently used header. It declares more functions than any other header of the Standard C Library.

The ANSI C committee decided to include only stream functions in stdio.h (fopen(), fclose(), fread(), etc.). The UNIX style I/O functions (open(), close(), read(), etc.) were not included in the C Standard. (The UNIX style I/O functions are older, simpler, and, in a sense, more primitive. They were not included in the C Standard because originally they lacked buffering, which had to be provided by the program. Many programmers had been using stream functions exclusively, because of the poor performance of the UNIX style I/O functions. Also, incorporating both sets of functions would have been undesirable. After all, a standard tries to impose some uniformity on how things are done.) Use stream functions whenever possible.

Stream functions are based on the FILE data object. Most of the stream functions accept a pointer to a FILE data object, which contains information on a given stream. This information includes a file position indicator, an error indicator, a pointer to and size of a buffer, and an end of file indicator. FILE data objects are created by the functions fopen() and freopen(). These functions return a pointer to FILE, which is then used by the other functions. Do not attempt to modify or use the contents of the FILE data object directly, even if you know its structure.

There are two types of files: binary and text. The UNIX system and the UNIX style I/O functions do not differentiate between these two types. Most other operating systems, however, treat these two types differently. For example, MS-DOS terminates lines in text files with both a carriage return and a line feed. At run time, C has to discard the carriage returns for text files, but keep them for binary files. You specify the type of a file when you open it. The default type is text.

Text files store data in *lines*. Each line consists of zero or more characters and a newline character. The Library functions may have to add, alter, or delete characters on input and output to support different conventions used by operating systems. Some implementations may not be able to represent partial lines at the end of the file (lines with no terminating newline). Text files may accept non-printable characters, but that is not guaranteed by the C Standard. To be able to read exactly what you wrote to a text file, follow a few precautions. Write only printable characters, horizontal tab, and newline. Do not write spaces at the end of the line. Make sure that the last character written is newline. Keep the maximum line length to under 510 characters.

Binary files store sequences of characters. Any character, printable or non-printable (including Ctrl-Z), can be stored in a binary file. No translation is performed on input or output. There is no explicit end-of-file character. Some operating systems do not maintain information about the exact length of a file. Do not assume that you will get back exactly as many characters as you wrote. Some implementations may pad the end of the file with null characters. If you need to know exactly where the file ends, keep your own file length information or use a terminating symbol.

When opening a file, you must specify whether you want to read only, write only, or read and write. If you do the latter, keep in mind that the C Standard does not support certain sequences of reads and writes. Do not read after you write, or write after you read, without a file positioning request in between. There is only one exception to this rule: writing is allowed if the end of file indicator has been set by a preceding read.

Streams are buffered. Do not assume that whatever you wrote will immediately be sent to the output device. The data may not be written to the output device until you close or flush the file.

I/O operations frequently result in errors. On error, some of the functions in stdio.h set errno to an implementation dependent non-zero value. Use ferror() to determine whether there has been an error for a particular stream. To reset the error indicator for a stream, use clearerr().

Three standard streams are available as soon as the program starts. They are standard input, standard output, and standard error. stdio.h defines three macros that expand to expressions of type FILE * to refer to these streams: stdin, stdout, and stderr. Some functions in stdio.h accept a pointer to FILE to specify what file to access and some functions use standard input, output, or error.

stdio.h provides two families of functions to deal with formatted I/O. The printf() family formats values for output. These functions are very powerful and are widely used. There are six functions in this family. Two write to standard output, two to a specified stream, and two to a string. Of the two functions of each type, one takes a variable number of arguments and the other takes a fixed number of arguments. In this second function, the last argument is a list of values (its type is va_list) to be used with functions of variable number of arguments.

The scanf() family reads values in various formats. Unlike the printf() functions, these functions are not used very often. There are three functions in this family. One reads from standard input, one from a specified stream, and one from a string. Whenever possible read the input first into a string, then use sscanf() to decode it. This provides more flexibility for error recovery and error reporting.

The printf() and scanf() families use complex format specifications. Keep in mind that the notation for the two families is similar but not exactly the same. There are many subtle differences between them. Keep a table of printf() and scanf() format specifications handy.

The functions sprintf(), vsprintf(), and sscanf() are the only three functions declared in stdio.h that do not act on files. These three functions are not used often. This is strange, since they are very useful. Use them whenever you need to encode or decode data.

stdio.h contains the only two functions in the Standard C Library, getc() and putc(), which when implemented as macros can evaluate a parameter more than once. This parameter is the stream on which they operate.

17.12 Use `stdlib.h` effectively

- `stdlib.h` provides an assortment of miscellaneous capabilities.

- `stdlib.h` declares four types: `size_t`, `ldiv_t`, `size_t`, and `wchar_t`; defines four macros: `EXIT_FAILURE`, `EXIT_SUCCESS`, `MB_CUR_MAX`, and `RAND_MAX`; and declares many functions: `abort()`, `abs()`, `atexit()`, `atof()`, `atoi()`, `atol()`, `bsearch()`, `calloc()`, `div()`, `exit()`, `free()`, `getenv()`, `labs()`, `ldiv()`, `malloc()`, `mblen()`, `mbtowc()`, `mbstowcs()`, `qsort()`, `rand()`, `realloc()`, `srand()`, `strtod()`, `strtol()`, `strtoul()`, `system()`, `wctomb()`, and `wcstombs()`.

- Use `exit()` to terminate programs. For maximum portability, use the constant `EXIT_FAILURE` or `EXIT_SUCCESS` as its argument.

- Use `atexit()` to install functions to be called on program exit.

- Use `abort()` only when there is a serious error; otherwise use `exit(EXIT_FAILURE)`.

- Use the type `size_t` to hold the result of the `sizeof` operator and for any index that will be used with arrays of arbitrary size.

- Use `abs(x)` or `labs(x)` to obtain the absolute value of an expression. They are often faster than `(x < 0 ? -x : x)`, and they evaluate `x` only once.

- `itoa()`, `ltoa()`, and `ftoa()` are not included in the Standard C Library; use `sprintf()` instead.

- Use `bsearch()` to search and `qsort()` to sort.

- Use the `malloc()` family when appropriate, but do not overuse.

- Use `div()` or `ldiv()` to obtain a quotient that truncates toward zero or the corresponding remainder. The operators / and % might truncate toward or away from zero for negative numbers (implementation-dependent).

- Do not parse the environment string to obtain values. Use `getenv()` instead.

- Use `mblen()`, `mbstowcs()`, `mbtowc()`, and `wcstombs()` to convert multibyte characters and strings to wide characters and wide character strings.

■ An implicit srand(1) is simulated at program startup. Unless you explicitly call srand(), you will always get the same sequence of pseudo-random numbers.

■ Do not call srand() too often; you will obtain numbers that are not distributed evenly over the interval from 0 to RAND_MAX.

■ Use strtod(), strtol(), and strtoul() to obtain numbers from text. They provide a pointer to the first character that is not part of the number.

■ Use system() to perform operating system commands.

Instead of:
```
main()
{   srand(rand());
    for(i=0; i<MAX; i++)
    {   n = rand();
        srand(n+i);
        process(n);
    }
}
```

Use:
```
main()
{   for(i=0; i<MAX; i++)
    {   if((!i%1000)) srand(clock()%RAND_MAX);
        n = rand();
        process(n);
    }
}
```

Notes:
In spite of its appearance, the first form is very ineffective. First, it will always generate the same sequence of numbers. (Since srand() is not executed before rand(), the first generated pseudo-random number will be always the same, causing srand() to be called always with the same value.) Second, calling srand() on every iteration does not make the numbers more random. Quite the contrary, it interferes with the generating mechanism and may yield numbers that are not uniformly distributed.

The header `stdlib.h` declares a variety of functions. Anything that does not belong in any other header is in `stdlib.h`. This header provides functions in several areas: text to number conversion, execution control, random number generation, integer arithmetic, searching and sorting, multibyte to wide character conversion, and storage allocation.

There are six text to number conversion functions: `atof()`, `atoi()`, `atol()`, `strtod()`, `strtol()`, and `strtoul()`. The last three functions are more general. They return a pointer to the first character that is not part of the number. This pointer is very useful when parsing complicated text. `strtol()` and `strtoul()` allow you to specify a base (between 2 and 36). The inverse functions (`itoa()`, `ltoa()`, and `ftoa()`) are not part of the Standard C Library, although many implementations provide them. The only functions in the Standard C Library that convert numbers to text are `sprintf()` and its relatives.

There are five functions that interface with the execution environment: `abort()`, `atexit()`, `exit()`, `getenv()`, and `system()`. Two of them allow you to terminate execution: `abort()` and `exit()`. Use `exit()` whenever possible. `exit()` causes normal program termination. It calls all functions registered with `atexit()`, closes any open streams, removes any temporary files, and returns control to the environment. A success code or an error code can be returned.   `stdio.h` defines two macros: `EXIT_SUCCESS` and `EXIT_FAILURE`. If possible, use `exit()` with one of them. `atexit()` allows you to register functions to be called on program exit. They will be called, without arguments, by `exit()`.   The C Standard guarantees that an implementation will allow you to register at least 32 functions.

`abort()` causes abnormal termination of your program. `abort()` does not necessarily close open files or remove any temporary files, and does not call the functions registered with `atexit()`. If a signal handler has been installed for `SIGABRT`, it will receive control instead. The handler might terminate your program or continue execution with a `longjmp()`.

`getenv()` searches the environment list. It returns the text associated with an environment variable name. Notice that the inverse function, `putenv()`, supported by some implementations, is not part of the C Standard. `system()` accepts a string and passes it to the environment's command processor. It can also be used to determine whether there is a command processor available. The effect of passing the string to the command processor is implementation-dependent.

`stdlib.h` provides two functions for random number generation: `rand()` and `srand()`. `rand()` returns a pseudo-random number between 0 and `RAND_MAX` (inclusive). Use `RAND_MAX`, which is guaranteed to be at least 32,767, to scale random numbers to any range. For example, the expression `a+(b-a)*(double)rand()/RAND_MAX` will generate doubles in the range [a,b]. Use `srand()` to provide a starting value (seed) for the sequence of pseudo-random numbers.   The same seed will generate the exact same sequence. The ability to generate a repeatable sequence is sometimes very important. If you want to generate different sequences somewhat randomly, use the time or any other data external to the program to create the seed. If you call srand() too often, you will upset the mechanism for generating pseudo-random numbers. The resulting sequence may not be evenly distributed over [0,RAND_MAX]. The equivalent of an implicit srand(1) is performed on program startup. You will obtain the same sequence every time you run your program, unless you call srand() with diverse values.

stdlib.h provides the functions abs(), labs(), div(), and ldiv(). The first two return the absolute value of, respectively, an int or a long. The last two return the quotient and remainder of a division of, respectively, two ints or two longs. The quotient truncates toward zero, and the remainder has the sign of the quotient. div() and ldiv() have the advantage over / and % that they guarantee a truncation direction for negative numbers. They also give quotient and remainder in one operation.

stdlib.h provides a function for sorting, qsort(), and a function for searching, bsearch(). Use them whenever possible. Writing your own takes time and is more likely to introduce bugs. In spite of its name, qsort() might not always be implemented as a quicksort. Quicksort is not a stable sort. That is, elements that compare equal might be swapped. Keep in mind that quicksort has very good average time but a very bad worst-case time. The same might be true of qsort().

stdlib.h provides the functions mblen(), mbtowc(), wctomb(), mbstowcs(), and wcstombs(). These functions convert multibyte characters and strings to wide characters and wide character strings, and vice versa. Wide characters have the type wchar_t. A wide character can represent any code of an extended character set. Multibyte characters can also represent codes of extended character sets. A multibyte character is a sequence of characters from the C character set used to represent an extended character.

stdlib.h also provides four functions for storage allocation: calloc(), free(), malloc(), and realloc(). These functions allocate and release memory blocks. Both calloc() and malloc() allocate storage. They differ in two aspects. malloc() does not initialize the allocated memory; calloc() sets all bits to 0. malloc() takes one parameter: block size; calloc() takes two: the number of elements to be allocated and element size.

free() releases a memory block. realloc() changes the size of the allocated memory block. realloc() returns a pointer to the new memory block. realloc() preserves the values of the memory block up to the minimum of the two sizes. Do not use a pointer after the memory to which it points has been freed or reallocated.

17.13 Use `string.h` effectively

- `string.h` provides functions to manipulate fixed-size memory blocks and null-terminated memory blocks

- `string.h` defines one macro: `NULL`; declares one type: `size_t`; and declares many functions: `memchr()`, `memcmp()`, `memcpy()`, `memmove()`, `memset()`, `strcat()`, `strchr()`, `strcmp()`, `strcoll()`, `strcpy()`, `strcspn()`, `strerror()`, `strlen()`, `strncat()`, `strncmp()`, `strncpy()`, `strpbrk()`, `strrchr()`, `strspn()`, `strstr()`, `strtok()`, and `strxfrm()`.

- Functions starting with `mem` operate on buffers that might contain nulls.

- Functions starting with `str` operate on null-terminated strings.

- Functions starting with `strn` operate on the first n characters of null-terminated strings of more than n–1 characters, or on full strings for strings of less than n characters.

- Use `memmove()` when source and destination may overlap.

- `strncpy()` does not append a null at the end of the destination string if the source string is more than n characters long.

- `memcmp()`, `strcmp()`, and `strncmp()` return 0 (`FALSE`) when the two buffers being compared are equal.

- `strcoll()` compares two strings according to the collating sequence defined in `LC_COLLATE`.

- Use `strchr()` to determine whether a character is in a given set of characters.

- Use `strspn()` to obtain the longest possible string whose characters are in a given set of characters.

- Use `strcspn()` to find the first character in a string that belongs to a given set of characters.

- Use `strtok()` to obtain tokens delimited by any number of characters belonging to a given set of delimiter characters.

- Use `strstr()` to determine whether a string is in a set of strings.

Instead of:

```
if(c=='.' || c==',' || c=='-' || c=='+')
    process(c);
```

Use:

```
if(strchr(".,-+",c)) process(c);
```

Notes:

The second form is simpler and, usually, faster. It is also easier to change the list of characters that should cause process() to be called.

It works by attempting to find the character c within a string composed of all the characters that should be tested against c and result in a true condition on a match.

If c is not found in the string, strchr() returns a NULL pointer, which is interpreted as false. If c is found in the string, strchr() returns a non-NULL pointer, which is interpreted as true.

Instead of:

```
char *m[] = { "jan","feb","mar","apr",
              "may","jun","jul","aug",
              "sep","oct","nov","dec" };

int nmonth(char *month)
{ int i;
   for(i=1; i<13; i++)
      if(!strcmp(m[i], month)) return i;
   return 0;
}
```

Use:

```
char m[] = "jan feb mar apr "
           "may jun jul aug "
           "sep oct nov dec ";

int nmonth(char *month)
{ char *p=strstr(m, month);
   return p && p[3]==' ' ? (p-m)/4+1 : 0;
}
```

Notes:

The second form is simpler and faster. It uses strstr() to search for the name of the month within a string composed of all the month names. If strstr() finds a match, it returns a pointer to that month's name. This pointer is then used to calculate the month's number. If p is NULL, the function returns 0. If p[3] is not a space, an invalid portion of the month's name has been found, and the function also returns 0.

The C language, unlike many others, provides minimal support for strings. The language itself supports only the creation of string and character constants. A constant such as "abcd" causes the compiler to store five characters in memory (one for the terminating null). A pointer to the first of those characters is then generated. Strings are arrays of characters. A statement such as s = "abcd"; will not copy the string "abcd" into s. Rather, the address of the first character of "abcd" is assigned to s. In this example, s must be a pointer to char. A string constant is equivalent to an unnamed, initialized, character array.

The omission of string operators from the language is intentional. The C language was designed to be small and simple. String operations are provided instead by functions of the C Library. These functions are declared in the header string.h. This header provides functions to copy, concatenate, compare, search, and parse character arrays, in addition to three miscellaneous functions. Most of these functions are very fast, and some compilers replace calls to them with inline code.

The functions in string.h can be divided into three broad categories. The functions starting with mem manipulate character buffers of a given length without treating nulls in any special way. Those starting with str operate on strings, that is, on character buffers terminated by a null. And those starting with strn operate on null-terminated strings, but also accept a maximum length constraint.

The copy functions are memcpy(), memmove(), strcpy(), and strncpy(). memmove() is the only one that can handle overlapping source and destination buffers. memmove() is very useful, not just with character arrays but with arrays of any type. Use it to shift part of an array up or down (e.g., when inserting or deleting elements). Notice that strncpy() will insert a null into the destination only if the end of the source string is reached. And in that case, it will supply additional nulls until n characters have been written.

The concatenation functions are strcat() and strncat(). In both of them, the initial character of the second string overwrites the null character of the first string. strncat() always adds a terminating null to the resulting string. (In this it differs from strncpy().)

The comparison functions are memcmp(), strcmp(), strncmp(), and strcoll(). They return a negative, zero, or positive value depending on whether the first string is smaller than, equal to, or greater than the second. strcoll() compares strings based on the collating sequence defined by LC_COLLATE.

strxfrm() transforms a string based on LC_COLLATE. The result of strcmp() on two strings so transformed is equal to the result of strcoll() on the two original strings.

The search functions are memchr(), strchr(), strrchr(), and strstr().
The first three search for a character within a character array or string. The
last one, strstr(), searches for a string within a string. These four functions
are very useful. They can be used to determine whether a character or a string
is a member of a given set.

Instead of: (c=='a' || c=='b' || c=='c' || ...),

Use: strchr("abc...",c).

It is shorter, and easier to read and modify.
Similarly,

Instead of: (!strcmp(s,"abc") || !strcmp(s,"def") ||
              !strcmp(s,"ghi" || ...),

Use: strstr("abc,def,fgh,...",s)

when s contains three characters and no commas.

The parsing functions are strspn(), strcspn(), strpbrk(), and
strtok(). strspn(s1, s2) (string span) finds the first character in s1 not
contained in s2. That is, it finds the longest span of characters in s1 belonging
to the set s2. strcspn(s1, s2) is the complement. It returns the first
character in s1 that is in s2. Both return an index instead of a pointer, and
both return an index to the terminating null if s1 is exhausted. strpbrk() is
similar to strcspn() but returns a pointer or NULL. strtok() is the most
complex of these functions. It can be called several times to parse a string.
strtok() returns tokens from the string separated by any of a set of specified
delimiters. Tokens can be separated by one or more delimiters. strtok()
maintains some static memory and therefore cannot be used to alternate
parsing of two strings. You can obtain similar functionality by using strspn()
and strcspn(): strspn() to skip the delimiters, strcspn() to find the end
of the token.

string.h provides three additional functions: memset(), strlen(), and
strerror().

memset() initializes memory blocks to a repeated character.

strlen() returns the length of a string. Notice that because of C's string
convention, strlen() must traverse the whole string to find the terminating
null. This is usually a fast operation, but it can take some time on long strings.
When possible, code so as not to call strlen() too often for long strings. In
many cases it is not necessary to determine the length of the string explicitly.

strerror() returns the error message corresponding to errno (see Rule
17.3). The text of the error message is implementation-dependent.

17.14 Use `time.h` effectively

■ `time.h` provides the ability to obtain and print time and date.

■ `time.h` defines two macros: `NULL` and `CLOCKS_PER_SEC`; declares four types: `size_t`, `clock_t`, `time_t`, and `struct tm`; and declares several functions: `asctime()`, `clock()`, `ctime()`, `difftime()`, `gmtime()`, `localtime()`, `mktime()`, `strftime()`, and `time()`.

■ Only two functions return current time: `clock()` and `time()`. The rest of the functions convert time from one format to another.

■ The precision of `clock()` and `time()` is implementation-dependent and might be very low. Check your implementation before relying on `clock()` or `time()`.

■ `clock()` provides the time elapsed since program start and presumably has a higher resolution than `time()`. `clock()/CLOCKS_PER_SEC` gives the time in seconds.

■ `time()` provides calendar time.

■ The functions in `time.h` use five different types to hold time information: `clock_t`, `time_t`, `struct tm`, `double`, and `char[]`.

■ Use `strftime()` to format time as desired. `strftime()` provides a format specifier similar to `printf()`.

■ Use `difftime()` to calculate the difference between two calendar times in `time_t` encoding.

■ Use `mktime()` to convert from a time separated into components (`struct tm`) to calendar time (`time_t`).

Example:
```
char *sortable_date_time(char *dest)
{ time_t t;
  time(&t);
  strftime(dest, 18, "%y/%m/%d %H:%M:%S",
                      localtime(&t);
  return dest;
}
```

Notes: This function returns the date and time in the format "`yy/mm/dd hh:mm:ss`".

The header `time.h` defines one new macro: `CLOCKS_PER_SEC`; three new types: `clock_t`, `time_t`, and `struct tm`; and several functions. `time.h` also defines the macro `NULL` and the type `size_t`, which are also defined in several other headers. `time.h` provides two functions to obtain the time: `clock()` and `time()`; and several functions for format conversions. The C Standard does not guarantee any given precision for the time function. An implementation is free to return time to a resolution of one hour or even always to return the same time. Check your implementation before relying on `clock()` and `time()`.

The functions in `time.h` use five different types for time representation: `clock_t`, `time_t`, `struct tm`, `double`, and `char []`. `clock_t` holds processor time as returned by `clock()`. `time_t` is the calendar time as returned by `time()`. `struct tm` contains the calendar time broken into components. `struct tm` contains at least the following members (all of type `int`): `tm_sec`, `tm_min`, `tm_hour`, `tm_mday`, `tm_mon`, `tm_year`, `tm_wday`, and `tm_isdst`. Time differences are represented as `double`. Several functions return time and date as text.

`clock()` returns the processor time (i.e., the time since execution start). The return type is `clock_t`. `clock()/CLOCKS_PER_SEC` gives the time in seconds. `time()` returns the calendar time. The return type is `time_t`. The encoding of `time_t` is unspecified.

`difftime()` returns the difference between two calendar times in `time_t` format. The return type is `double`. `mktime()` converts a calendar time in a structure of type `struct tm` to the type `time_t`. `mktime()` accepts values out of the normal ranges (i.e., `tm_sec` can contain 1230). It can be used to convert any number of seconds, hours, years, etc., to a calendar date. `localtime()` and `gmtime()` convert calendar times from `time_t` to `struct tm`. The first returns the local time, and the second returns the Coordinated Universal Time (UTC, previously known as Greenwich Mean Time). The local time might be in Daylight Saving Time.

Three functions return the time as text: `asctime()`, `ctime()`, and `strftime()`. `asctime()` and `ctime()` both return the same text. `asctime()` accepts a `struct tm` time, and `ctime()` accepts a `time_t` time. `ctime(&t)` is equivalent to `asctime(localtime(&t))`. `strftime()` accepts a format specifier as `printf()` does. It allows you to format the time to suit your needs. These three functions are affected by the `LC_TIME` category of the locale.

The functions returning `struct tm` share a common static data object. So do the functions returning text. If you need to preserve the `struct tm` time or the text representation, copy the value to your own variable. Beware of complicated expressions where later calls to one of the five time conversion functions can alter the values returned by an earlier call to one of them.

Exercises

1.   Rewrite: `while('0'<=*s && *s<='9') *d++ = *s++;`

2.   Rewrite:
```
if(c=='a' || c=='e' ||
    c=='i' || c=='o' || c=='u') vowel++;
```

3.   Rewrite:
```
#define E 2.718281828
nd = pow(E,-pow(z,2));
```

PART V: **Miscellaneous**

CHAPTER 18: Coding for Non-C Programmers

In most cases your readers will be C programmers. Sometimes, however, you might need to write your program so that it will be readable by non-C programmers. We call non-C programmers those programmers who do not have much experience in using the C language. It is a difficult (if not impossible) task to write programs in a language so that programmers with absolutely no knowledge of the language can understand them. We do assume that non-C programmers will have an understanding of the basics of C.

The C language shares many concepts with other popular languages. It also has some useful features that are very different from those offered in other languages. When coding for non-C programmers, the goal is to minimize use of the unusual features and maximize use of features that are shared by most languages. For this reason, much of the advice given in this chapter seems to contradict advice given in the rest of this book. There is no contradiction; the advice depends on your audience.

Which features are familiar and which features are not depends on what language or languages your readers know. The advice in this chapter assumes that the non-C programmer is fluent in one or more of the most commonly used high-level languages: ALGOL, BASIC, COBOL, FORTRAN, Pascal, or PL/1. In the rest of this chapter we will say "most programmers" when we mean "most programmers fluent in one of the high level-languages listed above." There is, however, the possibility that a reader might be highly proficient in some other, exotic language, rendering some of the advice in this chapter less usable. We do not address the cases where the readers are Assembler programmers either.

Some of the advice provided here can be applied when the audience is mainly C beginners. However, it is debatable whether to avoid some features because beginners might not know them, or whether to use those features so that beginners become acquainted with them.

The unusual features of C (from the point of view of "most programmers") include: a large number of operators, use of assignment *operators* instead of an assignment *statement*, lack of a boolean type, the presence of a preprocessor, extensive support for pointer operations, and extensive reliance on a library external to the language.

18.1   Minimize use of the value of assignment expressions and of the value of ++ and −− operations.

- Modify only one data object per statement, unless the modification is done by a function or macro.

- Do not use ++ or −− within larger expressions.

- Do not use assignment expressions within larger expressions.

- Most other languages provide an assignment *statement* instead of assignment *operators*.

Instead of: `if(x = a[i++]) adjust();`

Use:
```
x = a[i];
i++;
if(x!=0) adjust();
```

C differs from most other languages in that it provides several assignment *operators* instead of an assignment *statement*. Assignments can therefore be part of larger statements. In C, in contrast to most other languages, several data objects can be modified in one expression with no function calls. (In C and in most other languages, several data objects can be modified when passed by reference to a function.)

C also offers two unusual operators: ++ and −−. Like assignment operators, ++ and −− modify data objects and also can be used within larger expressions. They have the useful but confusing capability of behaving in two different ways, depending on whether they are used as prefixes or as postfixes (i.e., ++a or a++).

In most other languages, assignments are statements. Assignment statements in other languages allow modification of only one data object. Also, since assignments are not expressions, they cannot be used as parts of larger expressions.

To minimize confusion, do not use the operators ++ and −−, or the assignment operators, within larger expressions. This implies that no more than one data object should be modified per statement.

18.2   Minimize assignments within expressions controlling flow

■ Assignments within expressions controlling flow control statements will often be confused with tests for equality.

Instead of: `while( (c = getchar()) != EOF) putchar(c);`

Use:
```
for(;;)
{   c = getchar();
    if(c==EOF) break;
    putchar(c);
}
```

C programmers often use assignments within expressions that control execution flow (if, switch, for, while, and do ... while). This is a specific instance of using the value of an assignment expression (Rule 18.1). This case is treated here explicitly (as a separate rule) because it is particularly dangerous.

One of the few bad features of C is the use of a single equal (=) for assignment and a double equal (==) for equality testing. This feature, in conjunction with the fact that C provides assignment *operators* instead of an assignment *statement*, can lead to confusion and can cause bugs that are difficult to spot.

An assignment within an expression controlling a flow control statement is often mistaken for a test for equality. While using assignments in this context is a powerful technique, it should be used only for an audience of C programmers (Rule 11.4). The potential for confusion is too great when the readers are non-C programmers.

18.3   Use parentheses when evaluation order might be unclear

- C offers more operators than most other languages.

- Non-C programmers seldom (if ever) know the precedence level of all operators.

- Use parentheses whenever operators of different precedence levels are involved (especially if they are operators peculiar to C).

Instead of: `a = x>>4 & 0x0f;`

Use: `a = (x>>4) & 0x0f;`

C provides many operators, more than most other languages do. It is difficult enough for non-C programmers to remember what each operator does. Do not expect them to know the operators' precedence levels. While in some cases precedence is obvious (e.g., * is evaluated before +), in some other cases it is not (e.g., >> is evaluated before &). Use parentheses to clarify matters whenever precedence might be unclear. This usually happens when there are operators with different precedence levels, or when operators peculiar to the C language (such as >>) are used.

18.4   Do not use a instead of a!=0 and a!=NULL; do not use !a instead of a==0 and a==NULL

- In many languages there is a boolean type; an integer expression cannot be used as a substitute.

- Lack of a relational operator will most likely confuse the non-C programmer.

- When a data object is used as if it were boolean, do avoid explicit comparisons (e.g., use a instead of a==TRUE).

Instead of:
```
for(count=0,i=0; i<n; i++)
    if(a[i]) count++;
```

Use:
```
for(count=0,i=0; i<n; i++)
    if(a[i]!=0) count++;
```

C does not have a boolean or logical type. Wherever a true or false value is required, any expression can be used. A zero value is interpreted as false, and a non-zero value is interpreted as true. It is therefore not necessary to use a comparison with zero or NULL to check whether the value is non-zero (e.g., if(a) can be used instead of if(a!=0)). To check whether the value is zero, a not operator (!) can be used (e.g., if(!a) instead of if(a==0)).

While the practice of not providing an explicit comparison is recommended for an audience of C programmers (Rule 11.3), it can be very confusing for non-C programmers. For non-C programmers, provide an explicit comparison.

Sometimes, however, data objects are used to hold boolean values. Since in C there is no boolean type, they are usually declared as int. Zero is used for false, non-zero for true. When a data object is used as if it were of boolean type, it is not necessary to provide an explicit comparison (e.g., use if(stop) instead of if(stop==TRUE)). (This last comparison will fail if stop is non-zero (true) but different from TRUE.)

18.5   Use indexes instead of pointers when operating on arrays.

- Pointers are used much more extensively in C than in most other languages.

- Most other languages treat pointers and arrays differently.

- When dealing with arrays, index operations are often clearer than pointer operations.

Instead of: `for(s=0,p=a; n; n--,p++) s += *p;`

Use: `for(s=0,i=0; i<n; i++) s += a[i];`

Pointers are used extensively in many C programs. Most other languages either do not support pointers or do not provide as much support as C does. Even those languages that do support pointers usually do not support pointer arithmetic or do not treat pointers and arrays similarly. As a result, programmers in languages other than C either do not use pointers or do not use them as much as C programmers.

In particular, C offers the extraordinary feature (among high-level languages) of allowing access to array elements by simple pointer arithmetic. Programmers from other languages might not be used to the extensive utilization of pointers seen in many C programs. For them, use of pointers instead of indexes to access array elements might be especially confusing.

Whenever possible use indexes to access array elements when writing for an audience of non-C programmers (compare Rule 14.4). Most good optimizing compilers will, in most cases, generate code for indexes that is as efficient or almost as efficient as code using pointers. However, it is bad practice to rely on compiler optimizations. If high performance is required and can be obtained by using pointers, use them.

18.6 Minimize use of C idioms

- C idioms usually rely on unique features of the C language.

- C programmers are used to C idioms; non-C programmers are not.

- Replace idioms with more straightforward code, with functions, or with macros.

Instead of: `x = *--stack;`

Use:
```
double pop(void)
{   --stack;
    return *stack;
}

x = pop();
```

    C idioms, like idioms in ordinary languages, are difficult to understand for those who are new to the language. Use C idioms as sparingly as possible. Often, idioms can be replaced by simpler but longer code. Whenever possible, make the replacement. The small loss of conciseness or efficiency will often be more than compensated for by the enhanced readability. Remember, idioms are clear only to those who know the language well.

    If you cannot replace an idiom by simpler code, replace it with a function or macro. Unless efficiency is very important, use simpler language within the macro or function. However, even if the idiom is still used within the macro or function, it will at least be isolated to one point in the code (and should be clearly documented).

18.7   Minimize use of `longjmp()`

- `longjmp()` operates in a very peculiar way. Most languages do not have anything similar.

- If you must use `longjmp()`, either encapsulate it in a clarifying macro or use it strictly as a non-local `goto`. (I.e., use a different buffer for every `setjmp()` so that every `longjmp()` can jump to only one place.)

C does not provide inter-function `goto` as a few other languages do. Instead, two functions are provided in the Standard Library to achieve a similar effect: `setjmp()` and `longjmp()` (Rule 17.7). These functions can be useful and should be used on a very few special occasions when writing for an audience of C programmers (Rule 12.14).

However, these two functions work in a way that is different from the way non-local `goto`s work in most languages. A `longjmp()` does not always transfer control to the same location. Rather, it transfers control to the `setjmp()` that operated last on the buffer supplied to `longjmp()`. Restoration of local variables is somewhat unreliable unless the keyword `volatile` is used. Also, special care must be taken with the value returned by `setjmp()` since it can be used only in a few limited contexts.

For all these reasons, you should be even more reluctant than usual to use `longjmp()` when writing for non-C programmers. If you absolutely must use it (and this rarely, if ever, happens), try to use it strictly as a non-local `goto`. That is, use a different environment buffer for every `setjmp()` to ensure that every `longjmp()` will always go to the same place. Or encapsulate `setjmp()` and `longjmp()` in macros for a specific purpose. These macros should have a clear and straightforward role, such as exit to a higher-level function.

18.8   Minimize use of complicated macros

- Many languages do not include a preprocessor.

- Macros can be very confusing to non-C programmers; they might not be used to distinguishing between preprocessing time and compile time.

- The preprocessor has its own, peculiar language.

- Whenever possible, replace complicated macros with functions.

- If you must use a complicated macro, document it clearly.

Instead of: `#define   POPVF (assert(astack<stack),*--stack)`

Use:
```
double popvf(void)
{   assert(astack<stack);
    stack--;
    return *stack;
}
```

Notes: Both forms pop an element from the top of the stack, reporting an error if the stack is empty. The second form, however, is much more readable for non-C programmers.

C includes a preprocessor, which has its own small, independent language. While the preprocessor is great for C programmers, it can confuse non-C programmers. Many other languages do not include a preprocessor. The non-C programmer is likely to be unfamiliar with many of the key aspects of preprocessing (starting with the most basic fact, that there two distinct phases: preprocessing and compilation).

Complicated macros are likely to create confusion. Use them only when there is no alternative. In many cases they can be replaced by functions without much loss of efficiency.

Exercises

Modify the following code fragments for an audience of non-C programmers.

1.   Rewrite: `if(p = malloc(size)) return ERR_SPACE;`

2.   Rewrite: `c = *p++;`

3.   Rewrite:
```
double a[MAXS],b[MAXS],c[MAXS];
double *p,*q,*r;
...
for(p=a,q=b,r=c; n; n--)
    *r++ = *p++ * *q++;
```

4.   Rewrite: `a[i++] = c;`

CHAPTER 19: **Idioms and Techniques**

This chapter presents several code fragments. They show solutions to common problems. They also demonstrate compact, efficient, and elegant C code. The first five are so common that they are considered idioms. To the beginning C programmer, they might look obscure. The experienced C programmer has seen them often enough to know their function without analyzing them in detail.

This chapter includes just a handful of idioms and techniques to provide good examples of C programming. We have included only code that demonstrates features of the C language and solves programming needs arising frequently. This is by no means an exhaustive study. Many useful and clever techniques have been left out.

19.1   Stack push and pop

```
int s[SIZE],*p=s;

ps++ = v          /* push */
v       = *--p    /* pop  */

/***** Generic push and pop with bounds check *****/

#define   POP(p, s)      (assert((s)<(p),*--(p))
#define   PUSH(p, s, v)  (assert((p)<(s)+sizeof(s)), \
                          *(p)++=(v))
```

The C idioms for stack push and pop are, respectively, *p++ and *--p. p
is a pointer to whatever type you need. To create and manipulate a stack of
ints, for example, you should define an array of ints (s) and a pointer to int
(p). Initially, p should point to the beginning of s. This represents an empty
stack. To push a value, you must copy the value into the location pointed to
by p, then increment p. *p++ = v neatly accomplishes this. Notice that p
always points to the first element *after* the top of the stack. To pop a value,
you must decrement p, then retrieve the value at that location. *--p does
this.

Use *p++ and *--p directly in your code. There is no need to replace
them with macros. They do not, however, check for stack overflow or
underflow. If you want to include checking for underflow and overflow, use
macros to push and to pop. To avoid overflow, you must verify that p is
pointing to an element of the array s before pushing a value. The following
condition must hold: p < s+sizeof(s). To avoid underflow, you must verify
that there is something in the stack. That is, p should be pointing somewhere
after the first element of s. The following condition must hold: s<p. The
macros will need the pointer and the array as parameters, unless they work
only with two predefined variables.

19.2   String copy, comparison, and length

```
while(*d++ = *s++);                     /* Copy (strcpy(d,s))  */

for( ; *s; s++)                         /* Copy subset         */
    if(strchr("0123456789+-.,", *d)) /* Any condition       */
        *d++ = *s;
*d = 0;

while(*s1==*s2 && *s1) s1++,s2++; /*Compare (strcmp(s1,s2))*/
return *s1 - *s2;


for(p=s; *p; p++);                      /* Length (strlen(s))  */
return p-s;
```

The idiom for string copy takes advantage of two C features. First, the value of an assignment expression is the value being assigned to the left operand. Second, non-zero is true, zero is false. The expression *d++ = *s++ will evaluate to the character just copied from s to d. If the character just copied is not a null, the value of the expression will be true, and the loop will continue. The loop will end when the character copied is a null.

To copy a subset of the string, use a for statement. Copy to and increment d only when a certain condition holds. To control the loop, use *s; it will evaluate to false at the end of the string. *s is the C idiom for "s is not pointing to the end of the string."

To compare two strings, compare the first character of one string to the first character of the other. If they are equal, increment the pointers and compare the next pair. Continue until the characters being compared differ or until one of them becomes null. You must do this last check. Otherwise, two strings will never compare equal (the comparison will continue beyond their end). It is sufficient to check only one of the strings for termination. If the other one ended, one of the conditions *s1==*s2 or *s1 will fail. On reaching the end of a string or a different character, *s1 - *s2 will be negative if s1<s2, zero if s1==s2, or positive if s1>s2.

To obtain the length of a string, find the location of the terminating null. The index of the null within the string is the length of the string. For example, if s[23]==0, the length of the string is 23 (provided no nulls occur in s before s[23]).

19.3   Number parsing

```
for(n=0; isdigit(*p); p++) n = 10*n + *p-'0';
```

To obtain a number from a sequence of digits in text, initialize the number to zero. Then take one digit at a time and loop until there are no more digits.

Convert every digit to its numeric value (*p-'0'). Shift the number obtained so far one decimal position to the left (10*n). Add in the digit being processed to obtain the number corresponding to the digits read so far.

19.4   Linked list walk

```
struct Tnode {   ...
                 struct Tnode    *next;
             };
for( ; p->next; p=p->next) process(p);
```

To traverse a linked list, loop until there is no next element. On each iteration, process the current item, then go to the next element. p->next will be false (NULL) when there is no next element. p=p->next assigns the address of the next element to p.

19.5   File copy and file filter

```
while((c=getc(fin))!=EOF) putc(c, fout); /* Copy all       */

while((c=getc(fin))!=EOF)                /* Copy some     */
    if(isspace(c) || isalnum(c))         /* Any condition */
        putc(c, fout);
```

To copy a file, obtain one character from the input file and write it to the output file. Continue until the character read is EOF. To copy only some characters, write to the output file only the characters that fulfill some condition. The expression (c=getc(fin)!=EOF) does most of the work. It obtains a character, assigns it to c, then tests it against EOF. The whole expression evaluates to true if c is not EOF. Notice that there is only one equal sign between c and getc(fin). It is an assignment, not a test for equality.

19.6   Data driven switch

```
double stk[MAX_STK],*pstk=stk;
char *sym  = "+-*/^";
double (*func)(double,double) =
       { tadd, tsub, tmul, tdiv, texp };

double dosym(char c)
{   char *p;
    double v1,v2;
    p = strchr(sym, c);     /* Find operator number */
    assert(c && p);         /* Abort if invalid     */
    v1 = *--pstk;           /* Pop v1               */
    v2 = *--pstk;           /* Pop v2               */
    return *pstk++ = func[p-sym](v1,v2);
}
```

This function demonstrates the use of a table of function pointers as an alternative to a case statement. This function accepts as a parameter a one-character operator. It then performs the indicated function on the two topmost stack elements and leaves the result on the top of the stack. To accomplish this, it first uses strchr() to determine an operator number (0 through 4). If the operator is invalid, it aborts. Notice that the test that c is not '\0' in the assertion (c && p) is necessary because strchr() returns a pointer to the end of the string for a null character.

Two values are then popped from the stack and assigned to v1 and v2. The values cannot be popped directly as arguments to the function because the order of evaluation of function arguments is not defined. The function whose index is p-sym (the operator number) is then called with v1 and v2 as parameters. The result is pushed onto the stack.

This code fragment is more compact and easier to maintain than an equivalent version using switch.

19.7 Queue

```
#define QLEN 100

char queue[Q_LEN],*qin=queue,*qout=queue;

void putq(char c)
{   *qin++ = c;
    if(queue+QLEN<=qin) qin=queue;
    assert(*qin!=*qout);
}

void getq(void)
{   char c;
    assert(*qin!=*qout);
    c = *qout++;
    if(queue+QLEN<=qout) qout=queue;
    return c;
}
```

These two functions write to and read from a queue. The queue is implemented as an array and two pointers. The input pointer indicates the position of the next character to be read. The output pointer indicates the position of the next character to be written. Both move through the array in a circular fashion: after reaching queue[QLEN-1], they move to queue[0]. The queue can hold up to QLEN-1 elements.

Notice that the elements do not move within the array. Instead, the pointers to the start and end of the queue are adjusted; this is more efficient. When these two pointers run into each other, there is either an empty queue or a completely full queue. These conditions are detected by the assert() expressions.

19.8   Lookahead input

```
#define AHEAD 10
#define EXTRA 20
int bf[AHEAD+EXTRA+1],*a=bf;

int agetchar(void)
{   a++;
    if(bf+EXTRA<ahead)
    {   memmove(bf, a, AHEAD);
        a = bf;
    }
    a[AHEAD] = getc(fl);
    return *a;
}
```

This function provides one character from the file fl at a time. Besides the current character, it also provides AHEAD characters ahead in the global array bf. The n-th character ahead is provided at a[n].

To avoid moving the contents of the buffer on every read, EXTRA extra characters are allocated. The contents of the buffer will be shifted only every EXTRA reads.

By providing several characters ahead, this function greatly simplifies parsing of complicated constructs.

19.9   Command line parsing

```
for( ; *argv; argv++)
{  if(**argv=='-')
      for(p=*argv+1; *p; p++)
         switch(tolower(*p))
            {  case 'b':   f_binary = TRUE;        break;
               case 'c':   f_convert = TRUE;       break;
               case 'f':   strcpy(file, *++argv);  break;
               case 't':   strcpy(text, *++argv);  break;
               default :   print_usage();
                           exit(EXIT_FAILURE);

            }
   else
   {  if(strchr(*argv,".c")) strcpy(srcfile,*argv);
      else
         if(strchr(*argv, ".obj")) strcpy(objfile, *argv);
   }
}
```

This code fragment parses a command line. The command line consists of words separated by spaces. Each word can be either a set of one or more one character options, or a value. Option words start with '-' and are followed by options. Options can be grouped together in one word, or can be specified separately. The following command lines are all equivalent: "-b -c data.c", "data.c -bc", "-c data.c -b".

An option might have an associated value. This associated value is the next word. If several options in the same option word have associated values, the values follow the option word in the same order as the options appear. This code fragment does not require any other ordering of the command line.

To parse a command line, this code fragment loops through each parameter. If a parameter starts with '-', indicating one or more options, it loops through each character, starting with the second, and branches on every character to the appropriate case. If an option has an associated value, it reads the next word. If a word does not start with '-', it is presumed to be a value.

This fragment identifies two values in a position-independent manner. (If the functional requirements insist on a positional parameter at position n, you can obtain it at argv[n].)

If an option is invalid, print_usage() is called to print a short message on correct usage.

19.10 Arrays of variable length strings

```
char    dt[MAX_DATA];    /* text buffer                      */
char    *str[MAX_STR];   /* array of pointers to strings     */
char    *pdt=dt;         /* next free location               */

void    add(int i,char *s)
{   char *p = pdt+strlen(pdt)+1;   /* Prospective next        */
                                   /* free location           */
    assert(p<=dt+sizeof(dt));
    *str[i] = pdt;
    strcpy(pdt, s);
    pdt = p;
}
```

This function adds a word to str[i] (an array of pointers to strings). Each word can have a different length. To avoid wasting space, this function stores the words one after another in a separate buffer, dt, which can hold up to MAX_DATA characters. (Dynamically allocating each word is not as efficient. Words can be small; the overhead of mallocing each word is too high.)

Each element in str either is a NULL pointer or points to some place within dt. pdt points to the next free location. An assertion aborts the program if the end of the array is about to be passed.

Appendices

Answers to Exercises

In this appendix, we provide answers to the exercises included at the end of most chapters. Chapters 1, 4, 5, and 19 do not have exercises. The exercises were designed so as to emphasize the rules learned in each chapter. In general, the solutions provided here do not contemplate alternative ways of rewriting the code in a given exercise, other than by direct application of the rules in the corresponding chapter.

There are several correct ways to solve each exercise. Here, we generally provide just one of them. If you have a different answer which is not inferior to the solution presented here, and which involves application of the rules in the corresponding chapter, consider it correct.

When necessary, we provide line numbers next to each line of source code, and we use those numbers to organize the corresponding text. Since we do not cover every line of the code, you will see gaps and repetitions in the line numbers for the text.

A.2   Program Design

Exercise 1

Your specification should describe the parameters and the return value. Also, these four points have to be explicitly mentioned in your specification:

1. The string pointed to by s should be null-terminated.
2. A pointer to the *first* occurrence of c in s is returned.
3. If c is not found, a NULL pointer is returned.
4. If c is '\0', a pointer to the '\0' terminating s is returned.

None of these points cannot be inferred from the others. A functional specification that misses one of them is incomplete. Even though some of these points might seem obvious, a functional specification should not rely on "obvious" knowledge, but rather should spell out functionality in all its boring detail.

A.3   Testing

Exercise 1

```
#include <assert.h>
#include <stdio.h>
#include <string.h>

int main()
{   static char *s = "abcdefabdfg";
    assert(strstr(s,"ab")==s);
    assert(strstr(s,"abd")==s+6);
    assert(strstr(s,"")==s);
    assert(!strstr(s,"abcdefg"));
    assert(!strstr(s,"h"));
    printf("\nSuccess: strstr() tested OK.");
    exit(EXIT_SUCCESS);
}
```

Exercise 2

```
#include <assert.h>
#include <stdio.h>
#include <string.h>

int main()
{   static char bf[100],bf2[100];
    static char *s="abcdefghijk";
    strcpy(bf,s);
    memmove(bf,bf+5,0);
    assert(!strcmp(bf,s));
    memmove(bf2,bf,strlen(s)+1);
    assert(!strcmp(bf,s) && !strcmp(bf2,s));
    memmove(bf+1,bf,5);
    assert(!strcmp(bf,"aabcdeghijk"));
    memmove(bf+1,"xyz",2);
    assert(!strcmp(bf,"axycdeghijk"));
    printf("\nSuccess: memmove() tested OK.");
    exit(EXIT_SUCCESS);
}
```

Exercise 3

```c
#include <assert.h>
#include <floats.h>
#include <math.h>
#include <stdio.h>

#define LE_TEST(x)      assert((x)<=ceil(x))
#define EQ_TEST(x,y)    assert(ceil(x)==(y))

int main()
{   LE_TEST(DBL_MAX-1.0);
    LE_TEST(DBL_MIN);

    EQ_TEST(-1.0, -1.0);
    EQ_TEST(0.0, 0.0);
    EQ_TEST(1.0, 1.0);
    EQ_TEST(1.0+DBL_EPSILON, 2.0);
    EQ_TEST(DBL_MIN, 1.0);
    EQ_TEST(-1.0-DBL_EPSILON, -1.0);

    printf("\nSuccess: ceil() tested OK.");
    exit(EXIT_SUCCESS);
}
```

A.6   Visual Organization

Exercise 1

```
1   void prevrec(void)
2   {   short dec;
3       char pnext = pbfnext;
4       recno--;
5       if(recno<0 || task[ntask].trecs-1<=recno) return;
6       if(pbf=='|') nopt--;
7       pbfnext = pbf--;
8       do
9       {   if(--pbf<bf)
10          {   dec = min(txpos-txoff, sizeof(bf)+bf-pbfnext);
11              if(dec<=0)
12              {   pbf = bf;
13                  return;
14              }
15              txpos   -= dec;
16              pbf     += dec;
17              pbfnext += dec;
18              errseek(txpos);
19              errread(bf, (unsigned)min(sizeof(bf),
20                                        txlen+txoff-txpos));
21          }
22      } while(*pbf!='\n');
23      pbf++;
24  }
```

  1   `PrevRec` was changed to `prevrec` for consistency. (Rule 6.4)
  2   `DECRM` was changed to `dec`. (Rules 6.4 and 6.6)
  5   `task_table` was changed to `task` for brevity. (Rule 6.5)
  6   `n_opt` was changed to `nopt` for consistency. (Rule 6.4)
  6   braces around `nopt--` were removed. (personal preference)
  7   `pbuff` was changed to `pbf` for consistency with `pbfnext`. (Rule 6.4)
  9   `buffer` was changed to `bf` for consistency with `pbfnext`. (Rule 6.4)
 10   `text_pos` was changed to `txpos` for consistency. (Rule 6.4)
 11   `TextOfs` was changed to `txoff` for consistency. (Rules 6.4 and 6.6)
 12   The opening brace was moved to the beginning of the next line for consistency. (Rule 6.1)
 13   `return` was moved to a separate line. (Rule 6.8)
 18   `err_seek` was changed to `errseek` for consistency. (Rule 6.4)
 19   `err_read` was changed to `errread` for consistency. (Rule 6.4)
 22   `while` was moved to immediately after the closing brace. (Rule 6.7)

Several blank lines were deleted. (Rules 6.3 and 6.4)

We decided to use only lowercase, and not to use '_' for identifiers that are not macro names. Other consistent conventions are acceptable.

A.7   Comments

Exercise 1

```
/* prime(int n): check n to see if it is prime.

   return:  1 if n is prime
            0 if n is not prime

   Try every number up to about the square root
   of n.  If one of those numbers divides n
   evenly, return 0.  If none of them divides n,
   return 1.
*/
```

```
1  int prime(int n)
2  {   int i;
3      for(i=2; i*i<=n; i++)
4          if(n%i==0) return 0;
5      return 1;
6  }
```

Comments were removed from the code. (Rule 7.4)

4   n%i==0 was not changed to !(n%i) because that would have required an additional set of parentheses. (Rule 11.3)

Exercise 2

```
1  for(i=0; i<n; i++)    /* loop through m    */
2      if(0<m[i])
3          a[j++] = m[i]; /* store pos.number */
4      else
5          b[k++] = m[i]; /* store 0 or neg.number */
```

5   The comment was changed to reflect the code. (Rule 7.6)

Exercise 3

```
1   int atoi(const char *s)
2   {   int sign=1;
3       int n;
4       while(isspace(*s)) s++; /* skip white space */
5       if(*s=='-')             /* if negative       */
6       {   sign = -1;          /* set sign to neg. */
7           s++;                /* skip sign         */
8       }
9       else
10          if(*s=='+') s++;            /* if pos., skip sign  */
11      for(n=0; isdigit(*s); s++) /* for every digit:     */
12          n = n*10 + *s-'0';      /*     append it to n   */
13      return s*n;                 /* return sign and number */
14  }
```

2   The unnecessary comment was removed. (Rule 7.5)
6   The comment was modified. (Rule 7.1)
10 + was changed to pos. for consistency. (Rule 7.3)
12 The comment was changed to provide more information. (Rule 7.1)
13 The comment was changed to provide more information. (Rule 7.1)

A.8   Data Objects

Exercise 1

```
char days[7][4]   = { "Mon","Tue","Wed","Thu","Fri",
                      "Sat","Sun" };
int  hours_day[7] = {  8,    8,    4,    8,    8,
                       4,    0 };
```

The data in hours_day[] are now aligned with days[]. (Rule 8.1)

Exercise 2

```
#include <limits.h>
#include <stdio.h>

main()
{   static int count[UCHAR_MAX+1];
    static int c,*p;
    while((c=getchar())!=EOF) count[c]++;
    for(c=0; c<=UCHAR_MAX; p++)
        if(count[c])
            printf("\nCharacter \'%c\' count %5i",c,count[c]);
}
```

The character c is used directly as an index into an array containing the count. (Rules 8.3 and 8.4)

Exercise 3

```
1  int hash(char *code)
2  {   int h;
3      for(h=0; *code; code++) h += *code;
4      return h & 0xff;
5  }
```

4   An *and* (&) operation was used to force the code into the range 0 to 255. (Rule 8.6)

A.9   Numbers

Exercise 1

```
/* binomial(): calculate binomial coefficients
   for n<13 and any k.
*/

int binomial(int n,int k)
{  long a,b;
   if(k<0 || n<k) return 0;
   for(a=1,b=1; 0<k; n--,k--)
      a*=n,b*=k;
   return (int)(a/b);
}
```

a and b were changed to long to avoid overflows. (Rule 9.1)

Exercise 2

```
/* same_frac(): return true if the fraction
   represented by the numerator n1 and the
   denominator d1 is equivalent to the
   fraction represented by the numerator n2
   and the denominator d2.
*/

int same_frac(int n1,int d1,int n2,int d2)
{  return (long)n1*d2==(long)n2*d1;
}
```

In the exercise, the divisions are perfomed on ints, yielding int. This gives an incorrect result because of truncation. Performing the division on doubles would have been better, but would have required a complicated test for equality. A better approach is the one presented here, which avoids division altogether. This approach not only avoids the problems caused by numbers that can not be represented exactly as one double, but also works correctly when one or both of the denominators is zero. (Rules 9.2, 9.4, and 9.5)

Exercise 3

```
unsigned long t;
int i;
...
if(i<0 || i<t) return;
```

A test for i<0 was added to cover the case when i is negative and would be converted to a high unsigned value. (Rule 9.3)

A.10 Input and Output

Exercise 1

```
1   #define MAX_LEN
2   int nwords,wc[MAX_LEN];
3   ...
4   void count_len(void)
5   {   int len;
6       nwords = 0;
7       do
8       {   while(!isalpha(c=getchar()))
9              if(c==EOF) return;
10          nwords++;
11          for(len = 0; isalpha(c=getchar()); len++);
12          if(len<MAX_LEN) wc[len]++;
13          else            wc[0]++
14      } while(c!=EOF);
15      return;
16  }
```

The original program misbehaved if a word was too long.

13   An `if ... else` was added to handle the case where `len` is greater than or
     equal to `MAX_LEN`. (Rule 10.3)

Exercise 2

```
1   int mdays[12] = { 31,29,31,30,31,30,
2                     31,31,30,31,30,31 };
3   void check_date(int y, int m, int d)
4   {   if(y<0 || 99<y)  error("Bad year");
5       if(m<1 || 12<m)  error("Bad month");
6       if(d<0 || 31<d)  error("Bad day"); else
7       if(1<=m && m<=12 && mdays[m]<d)
8           error("Day beyond end of month"); else
9       if(m==2 && d==29 &&
10          (y%4 || (y%100==0 && y%400)))
11          error("February 29 of non-leap year");
12  }
```

The original program incorrectly reported "Bad day" when the day was inconsistent with the month. In those cases, the day might have been correct, and the month wrong.

6   "Bad day" is now reported only when the day is over 31. (Rule 10.2)
8   "Day beyond end of month" is now reported when the day is too big for a given month but not over 31. (Rule 10.2)
11   "February 29 of non-leap year" is now reported when appropriate. (Rule 10.2)

Exercise 3

```
 1  int n=0,s=1;
 2  ...
 3  c = getchar();
 4  if(c=='-')
 5  {   s=-1;
 6      c = getchar();
 7  }
 8  while(isdigit(c))
 9  {   if(MAX_INT/10 < n || MAX_INT-(n*=10) < c-'0')
10      {   error("Number is too big");
11          break;
12      }
13      n += c-'0';
14      c = getchar();
15  }
16  n *= s;
```

The original program could evaluate a number incorrectly because of integer overflow, without detecting this condition.

9   An if statement was introduced to detect possible overflows. (Rules 10.1 and 10.3)

A.11 Expressions

Exercise 1

```
1   #define OP(q) case ' ## q ## ': val q ## = num; break
2   char *s;
3   int n, val, num;
4   ...
5   for(n=0; *(s = get_term()) && n<MAX_OPS); n++)
6   {   if(isdigit(*s))  num = atoi(s)
7       else             num = value(s)
8       op[n] = get_oper();
9       switch(op[n])
10      {   OP(+);
11          OP(-);
12          OP(*);
13          OP(/);
14          OP(%);
15          OP(|);
16          OP(&);
17      }
18  }
```

1 The macro OP() is used to avoid repetitions in lines 9 to 15. (Rule 11.5)
5 *s!='\0' was simplified to *s. (Rule 11.3)
5 s = get_term() was incorporated into the test within the while.
   (Rule 11.4)
5 Parentheses around *s!='\0' and MAX_OPS>n were eliminated.
   (Rule 11.1)
5 MAX_OPS>n was changed to n<MAX_OPS to avoid using >. (Rule 16.5)
5 The while was changed to a for. (Rule 12.5)

Exercise 2

```
return *++p + a*x*x + b*x*y + c*y*y +
       (yterm_xst && yterm <= MAX_YTERM ? yterm : 0);
```

Unnecessary parentheses were removed. (Rule 11.1)
?: was used to eliminate repetition of a long expression. (Rule 11.5)

Exercise 3

```
1   int find(int a[], int num_elem, int num)
2   {   int n,low=0,high=num_elem-1;
3       while(a[n = (high+low)/2]!=num && low<=high)
4           if(a[n]<num)  low  = n+1;
5           else              high = n-1;
6       return a[n]==num;
7   }
```

3   The assignment n = (high+low)/2 was incorporated into the expression controlling the while to avoid repetition. (Rules 11.4 and 11.5)

3   Unnecessary parentheses were eliminated. (Rule 11.1)

6   The value of the relational expression a[n]==num is now returned to the caller. (Rule 11.2)

A.12   Flow Control

Exercise 1

```
1   do
2   {   panel_move(message,get_key());
3       if(!*message)
4       {   error("Selection error");
5           return 0;
6       }
7   } while(strcmp("OK",message) || key!=K_ESC);
```

3   *message==0 was changed to !*message. (Rule 11.3)
7   The combination of a flag (x), if, and continue was replaced by do ...
    while. (Rule 12.3)
7   strcmp("OK",text)==0 was changed to !strcmp("OK",text). (Rule 11.3)

Exercise 2

```
1    if(DoForm(initp,nfields)!=FR_IO) return;
2    if(err_code)
3    {   error(err_msg);
4        return;
5    }
6    if(scr_num!=S_DEF && scr_num!=S_DEF2) return;
7    if(npass=3) verify();
8    if(*c=='@')
9    {   aflag = 0;
10       npass++;
11   }
12   return;
```

1   DoForm() was moved into the loop, eliminating the temporary variable rtn.
    (Rule 8.2)
1   The condition was reversed and return used to minimize nesting. (Rules
    12.4 and 12.12)
6   else was removed. (Rule 12.3)
6   The condition was reversed and return used to minimize nesting. (Rules
    12.4 and 12.12)

Exercise 3

```
1  if(!group) return NOT_FOUND;
2  i = NGROUPS;
3  cptr = sfind(group,fl);
4  if(!cptr) return NOT_FOUND;
```

1   The condition was reversed to minimize nesting. (Rules 12.1, 12.4, and 12.12)
1   group==NULL was changed to !group. (Rule 11.3)
4   cptr==NULL was changed to !cptr. (Rule 11.3)

Exercise 4

```
1  for(i=0,len=strlen(s); len; len--)
2     if(0<a[len])
3     {  data[i++] = s[len];
4        t = s[len]*a[len];
5        if(t<MIN_T) nmin++;
6        if(MAX_T<t) nmax++;
7        if(s[len]==a[len]) break;
8     }
```

1   The while was changed to for. (Rule 12.5)
1   len!=0 was changed to len. (Rule 11.3)
7   The flag stop was eliminated. break is now used instead. (Rules 12.4 and 12.13)

Exercise 5

```
for(t=x=1; t<=limit; x*=3, t+=x);
```

The while was changed to for. (Rule 12.5)

Exercise 6

```
1  do
2  {  get_data(s);
3     process_data(s, a, &len);
4     if(err) break;
5     for(nodd=i=0; i<len; i++) nodd += a[i]%2;
6  } while(nodd<MAX_ODD);
```

1   while was replaced by do ... while to avoid repetition of lines 2 and 3 in the solution. (Rule 12.11)

4   stop was eliminated, and break is used instead. (Rules 12.4 and 12.13)

5   while was changed to for. (Rule 12.5)

A.13   Functions, Parameters, and Variables

Exercise 1

```
1   double factorial(int n)
2   {   double f=1.0;
3       while(1<n) f*=n--;
4       return f;
5   }
```

1   Parameter declaration was changed to ANSI style. (Rule 13.1)
3   Recursion was changed to a simple loop. (Rule 13.3)

Exercise 2

```
1   int pack(char *dest,int src)
2   {   int d,u;
3       u = src[0]-'0';
4       d = src[1]-'0';
5       if(u<0 || 9<u || d<0 || 9<d) return 1;
6       *dest = u+10*d;
7       return 0;
8   }
```

1   The order of the parameters was reversed. (Rule 13.5)
5   The return value was changed to 1 for error. (Rule 13.6)
7   The return value was changed to 0 for success. (Rule 13.6)

Exercise 3

```
1   static FILE *fileout;
2
3   print_val(int n)
4   {  fprintf(fileout," %i ", n);
5   }
6
7   print_oper(int n)
8   {  fputs(oper[n], fileout);
9   }
10
11  print_expr(Tnode *nd)
12  {  if(nd->left)  print_expr(nd->left);
13     else              print_val(nd->value);
14     print_oper(nd->value);
15     if(nd->right) print_expr(nd->right);
16     else              print_val(nd->value);
17  }
18
19  main()
20  {  Tnode *root;
21     ...
22     fileout = fopen(filename, "w");
23     print_expr(root);
24     ...
25  }
```

  1   fileout is now used directly throughout this module, instead of being passed as a parameter. (Rule 13.4)

  1   static was added to limit the scope of fileout to this module. (Rule 13.4)

  3   Parameter declaration was changed to ANSI style. (Rule 13.1)

  7   Parameter declaration was changed to ANSI style. (Rule 13.1)

12   Recursion is fully justified in this case. (Rule 13.3)

15   Recursion is fully justified in this case. (Rule 13.3)

A.14   Pointers and Arrays

Exercise 1

```
1   void ascii_ebcdic(char *dest, char *src)
2   {   while(*src) *dest++ = tbl_ascii_ebcdic[*src++];
3   }
```

2   Pointers are used instead of indexes. (Rule 14.4)
2   Parameters are used as local variables. (Rule 13.2)
2   A while is used instead of a for. (It is more appropriate.)

Exercise 2

```
if(*context->field[nfld].text) return;
```

(*context). was changed to context->. (Rule 14.5)
...text[0] was changed to *...text. (Rule 14.2)

Exercise 3

```
buffer[*p++]  (Rule 14.1)
```

A.15   The Preprocessor

Exercise 1

```
#define MIN(a,b)   ((a)<(b) ? (a) : (b))
```

Parentheses were added around parameters and result. (Rule 15.1)

Exercise 2

```
#define SORT2(a,b,t) ((b)<(a) && SWAP(a,b,t))
```

The if was replaced by &&. (Rules 15.2 and 15.9)

Exercise 3

```
#define CALL(f) \
    (fprintf(fdbg,"\n%s(%i) %s", __FILE__, __LINE__, #f),f)
```

A.16   Operators

Exercise 1

```
ftable[2]()  or (*ftable[2])()
```

Both forms are equivalent.
In the first case, parentheses around `ftable[2]` are unnecessary, since `[ ]` and `()` have the same precedence and associate from left to right. (Rule 16.1)

Exercise 2

```
tree[n].count++  or  ++tree[n].count
```

Parentheses around `tree[n].count` are not necessary, since `[ ]` and `.` have a higher precedence than `++`. (Rules 16.1 and 16.2)

Exercise 3

```
 1  int gcd(int a, int b)
 2  {   int c;
 3      if(a<b) c=a,a=b,b=c;
 4      do
 5      {   c = a%b;
 6          a = b;
 7          b = c;
 8      } while(c);
 9      return a;
10  }
```

5   The sequence `c = a/b; c = a-b*c;` was changed to `c = a%b`. (Rule 16.3)

Exercise 4

```
if(age1<18 ^ age2<18) study_case();
```

The series of nested `if`s was replaced by exclusive or (^). `study_case()` will be called only if exactly one of `age1<18` and `age2<18` is true. (Rule 16.5)

Exercise 5

```
1   int a[MAX_ELEM];
2
3   for(i=0; i<MAX_ELEM && !a[i]; i++)
4   {  ...
5   }
```

3 The `if` was absorbed into the test within `for` by using `&&`. (Rule 16.5)

A.17   The Standard C Library

Exercise 1

```
while(isdigit(*s)) *d++ = *s++;
```
   (Rule 17.2)

Exercise 2

```
if(strchr("aeiou",c)) vowel++;
```
   (Rule 17.13)

Exercise 3

```
nd = exp(-z*z);
```
   (Rule 17.6)

A.18   Coding for Non-C Programmers

Exercise 1

```
1  p = malloc(size);
2  if(p==NULL) return ERR_SPACE;
```

1 The assignment was made into a separate statement. (Rule 18.2)
2 ==NULL was added. (Rule 18.4)

Exercise 2

```
c = *p;
p++;
```

The statement was broken into two statements, each modifying one data object. (Rule 18.1)

Exercise 3

```
double a[MAXS],b[MAXS],c[MAXS];
...
int i;
...
for(i=0; i<n; i++) c[i] = a[i]*b[i];
```

The pointers p, q, and r were replaced by the index i. (Rule 18.5)

Exercise 4

```
a[i] = c;
i++;
```

The statement was broken into two statements, each modifying one data object. (Rule 18.1)

Level	Operators	Associativity
1	() [] -> .	Left to right
2	! ~ ++ == + - * & (*type*) sizeof	Right to left
3	* / %	Left to right
4	+ -	Left to right
5	<< >>	Left to right
6	< <= > >=	Left to right
7	== !=	Left to right
8	&	Left to right
9	^	Left to right
10	¦	Left to right
11	&&	Left to right
12	¦¦	Left to right
13	?:	Right to left
14	= += -= *= /= %= &= ^= ¦= <<= >>=	Right to left
15	,	Left to right

APPENDIX C: **Keywords**

auto	double	int	struct
break	else	long	switch
case	enum	register	typedef
char	extern	return	union
const	float	short	unsigned
continue	for	signed	void
default	goto	sizeof	volatile
do	if	static	while

Index

ABOUT THE AUTHORS

JAY RANADE is Series Editor in Chief of *McGraw-Hill's J. Ranade IBM Series* and *J. Ranade Workstation Series* and Series Advisor to the *McGraw-Hill Series on Computer Communications*. He is the best-selling computer author of two VSAM books, two books on SNA, and the C^{++} *Primer for C Programmers*. He is a senior systems architect and assistant vice president with Merrill Lynch.

ALAN NASH has been programming in several languages for more than ten years. He is currently at Merrill Lynch where he does high-level design and manages three teams for the implementation of client/server systems.